VOLUME 519

JANUARY 1992

S0-ADX-549

THE ANNALS

of The American Academy *of* Political
and Social Science

RICHARD D. LAMBERT, *Editor*
ALAN W. HESTON, *Associate Editor*

CHINA'S FOREIGN RELATIONS

Special Editor of this Volume

ALLEN S. WHITING

University of Arizona
Tucson

Ⓢ SAGE PUBLICATIONS *NEWBURY PARK LONDON NEW DELHI*

THE ANNALS

© 1991 *by* The American Academy *of* Political *and* Social Science

Editorial Office: 3937 Chestnut Street, Philadelphia, PA 19104.

For information about membership* (individuals only) and subscriptions (institutions), address:

SAGE PUBLICATIONS, INC.
2455 Teller Road
Newbury Park, CA 91320

From India and South Asia, write to:
SAGE PUBLICATIONS INDIA Pvt. Ltd.
P.O. Box 4215
New Delhi 110 048
INDIA

From the UK, Europe, the Middle East and Africa, write to:
SAGE PUBLICATIONS LTD
6 Bonhill Street
London EC2A 4PU
UNITED KINGDOM

SAGE Production Staff: LINDA GRAY, LIANN LECH, and JANELLE LeMASTER
*Please note that members of The Academy receive THE ANNALS with their membership.
Library of Congress Catalog Card Number 91-61242
International Standard Serial Number ISSN 0002-7162
International Standard Book Number ISBN 0-8039-4477-2 (Vol. 519, 1992 paper)
International Standard Book Number ISBN 0-8039-4476-4 (Vol. 519, 1992 cloth)
Manufactured in the United States of America. First printing, January 1992.

The articles appearing in THE ANNALS are indexed in *Book Review Index, Public Affairs Information Service Bulletin, Social Sciences Index, Current Contents, General Periodicals Index, Academic Index, Pro-Views,* and *Combined Retrospective Index Sets.* They are also abstracted and indexed in *ABC Pol Sci, Historical Abstracts, Human Resources Abstracts, Social Sciences Citation Index, United States Political Science Documents, Social Work Research & Abstracts, Sage Urban Studies Abstracts, International Political Science Abstracts, America: History and Life, Sociological Abstracts, Managing Abstracts, Social Planning/Policy & Development Abstracts, Automatic Subject Citation Alert, Book Review Digest, Work Related Abstracts,* and/or *Family Resources Database,* and are available on microfilm from University Microfilms, Ann Arbor, Michigan.

Information about membership rates, institutional subscriptions, and back issue prices may be found on the facing page.

Advertising. Current rates and specifications may be obtained by writing to THE ANNALS Advertising and Promotion Manager at the Newbury Park office (address above).

Claims. Claims for undelivered copies must be made no later than three months following month of publication. The publisher will supply missing copies when losses have been sustained in transit and when the reserve stock will permit.

Change of Address. Six weeks' advance notice must be given when notifying of change of address to ensure proper identification. Please specify name of journal. Send address changes to: THE ANNALS, c/o Sage Publications, Inc., 2455 Teller Road, Newbury Park, CA 91320.

The American Academy of Political and Social Science

3937 Chestnut Street   Philadelphia, Pennsylvania 19104

Origin and Purpose. The Academy was organized December 14, 1889, to promote the progress of political and social science, especially through publications and meetings. The Academy does not take sides in controverted questions, but seeks to gather and present reliable information to assist the public in forming an intelligent and accurate judgment.

Meetings. The Academy holds an annual meeting in the spring extending over two days.

Publications. THE ANNALS is the bimonthly publication of The Academy. Each issue contains articles on some prominent social or political problem, written at the invitation of the editors. Also, monographs are published from time to time, numbers of which are distributed to pertinent professional organizations. These volumes constitute important reference works on the topics with which they deal, and they are extensively cited by authorities throughout the United States and abroad. The papers presented at the meetings of The Academy are included in THE ANNALS.

Membership. Each member of The Academy receives THE ANNALS and may attend the meetings of The Academy. Membership is open only to individuals. Annual dues: $39.00 for the regular paperbound edition (clothbound, $54.00). California residents must add 7.25% sales tax on all orders ($41.82 paperbound; $57.91 clothbound). Add $9.00 per year for membership outside the U.S.A. Members may also purchase single issues of THE ANNALS for $12.00 each (clothbound, $17.00). California residents: $12.87 paperbound, $18.23 clothbound. Add $1.50 for shipping and handling on all prepaid orders.

Subscriptions. THE ANNALS (ISSN 0002-7162) is published six times annually—in January, March, May, July, September, and November. Institutions may subscribe to THE ANNALS at the annual rate: $120.00 (clothbound, $144.00). California institutions: $128.70 paperbound, $155.44 clothbound. Add $9.00 per year for subscriptions outside the U.S.A. Institutional rates for single issues: $23.00 each (clothbound, $28.00). California institutions: $24.66 paperbound, $30.03 clothbound.

Second class postage paid at Thousand Oaks, California, and at additional mailing offices.

Single issues of THE ANNALS may be obtained by individuals who are not members of The Academy for $15.95 each (clothbound, $25.00). California residents: $17.10 paperbound, $26.81 clothbound. Add $1.50 for shipping and handling on all prepaid orders. Single issues of THE ANNALS have proven to be excellent supplementary texts for classroom use. Direct inquiries regarding adoptions to THE ANNALS c/o Sage Publications (address below).

All correspondence concerning membership in The Academy, dues renewals, inquiries about membership status, and/or purchase of single issues of THE ANNALS should be sent to THE ANNALS c/o Sage Publications, Inc., 2455 Teller Road, Newbury Park, CA 91320. Telephone: (805) 499-0721; FAX/Order line: (805) 499-0871. *Please note that orders under $30 must be prepaid.* Sage affiliates in London and India will assist institutional subscribers abroad with regard to orders, claims, and inquiries for both subscriptions and single issues.

THE ANNALS

of The American Academy *of* Political *and* Social Science

RICHARD D. LAMBERT, *Editor*
ALAN W. HESTON, *Associate Editor*

──────────── FORTHCOMING ────────────

WORLD LITERACY IN THE YEAR 2000
Special Editors: Daniel A. Wagner and Laurel D. Puchner
Volume 520   March 1992

DRUG ABUSE: LINKING POLICY AND RESEARCH
Special Editor: Eric Wish
Volume 521   May 1992

THE FUTURE: TRENDS INTO
THE TWENTY-FIRST CENTURY
Special Editors: Joseph F. Coates and Jennifer Jarratt
Volume 522   July 1992

───

See page 3 for information on Academy membership and
purchase of single volumes of **The Annals.**

CONTENTS

BOOK DEPARTMENT CONTENTS

SOCIOLOGY

ECONOMICS

PREFACE

This volume of *The Annals* focuses on China's foreign relations since the Beijing massacre of 4 June 1989. I use the term "foreign relations" rather than "foreign policy" deliberately. The basic contours of Beijing's foreign policy have not changed from its pre-Tiananmen outline, but China's foreign relations are substantially different in several areas, most notably with the United States. When the People's Liberation Army killed and wounded unarmed demonstrators and innocent bystanders by the hundreds, if not thousands, the regime's status dropped dramatically in Washington, London, and Paris, not to mention with the World Bank and other sources of capital, both governmental and private.

To be sure, much of the initial anger abroad and the reactive backlash in Beijing aroused by that anger have subsided. Loans suspended in the first year after the event were resumed in the second. Exchanges of state visits, never halted by any in the Third World, resumed piecemeal for most of the industrial world. Japan, which had spoken most softly among the critics, led the "renormalization" of relations. Beijing's artful manipulation of its Security Council vote during the successive U.N. resolutions condemning Iraq's invasion of Kuwait won a White House invitation for Foreign Minister Qian Qichen and President George Bush's renewal of most-favored-nation trade privileges.

Nevertheless the tenor of discourse between China and much of the international community had changed, as several of the articles in this volume testify. Most notably, the American mood manifested another of the swings in the love-hate syndrome that has characterized this relationship throughout its history. The cumulative agenda of issues, some long-standing, some recent, captured the attention of Congress and columnists. Their criticisms, in turn, sparked assertively nationalistic rebuttals in the Chinese media and from the leadership itself.

Reference to "the leadership" requires a small caveat. Use of the term "China" and "the regime" in this volume does not connote a single-minded set of decision makers, much less a one-person dictatorship under Deng Xiaoping. All foreign observers and most Chinese speaking unofficially agree that the leadership has been seriously divided over both domestic and foreign policy for several years. Analysts argue whether it is polarized into two groups or coalitions of various factions and whether the labels "conservatives" and "reformers" are appropriate. But a consensus holds that policy differences and personal power struggles underlie the monolithic image connoted by the terms "China" and "Beijing." That fact notwithstanding, for the sake of convenience these terms are used throughout the text in lieu of a more complicated analysis that, in any event, must remain largely speculative.

Several other caveats are also in order. Our coverage is not completely comprehensive. Latin America is omitted as a region because it has come last and least onto the foreign policy agenda for Beijing. More serious, the Korean peninsula is not covered, higher priority being given to its Soviet and Japanese neighbors. Suffice it to say that, unlike Moscow, Beijing has denied Seoul diplomatic recognition so as to keep in somewhat better favor with Pyongyang while nevertheless opening an official trade office in the south. That trade was estimated to exceed $5 billion in 1991, well above trade with the north and far above the Seoul-Moscow exchange.

Finally, there is no attempt to sum up more than forty years of the People's Republic in world affairs, previous issues of *The Annals* providing an excellent reference for the interested reader. Nor is there a general treatment of the determining factors in Chinese foreign policy as the twentieth century draws to a close. An excellent essay, "Chinese History and the Foreign Relations of Contemporary China," by Professor Albert Feuerwerker in the July 1972 issue of *The Annals* still serves the purpose twenty years later. His denial of any distinctively Chinese aspects dominating decisions and his placing the historical heritage secondary to contemporary considerations are implicitly subscribed to by our contributors. One might reorder his priority ranking of the factors: "(1) nationalism, (2) the politics of the international Communist movement, (3) China's domestic politics, (4) Marxist-Leninist-Maoist ideology, and (5) a strategic-political imagery based on a traditional spatial-ideological world order."[1] But none of these would be wholly irrelevant today.

Yet one overriding factor, largely absent in 1972, must be added to this list—the goal of economic modernization. As a top priority for the Beijing leadership since 1978, this goal has forced China's entry into the world community as a major member committed to the basic rules of that community. How the leadership can protect its sense of sovereignty and its definition of "Chinese characteristics" while contending with asserted community principles such as human rights is a source of contention within China as well as the world community. But aside from this aspect, dependence on trade, technology transfer, loans, and credit has radically transformed China's foreign relations from those of twenty years ago.

While our focus is primarily on the post-Tiananmen period, such background data and analysis as necessary for particular subjects are included. The time of writing was spring 1991, with final editing later that year. Some authors have projected into the post-Deng era; others have stayed close to the

1. Albert Feuerwerker, "Chinese History and the Foreign Relations of Contemporary China," *The Annals* of the American Academy of Political and Social Science, 402:1 (July 1972).

period of composition. All are aware of the uncertainties in Beijing as the largest and one of the last Leninist regimes attempts economic modernization under one-party rule. How this will be managed and by whom is for another volume of *The Annals*. We trust that what we have written will stand for at least a few years and be of use beyond that as a record of our time.

ALLEN S. WHITING

ANNALS, *AAPSS,* **519,** January 1992

China's American Dilemma

By HARRY HARDING

ABSTRACT: The Tiananmen crisis of 1989 stimulated the most intense debate over Chinese policy toward the United States since the rapprochement between the two countries in the early 1970s. One issue confronting Chinese leaders has been to weigh the benefits of close economic and cultural ties with America against the disruptive ideas and values that accompany them. A second issue has been to determine China's response to the improvement of the U.S. strategic position caused by the collapse of communism in Eastern Europe, the moderation of Soviet foreign policy, and the American victory in the Persian Gulf. In the future, Beijing may also have to decide how to deal with growing American sympathy for the Nationalist Chinese government in Taipei or increased pressure for Taiwanese independence. The evolution of Chinese policy toward the United States since the Tiananmen crisis suggests that Chinese leaders still prefer a stable and beneficial relationship with America but are trying to find ways to maximize their diplomatic leverage over Washington.

Harry Harding is a senior fellow in the Foreign Policy Studies Program at the Brookings Institution in Washington, D.C. Educated at Princeton and Stanford, he taught political science at Swarthmore College from 1970 to 1971 and at Stanford University from 1971 to 1983. He is the author of Organizing China: The Problem of Bureaucracy, 1949-1976; China's Second Revolution: Reform after Mao; *and* China and Northeast Asia: The Political Dimension *and is currently completing a book on U.S.-China relations since 1972.*

THE sanctions imposed on China following the huge antigovernment demonstrations in Tiananmen Square in June 1989 produced the sharpest debate over Chinese policy toward the United States since the Sino-American rapprochement of the early 1970s. The debate focused on two central issues, both of which predated the Tiananmen crisis but were vividly highlighted by it. The first concerned the risks to China's domestic stability that stemmed from close economic and cultural ties to the United States. The second involved the implications of the changing international strategic environment for China's relationship with America. In the background was a third issue, Taiwan, that had traditionally been the most controversial and problematic aspect of Sino-American relations. Together, these issues constituted a familiar conundrum for Chinese leaders: the dilemma of assessing the costs and benefits of dealing with a nation that could greatly promote China's economic modernization and military security but whose values and institutions posed a major threat to the legitimacy of the Chinese government.

THE DILEMMA OF THE OPEN DOOR

Ever since their first extensive contacts with the West in the late eighteenth and early nineteenth centuries, Chinese leaders have been apprehensive about the domestic consequences of an extensive relationship with the outside world. The more xenophobic among them have consistently feared that cultural and eco-

nomic ties with the West would subject the Chinese economy to foreign exploitation, introduce unorthodox new ideas into Chinese society, and thereby undermine the security of the Chinese state. First during the mid-Qing dynasty, and then during the late Maoist period, the Chinese government imposed strict limitations on economic and cultural relations with the West, in an attempt to insulate the country from these destabilizing influences from abroad.

In the post-Mao period, however, China's new leadership has acknowledged the limitations to such an approach. In 1984, Deng blamed China's backwardness on its past international isolation and warned that "any country that closes its door to the outside world cannot achieve progress."[1] He and his colleagues recognized that it would be necessary to expand economic, cultural, and scientific exchanges with the outside world, including the United States, for China to become a more prosperous and powerful nation. The resulting liberalization of China's policies on foreign economic and cultural relations produced a dramatic expansion of trade, investment, tourism, and academic exchanges with the United States throughout the 1980s.[2]

1. Xinhua News Agency, 31 Dec. 1984, in Foreign Broadcast Information Service, *FBIS Daily Report—China* (hereafter cited as *FBIS—Chi*), 2. Jan. 1984, p. K4.
2. Bilateral trade between the two countries increased twenty times, from $1 billion in 1978 to $20 billion in 1990. American investment in China, nonexistent in 1978, had achieved a cumulative total of nearly $2 billion by the end of 1990. More than 100,000 visas were issued between 1978 and 1990 to Chinese students and scholars wishing to visit the

Indeed, Chinese leaders and foreign policy analysts increasingly regarded economic and cultural ties with the United States as the emerging foundation for Sino-American relations. In the 1970s, the relationship between the two countries had been rooted primarily in their common opposition to Soviet expansionism, particularly in Asia. With the moderation in Soviet foreign policy undertaken by Mikhail Gorbachev, however, the strategic underpinning of the U.S.-China relationship had largely eroded. By the late 1980s, many Chinese were hoping that Sino-American relations could evolve from a geopolitical alignment into an economic partnership, with the United States providing the capital, markets, technology, and scientific know-how needed for China's modernization and reform.

But the Tiananmen crisis of 1989 provided graphic evidence that the dilemma of the open door had not yet been fully resolved. The huge antigovernment protests in Beijing, calling for greater "freedom" and "democracy," illustrated the disruptive impact of the liberal values that were accompanying China's burgeoning economic and cultural relations with America. Moreover, the economic and diplomatic sanctions imposed by the United States in June 1989, and the subsequent threat to revoke China's most-favored-nation trade status when it came up for renewal in mid-1990, suggested that American willingness to cooperate in China's modernization was much more tentative and conditional than Beijing had previously realized. Once again, Chinese leaders perceived that contacts with the West, although necessary to build a strong and prosperous nation, could simultaneously threaten China's stability and autonomy.

The Tiananmen crisis sparked a sharp debate in Beijing over whether to respond to the American sanctions with concessions, retaliation, or simply forbearance.[3] As the debate unfolded, two fairly distinct positions became evident. Conservative leaders viewed the Sino-American relationship from an ideological perspective, depicting it as an inherently antagonistic confrontation between socialism and capitalism. As they saw it, the United States had consistently tried to undermine Communist rule in China ever since the establishment of the People's Republic in 1949. In the 1950s and 1960s, Washington had attempted to do so through a mixture of diplomatic isolation, military encirclement, and economic embargo. When that policy failed, the United States sought to take advantage of China's opening to the outside world in the 1970s and 1980s, using cultural and economic exchange to encourage China's "peaceful evolution" from socialism to capitalism. Now, after the Tiananmen crisis, the United States had

United States for training or research. Before the Tiananmen crisis, more than 300,000 American tourists were visiting China each year.

3. This debate is analyzed in much greater detail in Harry Harding, "The Impact of Tiananmen on China's Foreign Policy," in *China's Foreign Relations after Tiananmen: Challenges for the U.S.*, NBR Analysis, no. 3 (Seattle, WA: National Bureau of Asian and Soviet Research, Dec. 1990), pp. 5-17.

shifted tactics once again, employing economic sanctions and diplomatic pressure to force changes in domestic Chinese policy. But whatever the strategy, the conservatives were convinced that the ultimate objective of American policy remained the same: to secure the replacement of the Communist government in China by one more sympathetic to American interests.[4]

Based on this analysis, the conservatives proposed several modifications in China's policy toward the United States. They suggested reducing academic and cultural exchanges with America, so as to restrict one of the primary channels through which unorthodox Western ideas and values entered China. For similar reasons, they also advocated a less accommodating attitude toward economic relations with the United States, in favor of a more "self-reliant" strategy of economic development. Third, they favored a more critical attitude toward American foreign policy, especially in the Third World, but possibly in Asia as well. Finally, they advised imposing countervailing sanctions against the United States, including sharp reductions of Chinese imports from America and the withdrawal of the Chinese ambassador from Washington, particularly if China's most-favored-nation status were revoked.

Taken together, these proposals represented an effort to put more "filters" over China's door to the outside world, so as to insulate China from the contaminating influences from the West.[5]

But this position did not go unchallenged in the debate over Chinese policy toward the United States. More moderate political leaders and foreign policy analysts, less prone to a conventional ideological analysis, viewed the contemporary world not as a struggle between socialism and capitalism but as a competition for "comprehensive national strength" among a growing number of countries with diverse economic and political systems. Only nations that were fully integrated into the international economy, maintained friendly relations with a wide range of trading partners, and minimized their expenditures on military preparations could engage in that competition successfully. If China responded to American sanctions by further isolating itself from the West, let alone by engaging in a renewed strategic confrontation with the United States, it would find itself severely handicapped in its search for national wealth and power. In their analysis, China would be better advised to try to stabilize Sino-American relations and to rebuild its economic and political ties with the United States as quickly as possible.

To that end, this second group of Chinese leaders and analysts advocated dealing with American sanc-

4. For representative criticisms of the policy of "peaceful evolution," see *Renmin ribao* [People's daily], 7 July 1989, p. 6, in *FBIS—Chi*, 11 July 1989, pp. 2-4; *Renmin ribao*, 9 July 1989, p. 4, in *FBIS—Chi*, 11 July 1989, pp. 4-8; *Renmin ribao*, 5 Aug. 1989, in *FBIS—Chi*, Aug. 1989; *Liaowang* [Outlook], 7 Aug. 1989, 32:46-47, in *FBIS—Chi*, 23 Aug. 1989, pp. 40-42.

5. This metaphor is drawn from *Guangming ribao* [Enlightenment daily], 16 Feb. 1990, p. 3, in *FBIS—Chi*, 15 Mar. 1990, pp. 23-25.

tions with patience, not retaliation. They opposed placing restrictions on economic and cultural ties with the United States. Instead, they apparently recommended that the Chinese government make concessions on some of the issues of particular concern to Washington, including releasing some of the political activists arrested after the massacre of 4 June, lifting martial law in Beijing, and making special efforts to increase China's imports of American commodities. Beyond this, they favored waiting for American emotions to cool as memories of Tiananmen faded.

This second position was strongly supported by many individuals and institutions that had acquired a stake in an extensive relationship with the United States in the decade since the normalization of Sino-American relations. Many intellectuals, particularly in Beijing and Shanghai, wanted to protect opportunities for academic exchange with their American colleagues. Most local officials and industrial managers, especially in China's coastal regions, wished to maintain access to American markets and capital. Many military officers hoped to preserve their chances to learn about advanced American technology and strategy. Perhaps most important, Deng Xiaoping proved to be personally committed to maintaining an open door to the West and to preserving a stable relationship with the United States.

The outcome of this debate was a compromise—but one that, on balance, favored the realists over the ideologues. To be sure, China did impose some of the counter-sanctions proposed by the conservatives immediately after the Tiananmen incident. These included jamming several frequencies of the Voice of America, suspending the Fulbright exchange program, shelving plans to receive Peace Corps volunteers, and reducing imports of American goods. But measures such as these did not constitute the main thrust of China's policy in the post-Tiananmen period. Instead, China showed that it was prepared to make some concessions to Washington in order to rebuild, or at least to preserve, its relationship with the United States.

China's willingness to make these compromises first became apparent in December 1989, when National Security Adviser Brent Scowcroft and Deputy Secretary of State Lawrence Eagleburger visited Beijing. At that time, the leaders of the two countries reportedly agreed on a rough timetable for the renormalization of Sino-American relations. The Bush administration promised to ease some of its economic sanctions, including those blocking Export-Import Bank trade financing and World Bank loans for China. For its part, the Chinese government apparently indicated its readiness both to foster a more relaxed political climate and to restore some of the cultural ties with the United States that had been suspended immediately after the Tiananmen crisis.

Unfortunately, the fall of the Ceausescu government in Romania postponed the implementation of this understanding. Chinese leaders hesitated to loosen political controls over their society at a time when Communist regimes in Europe seemed to be collapsing one after another. But they soon realized that, unless they did something to improve their human rights record, they might lose their most-favored-nation trading status with the United States when it came up for annual renewal in the summer of 1990. Ultimately, Chinese leaders chose to lift martial law, release some of the protesters they had arrested after the Tiananmen crisis, resume some academic exchange programs with the United States, and permit the exile of Fang Lizhi, the prominent Chinese dissident who had sought refuge in the American embassy in Beijing shortly after 4 June. Although Congress continued to criticize the remaining violations of human rights in China, it was unable to overturn the president's decision to continue most-favored-nation status for Beijing.

But twelve months later, in the spring and summer of 1991, the issue of China's most-favored-nation status rose once again. This time, the Bush administration, members of Congress, and the American press had an even longer list of concerns to raise with Beijing, including not just its failure to resume meaningful political reform but also its burgeoning trade surplus with the United States and its export of military technology to the Middle East. Compared with 1990, Chinese leaders seemed somewhat more reluctant to make any further concessions to Washington so as to preserve their preferential trading status. As one Communist newspaper in Hong Kong warned, another series of compromises with the

United States might simply encourage the Americans to try to "extort" even more from China in the future.[6]

In the end, however, Deng Xiaoping once again decided that China should make whatever gestures to Washington might be necessary to retain China's most-favored-nation treatment.[7] Thus Beijing sent a trade mission to the United States to boost its imports of American goods, promised to provide better protection for American intellectual property in China, pledged to tighten legislation to prevent unfair trade practices, and released two more dissidents who had been arrested in the aftermath of the Tiananmen crisis. This enabled the president to recommend extension of China's most-favored-nation status for yet another year and prevented Congress from attaching stringent conditions to further renewals.

Thus the Tiananmen crisis illustrated the enduring ambivalence of Chinese leaders toward extensive cultural and economic ties with the West. At the same time, it also demonstrated that the majority of them appreciated the costs of resuming a policy of confrontation, or even simply of isolation, toward the United States. As a result, China's policy since June 1989 has been to keep the doors to America open, even though placing a somewhat finer mesh across the passages through which academic exchanges with America flow. Beijing has even been willing, despite its protestations to the con-

6. *Wen wei po* (Hong Kong), 11 May 1991, p. 2, in *FBIS—Chi*, 13 May 1991, pp. 10-11.
7. On Deng's role, see *Cheng ming* (Hong Kong), 1 May 1991, 163:14-15, in *FBIS—Chi*, 30 Apr. 1991, pp. 6-7.

trary, to make timely concessions to Washington to preserve its most-favored-nation status.

THE CHANGING STRATEGIC ENVIRONMENT

The foreign policy debate of 1989-91 raised a second crucial issue for Chinese policymakers: the implications of the dramatic changes in the international environment for their relationship with the United States. To what extent did the end of the Cold War reduce Beijing's diplomatic leverage over Washington? To what degree did the American victory in the Persian Gulf imply the emergence of a unipolar world, centered on the United States, in which China would be placed at a severe disadvantage? Most important, if the United States was now emerging as the world's only superpower, what mixture of confrontation and accommodation should China adopt in dealing with Washington?

Although not a superpower itself, China had derived considerable strategic leverage in the 1970s and 1980s from the widespread perception that it could determine the outcome of the global confrontation between Moscow and Washington. Thanks to its size, autonomy, and strategic location, China was viewed as a geopolitical trump card, which could form the winning hand for whichever superpower was able to play it.

By the end of the 1980s, however, some Chinese strategists had begun to ask whether changes in the international environment were depriving their country of this kind of leverage. Some of them believed that the

collapse of communism in Eastern Europe and the severe internal difficulties of the Soviet Union gave Washington such a decisive strategic advantage over Moscow that the China card became virtually irrelevant to American geopolitical calculations. The massacre of antigovernment demonstrators in Beijing in June 1989—in such sharp contrast to the nearly simultaneous emergence of multiparty systems in Hungary, Poland, and Mongolia—cost China most of the sympathy that it had previously enjoyed in the United States. Emerging opportunities for trade and investment elsewhere in the socialist bloc distracted American business from China, where economic performance seemed sluggish and economic reforms seemed to have been placed on hold. Some Chinese analysts concluded, therefore, that their country was much less important in American calculations than before, that Beijing would have much less influence over Washington than in earlier years, and that China would therefore have to pay a higher price if it wished to preserve its relationship with the United States.[8]

Not all Chinese leaders accepted such a pessimistic analysis, however. A second line of interpretation insisted that, despite the decline of Soviet power, the influence of the United States was also eroding. The American economy was losing ground to the Germans and the Japanese. Washington was still competing with Moscow for global strategic

8. Chinese analysts were particularly impressed by an article by Nicholas Kristof, "Suddenly China Looks Smaller in the World," *New York Times*, 27 Mar. 1990.

advantage. The emergence of independent regional powers was creating a more multipolar international
system in which American power
would be less decisive. Because of all
these developments, China still enjoyed an "important position and influence in world strategy" that the
United States could not overlook.[9] In
the end, American policymakers
would realize that economic and strategic links to China would be a crucial
factor in maintaining the global position of the United States and therefore would make concessions to Beijing in order to preserve their
relationship with China.

The question of the relative leverage of China and America was of particular salience after the Tiananmen
incident, as Beijing debated its response to the American sanctions. At
first, China attempted to demonstrate its independence from the
United States. Beijing sent high-
level emissaries throughout the
Third World in 1989-90, to show that
it had not been completely isolated by
Western sanctions. It made contact
with other hard-line Communist
states, including Romania, Bulgaria,
North Korea, and Vietnam, even as it
continued the normalization of its relations with the Soviet Union. It established or reestablished diplomatic
ties with Indonesia, Singapore, and
Saudi Arabia and exchanged trade or

academic liaison offices with South
Korea and Israel.

But the limits to such a strategy
soon became apparent. The revolutions in Eastern Europe virtually eliminated the possibility of re-creating a
global Communist bloc. The Soviet
Union's continued rapprochement
with the United States and mounting
internal problems made it an unreli-
able partner for a renewed alignment
with China. The Third World had little
to contribute to China's drive for economic modernization. Finally, the developed Western countries, despite
some differences of perspective, remained remarkably united on the
issue of sanctions against China. By
the end of 1989, China had decided
that an assertion of independence from
the United States would be of little
avail.

Beijing then took a somewhat different approach, trying to show not
only that China remained an important global actor but also that it was
prepared to cooperate with the United
States on issues of common concern.
To this end, Chinese leaders participated constructively in the international negotiations over Cambodia,
temporarily suspending their shipments of supplies to the Khmer
Rouge as a sign of their flexibility and
goodwill. They pledged greater restraint in their sale of conventional
weapons in the Middle East and
promised to join in international efforts to combat environmental pollu-
tion and drug trafficking. They exchanged trade offices with Seoul and
hinted that they would accept South
Korean membership in the United
Nations. Some Chinese officials visiting the United States began to urge

9. *Liaowang*, overseas ed., 16 Apr. 1990,
16:4-6, in *FBIS—Chi*, 1 May 1990, pp. 1-5. On
an internal report containing this analysis, see
New York Times, 5 Oct. 1989. For an article
suggesting that China could use the continuing Soviet-American rivalry to "ensure [its]
invincibility," see *Shijie zhishi*, 16 Dec. 1989,
24:2-3, in *FBIS—Chi*, 26 Jan. 1990, pp. 1-2.

a renewed strategic alignment with Washington, against either a resurgent Soviet Union or a more assertive Japan.

The crisis in the Persian Gulf, which erupted with Iraq's invasion of Kuwait in August 1990, gave Beijing an even greater opportunity to demonstrate its geopolitical significance to the United States. Since China occupied a permanent seat on the U.N. Security Council, it had the power to veto any resolution placed before the Council. To the extent that the Bush administration chose to work through the United Nations as part of its effort to create a "new world order," China automatically gained considerable diplomatic leverage over the United States.

At first, Beijing used that leverage extremely skillfully. In an attempt to secure China's support for the U.N. resolution authorizing the use of force against Iraq, the Bush administration agreed to receive Chinese Foreign Minister Qian Qichen in the White House in December—the highest-level diplomatic contact between the two countries since the Tiananmen crisis. In the end, in the vote on the resolution the Chinese abstained, but they had utilized their place in the Security Council to obtain a significant relaxation of American sanctions.

As the situation in the Persian Gulf escalated, however, Beijing made a series of erroneous predictions about its outcome. First, Chinese analysts assumed that international mediation—whether by the Arab nations, by members of the Non-Aligned Movement, by the Soviet Union, or by China itself—would produce a negotiated settlement that would obviate the need for an attack against Iraq. That prediction having been refuted, Chinese observers then forecast that the United States would become enmeshed in a ground war of protracted duration and with heavy casualties, comparable to the indecisive conflict in Korea some forty years earlier.[10] Moreover, they also predicted that the anti-Iraqi coalition would quickly break apart, with its Western participants splitting from the United States over the human and economic costs of the war and with its Arab members defecting as Israel was drawn into the conflict.[11] As a result of these assessments, Chinese propaganda took on an increasingly anti-American tone as the war intensified, criticizing the heavy losses inflicted on Iraqi troops and civilians by American air strikes.[12]

The quick and decisive American victory against Iraq not only disproved these Chinese forecasts but also challenged some of the underlying assumptions on which they had been based. Instead of the multipolar international system that Chinese analysts had been predicting, there now seemed to be the possibility of a

10. See, for example, *Jiefangjun bao* [Liberation Army daily], 17 Dec. 1990, p. 3, in *FBIS—Chi*, 3 Jan. 1991, p. 1; *Ta kung pao* (Hong Kong), 6 Feb. 1991, p. 2, in *FBIS—Chi*, 7 Feb. 1991, pp. 3-4. For one of the few exceptions, which noted that a quick coalition victory was possible and would be conducive to regional stability, see *Gongren ribao* [Workers' daily], 22 Jan. 1991, p. 4, in *FBIS—Chi*, 5 Feb. 1991, pp. 4-5.

11. For instance, *Ta kung pao*, 16 Jan. 1991, p. 3, in *FBIS—Chi*, 16 Jan. 1991, pp. 3-4.

12. *Ta kung pao*, 1 Feb. 1991, p. 2, in *FBIS—Chi*, 1 Feb. 1991, pp. 2-3.

unipolar world centered around the United States. Nor was it so evident that American military force would be less relevant in a world obsessed with economics. Rather, the dynamics of the international system seemed to combine both geopolitical and economic rivalry, in which American military power would continue to play a prominent role.

Thus, when the Bush administration began to speak of forging a "new world order" to replace the international system of the Cold War era, some Chinese analysts and political leaders reacted with alarm. They feared that this "new world order" would be dominated by the United States, perhaps acting in concert with some of its closest allies. They worried that the promotion of human rights would become an important element of American foreign policy and that, given the dramatic progress of political liberalization in the Soviet Union and Eastern Europe, China would become the principal target of such efforts. Summarizing these apprehensions, one senior Chinese official reportedly characterized American proposals for a "new world order" as nothing less than an effort to achieve "world domination" and to promote China's "peaceful evolution" from communism to capitalism.[13] The clear, if unstated, implication of such an analysis was that China should seek to organize some kind of international united front to counterbalance resurgent American hegemonism, just as it had done against Soviet "social imperialism" in the

1970s and American "imperialism" in the 1950s and 1960s.

Within a month or so, however, Chinese analysts began to take a more sanguine view of the international strategic environment. Gradually, they concluded that the balance of power had not experienced such a decisive shift in America's favor. Despite the undeniable decline of the Soviet Union, the broader trends toward multipolarity—particularly the rise of new global economic powers like Japan and Germany, and the emergence of new regional powers such as India and China—had not been reversed. Nor had Washington's victory in the Persian Gulf halted the relative decline of American power. By the spring of 1991, Chinese analysts were reassuring their readers that the United States lacked the strength to achieve its "vaunting ambitions" and that the prospects of a "U.S.-dominated 'unipolar world' " were remote.[14]

Thus, rather than deciding to confront the United States, China chose once again to try to maximize its maneuverability by improving its ties with other countries. This time, however, it did not focus on other Communist countries or on the Third World, as it had done in 1989. Instead, it sought to strengthen its relations with its Asian neighbors. Beijing stopped its internal denunciations of Gorbachev's domestic economic and political reforms and continued to expand its political, economic, and even military ties with

13. *South China Morning Post* (Hong Kong), 4 Apr. 1991, p. 11, in *FBIS—Chi*, 4 Apr. 1991, p. 3.

14. *Liaowang*, overseas ed., 13 May 1991, 19:9-10, in *FBIS—Chi*, 21 May 1991, pp. 3-6; ibid., 8 Apr. 1991, 14:26-28, in *FBIS—Chi*, 17 Apr. 1991, pp. 7-9.

the Soviet Union. China muted its criticism of Japanese defense policy and invited the new Japanese emperor to make a state visit to Beijing. Chinese leaders made regular tours of neighboring states in Northeast, Southeast, and South Asia. And, although it continued to press Vietnam to accept a comprehensive political settlement in Cambodia, Beijing even seemed willing to reduce tensions with its regional rival in Hanoi.

Even as it tried to diversify its international contacts, however, China continued to find ways of cooperating with the United States on various international issues. It successfully encouraged North Korea to accept membership in the United Nations, together with South Korea. It expressed its willingness, after almost thirty years, to accede to the nuclear nonproliferation treaty. It agreed to participate in international negotiations to restrict the flow of arms to the Middle East, and it hinted that it might join similar efforts to limit the diffusion of missiles to Third World countries. All these steps suggested that China had chosen neither to confront the United States nor to accommodate it completely but was trying to find the diplomatic leverage to deal with Washington from as advantageous a position as possible.

THE ISSUE OF TAIWAN

For most of the past four decades, Taiwan has been the most serious impediment to stable Sino-American relations and has figured prominently in any crisis between the two countries. In the late 1980s, however, developments in the Taiwan Strait relegated the island to a secondary position on the diplomatic agenda between Washington and Beijing. Nor did the Taiwan issue assume a prominent role in Sino-American relations in the immediate post-Tiananmen period. Nonetheless, it could still reemerge to confound Chinese policy toward the United States in the years ahead.

The United States has maintained close ties with the Chinese Nationalist government ever since the latter retreated to Taipei after losing power on the Chinese mainland in 1949. The United States has been Taiwan's largest trading partner, a source of large amounts of military and economic aid, and the guarantor of the island's security. This long-standing relationship has consistently aroused suspicions in Beijing that the United States opposes the reunification of China, preferring that Taiwan remain a separate political entity closely aligned with Washington.

Beijing has periodically used the United States as a pressure point in its efforts to secure the reintegration of Taiwan with the rest of China. In the 1950s, it attacked some of the offshore islands held by the Nationalists, in an attempt to demonstrate to the United States the costs of a commitment to Taiwan's defense. In the 1970s, China insisted that the United States break its diplomatic ties with Taipei as the price for establishing normal relations with Beijing. A few years later, Beijing successfully demanded that Washington agree to reduce its supply of weapons to Taiwan, even while failing to secure explicit American endorsement for its formula for reunification. In each case, China's aim was to weaken American support for Taiwan, increase Taiwan's vulnerability, and therefore force it to accept a reconciliation on Beijing's terms.

If Taiwan was not an issue in Sino-American relations in the months following the Tiananmen crisis, this was partly because of the restraint shown by both sides. The United States did not upgrade its relations with Taiwan as a means of expressing its dissatisfaction with the violation of human rights in China. Nor did Beijing criticize the remaining American links with Taiwan as a way of signaling its displeasure with U.S. sanctions against China. Moreover, the economic and cultural ties across the Taiwan Strait, which had begun to develop rapidly after 1986, continued despite the instability and repression in China. The Taiwan government decided that, because such linkages served to reduce tensions between the two sides, it would be unwise to restrict them in response to the unhappy events on the mainland. Indeed, by early 1991, Taipei was prepared to announce an official formula for national reunification and to outline the process by which it might be realized.[15]

These developments enabled Beijing to conclude, at least for the moment, that the tendency toward national unity was stronger than the trends toward a permanent separation of Taiwan from the mainland. This sense of optimism made it un-

necessary for Chinese leaders to place further pressure on the United States to support Taiwan's reunification with the mainland.

Still, in the years to come, the Taiwan issue could easily reemerge to plague Sino-American relations under either of two circumstances. One would be if the tendencies toward independence appear to be gaining the upper hand over the tendencies toward reunification. This, in turn, could be the result of further turmoil and repression on the mainland, economic difficulties in China's coastal provinces, or troubles in Hong Kong during the transition to Chinese sovereignty in 1997, any of which would make a closer relationship with the mainland much less attractive to political and commercial leaders on Taiwan. It could also occur if the final stages of political reform in Taiwan, scheduled to be completed by the end of 1992, should give rise to more vocal demands for complete independence from the mainland of China.

Another occasion for tensions between Beijing and Washington over Taiwan would be the emergence of a more sympathetic American policy toward the island. As of the middle of 1991, there were a few signs that such a change was occurring. In July, as part of the Bush administration's strategy to prevent Congress from attaching conditions to the renewal of China's most-favored-nation status, the White House announced that it would support Taipei's application to rejoin the General Agreement on Tariffs and Trade (GATT), thus abandoning its earlier policy of waiting for Beijing to join the organization first.

15. For the text of the formula, see *Lien ho pao* [United daily news] (Taipei), 21 Feb. 1991, p. 2, in *FBIS—Chi*, 25 Feb. 1991, pp. 62-63.

Shortly after leaving his post, the former U.S. ambassador to China, James Lilley, paid a visit to Taipei, where he described China's formula for reunification as unrealistic and outdated. The reported sale of Soviet fighters to Beijing renewed speculation that the United States might agree to sell more advanced military aircraft, such as F-16s, to Taiwan.

Either of these two sets of developments would pose a new dilemma for Beijing. In the past, China would almost certainly have chosen to exert diplomatic pressure on Washington in order to discourage any demands for Taiwanese independence or to prevent any upgrading of American relations with Taipei. But recent events have made the United States more resistant to Chinese duress on these issues. The growing American sensitivity to violations of human rights on the Chinese mainland and the mounting respect for the process of democratization under way on Taiwan are removing any residual American sympathy for China's position toward Taiwan. Moreover, China's geopolitical leverage over the United States is now extremely low, thereby reducing the chances that the United States would capitulate to Chinese pressure in order to preserve its overall strategic position.

Under such circumstances, Chinese pressure on the United States, exerted in response to unfavorable developments on Taiwan, might prove to be ineffective or even counterproductive. It would certainly threaten other dimensions of Sino-American relations, such as the economic and scientific ties between the two countries. Moreover, it might

even strengthen, rather than attenuate, the American commitment to the peace and security of Taiwan. Unless China can regain some of its leverage over the United States, it will find it more difficult to use America as an effective pressure point against Taiwan.

CONCLUSION

In essence, the three issues discussed in this article boil down to one overarching dilemma: China's enduring ambivalence toward the United States as the leading Western power of the late twentieth century. On one hand, the United States has often been regarded as a nation that can exercise great military, economic, diplomatic, and cultural influence to pursue its own objectives in China, often to the detriment of China's own national interests. On the other hand, the United States has also been periodically perceived as a country that embodies such attractive values as democracy, justice, and prosperity and that can provide substantial assistance to China's modernization and security.[16]

During most of the Maoist period, Chinese leaders emphasized the ideological and military threat that the United States posed to the Communist revolution in China. Conversely, in the 1970s and 1980s they began to appreciate the opportunities that America presented them as a counterweight to Soviet and Japa-

16. For an overview of this ambivalence in recent times, see David Shambaugh, *Beautiful Imperialist: China Perceives America, 1972-1990* (Princeton, NJ: Princeton University Press, 1991).

nese power and as a source of technology, capital, and markets for China's economic development and reform.

More recent events, however, have once again symbolized the challenges that the United States poses to the Communist leadership in China. The continuing American involvement in Taiwan—along with a growing interest in developments in Hong Kong and Tibet—are regarded in Beijing as further evidence that the United States opposes the unification of China. The American victory in the Persian Gulf, together with the seeming collapse of Soviet power, raises the disturbing possibility that Washington may be closer to achieving its goal of global dominance than at any time since the end of World War II. Finally, the American reaction to the Tiananmen crisis reveals that the United States still seeks to transplant its economic and political system, as well as its cultural values, in China. This is the greatest threat of all, since it would involve the undermining of the Leninist order on which Communist rule in China rests.

Despite the renewed emphasis on the darker portrait of American intentions, the evolution of China's policy toward the United States since the Tiananmen crisis suggests that most Chinese leaders still place greater weight on the opportunities inherent in Sino-American relations. In part, this is the result of their own assessment of the relative costs and benefits of adopting a more hostile or rigid policy toward the United States. But in part, too, it is the consequence of the growing pressure from below—from provincial governments, economic enterprises, academic institutions, and even parts of the central bureaucracy—to maintain cooperative contacts with America.

Given Deng Xiaoping's crucial role in formulating this policy, it is possible that his death will change the way in which China addresses its American dilemma. If a new generation of leaders emerges that is committed to radical political and economic reform, then they will quite likely take a more positive attitude toward the United States than their predecessors. Even so, there would probably be continuing tensions between the two countries over economic issues, particularly if China's export drive persists. One could also anticipate at least moderate differences between Washington and Beijing over international security and environmental issues.

If, as unfortunately is more probable, China remains unstable and repressive in the post-Deng era, then its leaders will probably continue to view the United States with skepticism and ambivalence. The relationship between the two countries will be plagued with persistent tensions over human rights, global and regional issues, and possibly Taiwan. Nevertheless, the aftermath of the Tiananmen crisis suggests that China's policy toward the United States is unlikely to turn completely hostile. The cost to Chinese leaders, in terms of both their international position and their domestic political support, is now too great to allow a complete break with America.

Second Chance in China:
Sino-Soviet Relations in the 1990s

By STEVEN I. LEVINE

ABSTRACT: The normalization of Sino-Soviet relations in 1989 represents an important element in the evolving post-cold-war system of East Asian regional and global politics. Unlike the Sino-Soviet security alliance cum ideological partnership of the 1950s, the new relationship is both pragmatic and limited. The improved security atmosphere is evidenced by mutual force-reduction agreements and the resumption of military exchanges. Border and regional trade are an increasingly important element in the economic relationship, but centralized trade still predominates. Chinese leaders are very disturbed by the weakening of Communist Party control and the erosion of socialist values in the USSR. Political uncertainties in both countries, particularly in the USSR, require us to consider alternative scenarios for the future of Sino-Soviet relations. In any event, the relationship is less central to each country than in the past because of the altered international environment in the Asian-Pacific region.

Steven I. Levine received his B.A. from Brandeis University and his Ph.D. from Harvard University. He has taught at Columbia, the Defense Intelligence College, Duke, and the University of North Carolina. He is currently with Boulder Run Research, Hillsborough, North Carolina. The author of Anvil of Victory: The Communist Revolution in Manchuria *and coeditor of* China's Bitter Victory: The War with Japan, 1937-1945, *he has written widely on Chinese foreign policy.*

DURING the depths of the Sino-Soviet cold war, innocent travelers in Moscow, hoping to satisfy a craving for Chinese food, would venture on occasion into the nearly deserted restaurant of the dilapidated Hotel Peking, a relic from the heyday of Sino-Soviet cooperation. Seated in the cavernous dining room, where supernumerary Soviet waiters slouched in the shadows, the visitors endured the usual interminable delay after ordering. Finally, their own surly waiter would emerge from the kitchen and slam onto the table a trayful of doubtful-looking dishes concocted by Russian chefs who had obviously forgotten most of what they had learned from their long-departed Chinese mentors. It was a difficult time.

On 1 September 1989, a renascent Beijing Restaurant opened in Moscow. One of the first of the new Sino-Soviet joint ventures, this restaurant boasted a staff of Chinese chefs using authentic ingredients and equipment imported from their homeland. Its opening was just one of the innumerable signs that a new era had arrived in Sino-Soviet relations.

The significance of the restoration of amicable relations between China and the Soviet Union has been obscured by the internal upheavals in both countries, particularly in the USSR. Yet the normalization of Sino-Soviet relations in 1989 introduced an important new element into the evolving post-cold-war system of global and East Asian regional politics even as it signified the end of an era of Sino-Soviet conflict. That conflict, which erupted in the early 1960s, shattered the myth of international Communist unity and rewrote the terms of the global strategic equation. In the United States and elsewhere, it gave rise to an approach to foreign policy based on the concept of the strategic triangle that posited the United States, the Soviet Union, and the People's Republic of China as the decisive global actors. The intensity of Sino-Soviet hostility, expressed in the early years in bitter ideological polemics, and later in military confrontations and global geopolitical rivalry, convinced many observers that the conflict was a structural antagonism that would last indefinitely. This turned out not to be so.

Starting in the early 1980s, Soviet and Chinese leaders began to dismantle the costly and unproductive Sino-Soviet cold war.[1] With a minimum of fanfare, they slowly began to construct a new relationship that might prove more durable than the short-lived alliance of the 1950s. Finally, in May 1989, amid the turbulent hopes of China's democracy movement, leaders of the People's Republic of China (PRC) received Soviet President Gorbachev in Beijing for a summit meeting designed, in the words attributed to Deng Xiaoping, to " 'end the past and open up the future.' "[2]

Since that meeting, Sino-Soviet ties have continued to expand significantly in many areas, including economic relations, military and security relations, and cultural ex-

1. See, inter alia, Thomas G. Hart, *Sino-Soviet Relations: The Prospects for Normalization* (Aldershot, Hampshire, England: Gower, 1987).

2. *China Daily*, 17 May 1989, p. 1.

changes. Despite the determination of both sides to avoid the pitfalls of the past, many questions remain about the future of the relationship. The present uncertainty derives not so much from actual or potential disagreements between Moscow and Beijing over such past issues as ideology, foreign policy, security, and development assistance but from something much more fundamental, namely, whether or not China, and even more so the Soviet Union, will survive as centralized Communist party-states.[3] One can envision very different futures for the Sino-Soviet relationship depending on which of various conceivable alternate political scenarios comes to pass in the two countries.

This article comprises three sections. The first briefly reviews the process of Sino-Soviet normalization. The second discusses key developments in the last several years. The final section considers what impact alternate domestic political scenarios in China and the Soviet Union might have on their relationship.

SINO-SOVIET NORMALIZATION

Many contemporary observers were inclined to attribute the Sino-Soviet conflict to long-standing historical enmities, profound civilizational differences, and even racial animosities between the Russians and the Chinese. There was little basis for such views. In fact, the proximate causes of the conflict were the

3. At the time of writing, even the nomenclature of Soviet politics was in question; the names "USSR" and "Soviet Union" seemed likely to disappear.

real ones. Sino-Soviet disagreements over a series of issues concerning authority within the Communist bloc and bloc strategy escalated rapidly in the late 1950s and early 1960s due to the lack of any effective means of conflict resolution within the alliance. Nikita Khrushchev and Mao Zedong, faithful disciples of Lenin at least in this respect, each believed in the need to crush and humiliate his opposite number. That was the fundamental theorem of Communist politics. Until his death in 1976, Mao made opposition to the Soviet Union a touchstone of loyalty among his followers. Soviet leader Leonid Brezhnev was obsessed with the Chinese menace.

China's opposition to Soviet expansionism became the basis for the Sino-American strategic alignment of the 1970s that led to diplomatic relations in 1979 and access to Western markets, technology, investment, and loans. Once these benefits were more or less secured, however, there was less reason for China to continue to tilt so far toward the United States. Beijing's proclamation of an "independent" foreign policy in 1982 signaled Moscow that China was ready to improve relations. For both sides, the conflict between them had become an unnecessary burden, an expensive and ineffective means of pursuing their national security objectives. The program of economic reform and political revitalization that Deng Xiaoping introduced in 1978 downgraded ideology and implicitly acknowledged the dysfunctional character of the conflict with the USSR. The normalization of Sino-Soviet relations became the long-term goal of both sides, although Chinese leaders were as yet unwilling to admit this publicly.

Not wishing to jeopardize its vital connection to the United States, China carefully regulated the pace of Sino-Soviet normalization from 1982 to 1988, engaging in a kind of shuffle-step diplomacy that successfully allayed Washington's latent anxieties. Nonetheless, by the mid-1980s the incremental achievements were already considerable. High-ranking Soviet and Chinese diplomats met regularly to discuss issues of common concern; economic relations again assumed a substantial character, especially in the area of trade as the Soviet Union became China's fifth-ranking trading partner. Cultural, scientific and technological, academic, sports, and other exchanges were resumed. At first the numbers involved were very small, particularly in comparison to the much larger exchanges with the United States, Europe, and Japan, but more important than the numbers themselves was the construction of an institutional infrastructure for the subsequent expansion of Sino-Soviet relations.[4] Modes of cooperation slowly replaced the presuppositions and habits of the era of hostility. Finally, in 1988, by ending the Soviet intervention in Afghanistan, pressuring Vietnam to pull out of Cambodia, and drawing down Soviet troops

from Mongolia, Gorbachev convinced skeptical Chinese leaders that he had abandoned the expansionist policies of his predecessors. The stage was set for the first Sino-Soviet summit meeting in thirty years.

The summit itself turned out to be almost a sideshow to Beijing's swirling democracy of the streets that greeted Gorbachev as a harbinger of democratic change. That the summit produced no diplomatic or other breakthroughs, however, did not matter. Its importance consisted in the very fact that it took place. Gorbachev's meetings with senior Chinese leaders including Deng Xiaoping closed the book on the Sino-Soviet conflict, marking the normalization of state-to-state relations and the restoration of ties between the Soviet and Chinese Communist parties.[5] Since the summit, numerous delegations of visiting Soviet and Chinese government and Party officials at all levels have multiplied the connections between the two countries.

BUILDING THE
NEW RELATIONSHIP

The contemporary international environment within which the new pattern of Sino-Soviet cooperation is unfolding bears little resemblance to the bipolar cold-war world of the earlier Sino-Soviet alliance. At that time, the socialist bloc was a mostly self-contained, alternative international order counterposed to the U.S.-dominated system that both Moscow and Beijing viewed as their historical

4. For a more detailed exposition see Steven I. Levine, "Reprise or Transformation? Some Thoughts on Sino-Soviet Relations in the 1990s," in *The Soviet Union and the Asian-Pacific Region*, ed. Pushpa Thambipillai and Daniel C. Matuszewski, (New York: Praeger, 1989), 50-59.

5. Steven M. Goldstein, "Diplomacy amid Protest: The Sino-Soviet Summit," *Problems of Communism*, 35(5):49-71 (Sept.-Oct. 1989).

enemy. Now the socialist bloc is gone, and the Soviet Union and China are integrated into the world system they once condemned. The 1970s-era world of the strategic triangle, dominated by military security concerns, is also largely a thing of the past. Historical enemies and former ideological adversaries are elaborating new patterns of economic and diplomatic interaction, particularly in the Asian-Pacific region, where Soviet and Chinese interests directly intersect. Regional cooperation to address such issues as trade, development, ecology, arms control, and regional conflict resolution is under active consideration. If the renovated structure of Sino-Soviet relations is to endure, it must conform to these new zoning laws of regional and international politics. The multivalent diplomacy of the 1990s, which requires considerably more flexibility and imagination than that of the past, imposes much less of a burden on any particular bilateral relationship, including that of China and the USSR. But to a like degree it also diminishes the role that any bilateral relationship can play in the overall pattern of relations.

The new Sino-Soviet relationship is grounded in certain broad understandings between the two sides concerning the limits as well as the potentialities of the relationship. Moscow and Beijing have denied any interest in establishing a military alliance and have sworn off engaging in ideological disputes or interfering in each other's internal party affairs.[6] These Three Renunciations, as we

6. *Pravda*, 1 Mar. 1990, p. 5.

may call them, complement the time-honored Five Principles of Peaceful Coexistence, first enunciated by China and India in 1954—mutual respect for sovereignty and territorial integrity, nonaggression, noninterference in each other's internal affairs, equality and mutual benefit, and peaceful coexistence—which were invoked at the Sino-Soviet summit in May 1989 as well as subsequently. More than just diplomatic boilerplate, the Five Principles are an affirmation that the universal norms of international relations must be honored in Sino-Soviet relations as they were not in the past. Together the Five Principles and Three Renunciations constitute a compact for pragmatic coexistence and are an implicit repudiation of the sins of the fathers.

The turbulent events of 1989 sorely tested these new understandings. Democratic voices in the USSR, including most prominently Andrei Sakharov, decried the Chinese army's bloody suppression of the democracy movement.[7] Meanwhile, Soviet conservatives cheered the restoration of order by whatever means necessary. The official Soviet reaction, cued by Gorbachev himself, warily avoided comment on Chinese internal affairs. A senior Soviet scholar explained that this stance correctly reciprocated China's "ex-

7. On the first anniversary of the May 1989 student hunger strike in Beijing, students in 36 Soviet cities staged commemorative hunger strikes of their own. *Komsomolskaya pravda*, 12 May 1990, p. 2, in Foreign Broadcast Information Service, *FBIS Daily Report—Soviet Union* (hereafter cited as *FBIS—SU*), 14 May 1990, p. 27.

ceptional propriety and understanding" with regard to earlier Soviet army killings in Sumgait and Tbilisi.[8] Translated, this seemed to mean, "You shoot your troublemakers when you need to, and we'll shoot ours." Even so, an audible note of skepticism crept into mainstream Soviet reporting from China after Tiananmen. Should Soviet liberals ever manage to come to power, it would not be surprising if Chinese human rights abuses became an issue in Soviet-Chinese relations as they have been periodically in Sino-American relations.

Chinese leaders were soon given their own opportunity to practice the Confucian virtue of self-restraint. Soviet acquiescence to the collapse of communism in East Europe and the subsequent decision to abolish the privileged position of the Communist Party of the Soviet Union (CPSU) in the Soviet Constitution enraged senior leaders of the Chinese Communist Party (CCP), who privately condemned Gorbachev as a revisionist who had betrayed Marxism-Leninism. But they finally decided to refrain from public criticism of the Soviets and concentrate instead on combating ideological heresies within the ranks of the CCP.[9] In December 1989, CCP General Secretary Jiang Zemin told Valentin Falin, the head of the CPSU's International Department,

that China respected the "historic choices" made by the peoples of Eastern Europe.[10]

It was a Hobson's choice. Only a massive Soviet military intervention could have artificially prolonged the life of the dying East European Communist regimes, but given its past condemnations of Soviet military intervention, the PRC could hardly approve of such intervention in 1989. Thus Chinese Communist leaders were reduced to gnashing their teeth but holding their tongues. By the time of Premier Li Peng's visit to Moscow in April 1990, things had been smoothed over a bit, and Gorbachev's subsequent turn to the right raised Chinese hopes that a recognizable version of socialism—that is to say, a neoconservative regime of order—might yet survive in the USSR.

Meanwhile, Chinese democrats, bloodied from their own recent battles, took some comfort from events in the Soviet Union and Eastern Europe, particularly the ignominious execution of China's long-time favorite, Nicolae Ceausescu.[11] Clearly, the old division between "Chinese dogmatists" and "Soviet revisionists"— to use the language of the 1960s' polemics, or "hard-liners" and "reformers" in contemporary parlance—no longer runs along national lines. The increasing complexity of Soviet domestic politics and the almost certain reappearance of a broader political

8. Sergei Goncharov in *Moscow News*, 9 July 1989, p. 6, in *FBIS—SU*, 19 July 1989, p. 18.

9. *South China Morning Post*, 25 Nov. 1989, in Foreign Broadcast Information Service, *FBIS Daily Report—China* (hereafter cited as *FBIS—Chi*), 27 Nov. 1989, p. 7; ibid., 17 Jan. 1990, in *FBIS—Chi*, 20 Jan. 1990, p. 4.

10. Moscow International Service in Mandarin, 23 Dec. 1989, in *FBIS—SU*, 26 Dec. 1989, p. 5.

11. See Liu Binyan, *China's Crisis, China's Hope* (Cambridge, MA: Harvard University Press, 1990).

spectrum in China suggests that we need to think about Sino-Soviet relations in much more differentiated ways than we have hitherto been accustomed to doing. Under the right set of circumstances, persistent political instability, particularly in the adjacent, outlying areas of the USSR and China, may foster the creation of transnational political alliances, based on a variety of common interests. These could play significant roles in Sino-Soviet relations and in domestic politics.

SECURITY RELATIONS

The shadow of war between China and the Soviet Union, which haunted the world for a generation, has all but vanished during the past several years. The resumption of internal commerce and tourism along the lengthy Sino-Soviet border has revived the frontier towns that languished during the cold war. Meanwhile, significant progress has been made to settle the disputed boundary itself. Publicity-shy teams of working-level diplomats, cartographers, and surveyors are methodically providing a technical solution to what many had considered the particularly thorny issue of conflicting national territorial claims.

The normalization of Sino-Soviet security relations conforms to the new patterns of international relations in the Asia-Pacific region referred to earlier in this article and enhances the prospects for multilateral cooperation in resolving regional conflicts and tackling such issues as development and environmental protection. Renewed Sino-Soviet cooper-

ation in the sphere of military technology and arms transfers may, however, increase security concerns among smaller Asian states such as Taiwan.

Substantial, unilateral Chinese and Soviet force reductions in the 1980s lightened the burdens that the swollen military establishments of these countries placed on badly strained economies undergoing reform. These reductions reflected diminished mutual threat perceptions at a time when Soviet-Chinese diplomatic dialogue and economic transactions were intensifying and both countries were becoming increasingly preoccupied with problems of domestic reform. Soviet withdrawal of three-quarters of its 75,000-man ground force from Mongolia in 1989-90 along with air force and armored units responded to a long-standing Chinese demand. At the May 1989 summit in Beijing, the Chinese and Soviets pledged to settle their differences peacefully and refrain from the threat or use of force. In April 1990, Foreign Ministers Eduard Shevardnadze and Qian Qichen signed an agreement to reduce the number of armed forces along the Sino-Soviet border "to the lowest possible level" consistent with normal relations and to transform remaining forces into purely defensive units.[12] The agreement requires that military units slated for reduction be disbanded, and their equipment and installations be destroyed or converted to civilian use. This is an extraordinarily complex business, and negotia-

12. See *Vestnik* (Moscow), June 1990, pp. 25-26.

tions to convert the principles of the agreements into a detailed disarmament schedule are still going on. It will take some time to pare the forces and equipment down to or below the levels that prevailed before the huge military buildup that began in the mid-1960s.[13]

Meanwhile, the Soviet and Chinese military establishments have become reacquainted with each other. The first Chinese military delegation to visit the Soviet Union in thirty years arrived in Moscow in April 1990, and soon after a Soviet delegation visited Beijing. In June, General Liu Huaqing, vice-chairman of the CCP's Central Military Commission and a 1958 graduate of the Voroshilov Naval Academy in Leningrad, met in Moscow with Soviet Defense Minister Yazov and others, mapped out a program of regular military exchanges, and discussed cooperation in the fields of military technology and economy.[14] Thereafter, things moved more quickly than most observers had anticipated.[15] In the

fall of 1990, Moscow agreed to sell China two dozen troop-carrying helicopters suitable for use in such high-altitude climes as Tibet. Earlier, the United States had refused to permit the sale of comparable U.S. helicopters. Around this time, the PRC backed out of a $500 million avionics deal with the United States to upgrade People's Liberation Army fighters and neared agreement with Moscow to purchase advanced Mach-2 Soviet Su-27 jet fighters. This led Taiwan to express fears that PRC deployment of advanced Soviet aircraft could destabilize the military balance in the Taiwan Strait.[16]

The significance of amicable ties between the Chinese and Soviet military establishments extends beyond the realm of military-security affairs into that of domestic politics. The internal political role of the Chinese military has expanded since Tiananmen, and the Soviet army is likewise a key player defending the unified state system against separatists and secessionists. A further escalation of political strife could jeopardize the position of civilian leaders, leaving central and regional military elites as the only forces capable of holding together the fragments of collapsed Communist power. Even without such a scenario, military elites will continue to be significant actors in central and regional politics, pointing to the importance of good relations between senior Soviet and Chinese military leaders.

13. Reviewing changes in the Soviet military, China's army newspaper *Jiefangjun bao* acknowledged that the USSR had adopted a defensive strategy and would henceforth be more cautious in using military force, but it also noted that Soviet forces retained a powerful offensive military capacity. *Jiefangjun bao*, 10 Sept. 1989, p. 4, in *FBIS—Chi*, 26 Sept. 1989, p. 4. Two military establishments that regarded each other as primary adversaries for a generation are not likely to jettison their ingrained attitudes all at once.

14. Moscow International Service in Mandarin, 2 June 1990, in *FBIS—SU*, 4 June 1990, p. 35.

15. See "The Military Implications of Sino-Soviet Relations," in U.S., Congress, Senate, Foreign Relations Committee, Subcommittee on East Asian and Pacific Affairs and Congres-

sional Research Service, *Sino-Soviet Relations after the Summit* (Washington, DC: Government Printing Office, 1990), pp. 76-110.

16. See *Free China Journal* (Taipei), 22 Nov. 1990, p. 5.

In the international arena, neither the Soviet Union nor China, acting individually, can currently hope to balance the dominance of the United States in the early post-cold-war era. Both retain an interest in restraining the resurgence of American power, however, and both may soon discover the utility of coordinating their diplomatic activity in cases where their interests run parallel. Settlement of leftover regional conflicts such as Cambodia and Korea would facilitate such cooperation. Moscow's loss of its East European empire enhances Beijing's appeal as a diplomatic partner. At the same time, the balance-of-power logic that Mao Zedong and Zhou Enlai invoked in aligning China with the United States against the Soviet Union in the 1970s may again make Moscow an attractive partner for Beijing should Washington once more try to play the role of global hegemon. Of course, the international equation is considerably more complicated now than it was twenty years ago. This time around, a Sino-Soviet diplomatic partnership would at most be a limited, informal arrangement between sovereign equals, unlike the unequal alliance of the 1950s.

Even if they are able to coordinate policies in specific cases, Moscow and Beijing will very likely remain rivals for influence in South and Southeast Asia, the Middle East, and elsewhere, tugged in conflicting directions by their long-standing ties to such countries as India, Pakistan, and Vietnam, among others. Moreover, a new dimension has recently been added to this traditional rivalry, namely, competition for international economic resources including financial assistance, foreign investment, and technology.[17]

ECONOMIC RELATIONS

During the 1980s, burgeoning trade eased the way toward the overall normalization of Sino-Soviet relations. From an insignificant $275 million in 1981, total turnover grew to almost $2 billion in 1985, and by 1989 to $3.8 billion, making the Soviet Union China's fifth-ranking trading partner. Even so, Sino-Soviet trade was still only 3.5 percent of China's total foreign trade and only 1 percent of the USSR's. Moreover, by the beginning of the 1990s, the end of the period of double-digit expansion was in sight as staggering Soviet economic problems limited Soviet export capacity, compounding existing problems created by inadequate infrastructure and overregulation. Beginning in 1991, the changeover from settling accounts through barter to using convertible currency may have a negative impact on trade volume.

Three levels of economic relations exist between the USSR and China—central, regional, and border. The vast majority of trade still consists of commodity exchanges arranged on a barter basis through the two central governments. The USSR supplies China with industrial products such as power generators, steel, aircraft, locomotives, and autos in exchange for raw materials including food-

17. See the series of articles on this theme in *Tang-tai* (Hong Kong), 24 Feb., 3 Mar., 10 Mar. 1990, in *FBIS—Chi*, 28 Feb. 1990, pp. 7-8; 7 Mar. 1990, pp. 5-8; 16 Mar. 1990, pp. 6-8.

stuffs, nonferrous metals, and light consumer goods. Beginning in the mid-1980s, long-term trade protocols were worked out and an institutional framework established in the Soviet-Chinese Commission on Economics, Trade, and Scientific and Technological Cooperation, which meets regularly to review progress and identify opportunities for further cooperation.

Although it is true that both the Soviet Union and China must look to Japan and the West for advanced technology and capital to help solve many of their economic problems, this does not mean that there is little they can do for each other. Considerable opportunity exists for Sino-Soviet cooperation in energy, fuels, transportation, agriculture, metallurgy, mineral exploration, aviation, consumer industry, and so forth. In March 1991, China extended a $700 million credit to the USSR for the purchase of surplus Chinese agricultural commodities that are desperately needed in the Soviet Union. At the same time, this signaled China's preference for Gorbachev over his radical opponents.

In 1982, limited border trade was resumed between the Chinese provinces of Heilongjiang and Inner Mongolia and the contiguous Soviet republics. By the late 1980s, several additional Chinese provinces were authorized to engage in this trade. Although border trade still comprises less than 10 percent of total trade turnover, it has been the fastest-growing element.[18] Economic decentralization, particularly with respect

to foreign trade, has enabled local authorities to multiply their cross-border links. In addition to trade, other forms of economic interaction include the export of Chinese contract workers to chronically labor-short eastern Siberia and the Maritime Province, the establishment of various kinds of joint ventures, and the opening of new or expanded rail, road, air, and telecommunications links.[19]

Among the most interesting developments of recent years because of its political as well as its economic significance is the forging of regional economic connections between the increasingly autonomous-minded Soviet republics and Chinese provincial governments. Heilongjiang, on the Chinese side, and the Russian Republic, on the Soviet side, have been particularly active in conducting a kind of subnational diplomacy, often entirely bypassing the center, and establishing direct connections with each other. Furthermore, by virtue of its location and experience, Heilongjiang has established itself as a broker for interior Chinese provinces and municipalities trading with the Soviets. These transnational connections can be seen as elements in broader regional economic patterns, among which the Chinese identify the "Great Northeast Asian Circle"— including the Soviet Far East, Japan,

18. See Sharon E. Ruwart, "Expanding Sino-Soviet Trade," *China Business Review*, 18(2):42-50 (Mar.-Apr. 1991).

19. As of late 1990, approximately 20,000 Chinese workers were engaged in construction, the timber industry, agriculture, and so on in the Soviet Union, and the total demand for such workers was estimated at 200,000. In 1990, the through rail link between Xinjiang and Kazakhstan—first agreed to in 1956 but suspended because of the Sino-Soviet conflict —was completed with the help of a Soviet loan.

Korea, and China's northeastern provinces of Heilongjiang, Jilin, and Liaoning—and the "Great Islamic Circle," composed of Xinjiang, Soviet Central Asia, and the Middle East.[20]

The history of Sino-Russian relations suggests that, under certain circumstances, these transnational economic connections may contribute to the rise of political and military challenges to central authorities who have already been weakened. This is particularly true in border areas such as Xinjiang, where ethnic and religious minorities have resisted political control from the center on more than one occasion.

CULTURAL AND OTHER EXCHANGES

Following the resumption of Sino-Soviet cultural relations in the early to mid-1980s, long-term agreements were signed governing Sino-Soviet exchanges in the areas of culture, education, sports, and science and technology. Compared to China's exchanges with the West and Japan, the scale is still very modest. In 1990, some 900 Chinese exchange students were dispatched to the Soviet Union and 320 Soviet students to China. By 1995, when the number of Chinese exchange students in the Soviet Union is slated to increase to 2000, this will still be a small fraction of the roughly 30-40,000 Chinese students currently in the United States.[21] It is worth noting that many mid-level as well as high-ranking officials in contemporary China were trained in the Soviet Union during the 1950s, including both Premier Li Peng and General Secretary Jiang Zemin. A Chinese Association of Soviet Higher Educational Institution Graduates established in 1989 boasted 2000 members in Beijing alone, including a majority of the heads of major industrial enterprises and numerous government ministers and deputy ministers.[22]

The resumption of Sino-Soviet educational and scientific-technological relations serves after a fashion to revalidate the credentials of the PRC's powerful first-generation technocrats who were threatened by the tidal wave of interest that their successor generations displayed in Western and Japanese technology during the last decade. Those eminent mediocrities, Li Peng and Jiang Zemin, are appropriate representatives of the generation of the 1950s which has apparently held onto the core political values it acquired in that now-distant era.

But times have changed. To the dismay of China's hard-line leaders, "bourgeois liberalism," once a Western contagion, has attained pandemic proportions in the Soviet Union as well. In addition, long before this happened, the unruly weeds of global pop culture had overrun the stately gardens of Soviet socialist culture. One can easily imagine the bewilderment and fury of the generation of Deng Xiaoping, Wang Zhen,

20. See Gaye Christoffersen, "Xinjiang's Open Door Policy in Sino-Soviet Relations," *Pacific Affairs* (in press).

21. Moscow International Service in Mandarin, 6 Aug. 1989, in *FBIS—SU*, 21 Aug. 1989, p. 13; Leo A. Orleans, *Chinese Students in America* (Washington, DC: National Academy Press, 1988).

22. *Pravda, FBIS—SU*, 22 May 1990, p. 13.

Chen Yun, and others as they survey the moonscape of Soviet socialism. Yet for China to adopt the alternative of a North Korean-style isolationism is not only impossible but entirely inappropriate in light of China's present needs.

SOME ALTERNATIVE FUTURES

By way of conclusion, let us consider the potential impact of some alternative domestic political scenarios on the future of Sino-Soviet relations. The question is whether and, if so, how internal political changes in China and/or the Soviet Union would affect the relations between them. Is there any likelihood either that Sino-Soviet relations will relapse into hostility or that the relationship will become much closer than it is now?

The most likely outlook for Sino-Soviet relations over the next five years is more of the same. Within the present carefully constructed framework, we can expect to see the gradual expansion of the kinds of economic, cultural, and military relations already discussed. In both Moscow and Beijing, there appears to be a political consensus regarding the current state of bilateral relations, and no vocal advocates of alternate policies. Perhaps this is because the Sino-Soviet relationship is just not all that important to either side. A recrudescence of the Sino-Soviet conflict seems as unlikely as the possibility of a new Sino-Soviet alliance. If there are currently no pressing issues or active conflicts of interest between the two sides, there are also no compelling reasons for them to transcend the existing boundaries of their

relationship. China and the Soviet Union presently enjoy normal relations.

But these are not normal times. Let us very briefly consider the implications for Sino-Soviet relations of several alternative regime types, all but one involving changes in the USSR: (1) a post-Soviet federation of democratic republics; (2) post-USSR successor regimes; and (3) a post-Communist democratic regime in China.

The first alternative—a post-Soviet federation of democratic republics—envisions the emergence of a large post-Soviet state consisting of Russia, Belorussia, perhaps the Ukraine, and the Central Asian republics in a voluntary federation with a weak central government. The emergence of such a regime would probably have little impact on Sino-Soviet relations. The Russian Republic is already by far the most important partner for China and would continue to be so in this scenario, and China's connections with the Central Asian republics of Kazakhstan, Kirghizia, and so forth would likewise be unaffected. Such a federative republic might be more inclined to pursue relations with Taiwan, however, and this could cause some problems if the PRC chose to object.

The second alternative—post-USSR successor regimes—supposes a more drastic breakup of the USSR than the preceding scenario. China could be expected to establish relations with all of the successor regimes and pursue the various kinds of connections it now has with the USSR. An indeterminate period of Chinese adjustment to the emergent new reality would be required in order not to antagonize the largest of the successor regimes. Only if Siberia and the Maritime Province broke off from Russia to establish a separate state—an extremely remote but not completely impossible scenario—would this seriously affect Sino-Russian relations since new security arrangements would then have to be worked out between China and such a state.

In the unlikely event that a post-Communist democratic regime emerges in China following the passing of the older generation of Communist revolutionaries, China would presumably still remain a unitary state although Tibet might achieve genuine rather than spurious autonomy. Such a regime would be much more likely to accelerate China's full integration into the international system than to seek closer relations with the Soviet Union. In such a regime, the balance of power between the center and the provinces would likely tilt in favor of the latter. Transnational connections between Chinese provinces and adjacent Soviet or post-Soviet political units might then threaten national unity.

Whatever may be the value of such speculative calisthenics, they should not make us lose sight of what has already been accomplished in the real world of Sino-Soviet relations. For the first time in this century, the relations between Russia and China have been established on a balanced and firm footing devoid of excessive expectations, ideological fantasies, or nightmarish perceptions about security threats. Both the Sino-Soviet alliance of the 1950s and the Sino-Soviet conflict of the 1960s and 1970s were destabilizing elements in the international order, contributing to obsessive preoccupation by all parties concerned with security threats, real and imagined. The new Sino-Soviet relationship lacks the drama and excitement of these earlier incarnations, but it contributes to the hope that the conflicts and suspicions of the past can at last be subordinated to the multilateral tasks of prudent development, environmental protection, and long-term security that lie before us.

ANNALS, *AAPSS,* 519, January 1992

China and Japan:
Politics Versus Economics

By ALLEN S. WHITING

ABSTRACT: Sino-Japanese relations suffer from the heritage of Chinese bitterness over Japanese expansionism and aggression. This has put a political burden on economic complementarity that places Japan foremost in China's economic modernization in terms of trade, loans, and aid, and second in investment. In addition to the political burden, the economic interdependence is highly asymmetrical, being far more valuable for China than for Japan. Since the Tiananmen massacre, however, economic pragmatism has prevailed in Beijing as a result of Tokyo's muting its criticism of the event and moving to lift sanctions imposed by the Western industrial capitals. Yet Chinese memory and suspicion, heightened by a dispute over islands in the East China Sea, remain.

Allen S. Whiting is professor of political science and director of the Center for East Asian Studies, University of Arizona. His various works include China Crosses the Yalu; The Chinese Calculus of Deterrence: India and Vietnam; *and, most recently,* China Eyes Japan. *He served with the Department of State, first as director of the Office of Research and Analysis, Far East (1962-66) and then as deputy principal officer in the American Consulate General, Hong Kong (1966-68).*

THE Chinese Communist emphasis on contradictions, derived from Marxism, is well suited to Sino-Japanese relations. The historical heritage of many centuries gives the two peoples a common cultural legacy in Confucian and Buddhist values, art and architecture, and elements of writing, transferred from China to Japan as from teacher to student. But the historical heritage of the half-century from 1894 to 1945 leaves bitter hatred on the Chinese side as a result of repeated suffering from Japanese expansionism and aggression. Salt is rubbed into the wounds of memory as the victor now finds itself dependent on the former enemy for trade, investment, loans and technological modernization. This reversal of roles between teacher and student creates problems for each side, particularly on the Chinese mainland, where Japan's military domination has been succeeded by economic ascendancy, with all that this implies for China's sense of historical superiority.[1]

Beijing's 1950 alliance with Moscow explicitly defined Japan as the threat against which the two Communist capitals united. Twenty years later, Beijing's perceived threat from Moscow prompted it to welcome the Tokyo-Washington alliance to offset growing Soviet power in East Asia. But in the 1980s, as Soviet power waned relative to that of the United States and as Sino-Soviet détente normalized relations with Moscow, Beijing once again voiced concern over prospective Japanese militarism.

Given these past developments, it is understandable that Chinese views of Japan are highly ambivalent, with contradictory postures coexisting simultaneously in public analyses and private policy debates. The pull between economic pragmatism and political prejudice is exacerbated by similar contradictions in Japan, where official generosity, manifest in large loans at low interest rates, combines with unofficial insensitivity to past aggression. As a result, Sino-Japanese relations are less stable and solidly based than objective factors might warrant. Since the Beijing massacre of 4 June 1989, however, they have shown steady improvement, thanks to special handling on both sides. Indeed, Beijing and Tokyo are on better terms than at any point in the twenty years since the resumption of relations in 1972.

ECONOMICS:
PRIORITY OVER POLITICS

Deng Xiaoping's vaunted reputation for economic pragmatism laid the basis for Sino-Japanese relations over most of the past decade. An uneven tripod of trade, loans and aid, and investment supports the basic structure of relations, which has stood the test of political storms over different issues. Aside from Hong Kong, which serves as both an indigenous trading partner and an entrepôt for China's interaction with other countries, Japan consistently ranks first, with roughly one-fifth of

1. For fuller treatment of these aspects, see Allen S. Whiting, *China Eyes Japan* (Berkeley: University of California Press, 1989). Based on extensive interviews in China and Japan during 1986, this study provides detailed analysis of the developments in the years 1982-87 referred to in the present article.

China's total foreign trade. In 1990, the $18.18 billion worth of goods exchanged between the two neighbors left Beijing with a comfortable $5.9 billion surplus.[2] This fell 7.5 percent below the peak level of 1989 as Beijing attacked inflation and an overheated economy, with imports from Japan declining by 28 percent in the process. The past cyclical pattern of the economy suggested that the previous peak level would soon be surpassed, however.

While Japan's importance in Chinese foreign trade has remained consistent, the balance of trade has varied widely, depending on the mainland's import practices. Thus, during much of the 1980s, decentralization and the expansion of consumer purchasing power prompted coastal areas to order massive quantities of automobiles, washing machines, refrigerators, and television sets. The cumulative trade deficit with Japan surpassed $6 billion in 1986 and Beijing's foreign exchange reserves plummeted from $17 billion to $11 billion. This in turn sparked heated demands for Tokyo to remedy the imbalance by opening its market and facilitating Chinese exports, basically to no avail. Only when Beijing clamped down on the profligate importation of consumer goods and limited the availability of foreign ex-

2. Data from customs statistics of the Japanese Ministry of Finance, *China Newsletter*, (Japan External Trade Organization), Mar.-Apr. 1991, no. 91. Discrepancies between Japanese and Chinese figures result from different bases of computation, with further differences in Chinese data between customs calculations and compilations by the State Statistical Bureau.

change, together with improved quality control over export commodities, did trade shift in China's favor.

Sino-Japanese trade is certain to remain important, but its importance is inherently asymmetrical in both quantitative and qualitative terms. On one hand, China has the foodstuffs and natural resources, especially coal and oil, essential to the Japanese economy. It also has a growing market for the aforementioned consumer goods. For its part, Japan has the technology, machinery, chemical products, and steel and other metallic products essential to China's modernization. On the other hand, the China trade is unlikely to surpass 4-5 percent of total Japanese foreign trade, at least in this decade, as compared with Japan's continuing command of roughly one-fifth of the Chinese side. Furthermore, China's commodity exports to Japan—first and foremost, oil—are vulnerable to world price changes while modernization will demand more energy resources, reducing their availability for export. Finally, the limited purchasing power of 1.1 billion consumers will increase only incrementally.

Sino-Japanese trade benefits from many factors in comparison with China's other trading partners. Geographic proximity, seaborne commerce, linguistic complementarity, historical familiarity with local conditions, and the Japanese focus on long-term benefits rather than short-term returns all combine to advantage Tokyo over its competitors worldwide. The asymmetry of need and capability, however, makes unbalanced trade a recurring threat for Beijing as modernization increases demand for imports more quickly than it provides suitable and competitive exports. This in turn may burden the political relationship between the two countries should Beijing try to remedy the problem by pressuring Tokyo as it did in the 1980s.

To provide some control over this situation, the two sides have signed long-term trade agreements, with modest success. The initial agreement of 1978-85, extended for another five years, provided 110 million tons of Chinese oil and 39 million tons of coal.[3] Its original yearly commitment of 13-15 million tons of oil, however, proved unrealistic, to the dismay of Japanese refiners who had invested in special facilities to process the high-paraffin crude from the main wells in northeast China. The new five-year pact signed on 18 December 1990 targets 8.8-9.3 million tons of Chinese crude per annum together with 3.7-5.3 million tons of coal. In return, Japan is to deliver $8 billion in technology, sets of equipment, and construction equipment.[4]

The second leg of the economic tripod, loans and aid, is the strongest, as the Chinese are well aware. As the primary governmental source of such assistance, Tokyo has gone further than any other capital in underwriting Beijing's vast program of modernization. In 1988, Japan offered a five-year loan of 810 billion yen—$5.2-5.6 billion, depending on exchange

rates—for basic infrastructure projects in China. Tokyo suspended implementation of the loan after the June 1989 developments but reopened the window in late 1990 with $350 million, at 2.5 percent with a 30-year payback, for hydroelectric power stations, reservoirs, water-supply facilities, a chemical-fertilizer plant, and highways. In January 1991, Tokyo's minister of finance became the first Japanese cabinet official to visit Beijing since Tiananmen, signaling the mutually perceived importance of financial interaction. He announced that the Japanese Export-Import Bank window was open to China and pledged additional help through the World Bank and the Asian Development Bank. The following month, sources in Tokyo claimed Beijing was asking for another $6 billion loan, over and above the 1988 amount, to develop new oil fields and coal mines.[5] This same request had previously gone to the Export-Import Bank in early 1989 after the bank had provided roughly 1 trillion yen in two five-year untied loans in 1979 and 1984, but the request was shelved after the June events.

Japanese generosity has mixed motivations to which the Chinese are quite sensitive. When the American occupation of Japan ended, Washington forced Tokyo to establish diplomatic relations with the Chinese Nationalist regime that had fled to Taiwan instead of with the newly proclaimed Communist regime. For his part, Chiang Kai-shek renounced reparations from Japan despite the

3. Xinhua in Chinese, 18 Dec. 1990, in Foreign Broadcast Information Service, *FBIS Daily Report—China* (hereafter *FBIS—Chi*), 19 Dec. 1990, p. 8.

4. *FBIS—Chi*, 18 Sept. 1990, pp. 10-11; ibid., 19 Dec. 1990, p. 8.

5. Kyodo in English, 19 Feb. 1991, in *FBIS—Chi*, 19 Feb. 1991, p. 7.

eight years of invasion. Premier Zhou Enlai perforce followed suit in 1972 to facilitate Tokyo's transferring recognition from Taipei to Beijing. Thus, for many older Japanese, a sense of guilt over the death and destruction inflicted on China prompts loans and aid in lieu of reparations. On occasion the Beijing leadership tries to exploit this guilt in calling for trade concessions and long-range investment as recompense for past aggression.

In addition, Tokyo recognizes that loans and grants are likely to benefit Japanese contractors, especially since specific project approval comes through intensive interaction between experts and bureaucrats on both sides. There is no need for formal agreement on this score, an informal understanding implicitly underlying discussion on how and where the money is to be spent. Sometimes this can backfire against the Japanese when a badly designed project aborts, as with the first gigantic steel complex near Shanghai. More frequently, however, it provides an unbeatable advantage against other foreign competitors.

Last but not least, Japanese officials believe China is too large to ignore or isolate. Both publicly and privately they argued against Western sanctions imposed after the Beijing massacre. They felt that sanctions were likely to strengthen Chinese hard-liners and heighten a nationalistic reaction, thereby slowing if not thwarting necessary reforms. Political instability and economic stagnation on the mainland jeopardize a peaceful and prosperous Asia-Pacific region. Given the magnitude of China's economic problems, large loans and generous aid are seen as necessary to modernization, which in turn serves Japan's interest.

So far, the least developed leg of the economic tripod is Japanese investment. The official rationale for loans and aid does not apply to private capital, which is primarily responsive to profit and risk, although it is not wholly insensitive to government policy. Japanese business encounters many of the same obstacles that deter other foreign investors from underwriting large long-term productive enterprises, instead channeling capital to short-term service industries, such as hotels and restaurants, and to electronic assembly plants. China lacks a stable currency, guaranteed access to foreign exchange to purchase equipment and spare parts abroad, and managerial control over the hiring and firing of workers, while being burdened with a labyrinthine bureaucracy rife with corruption. Under these circumstances most Japanese entrepreneurs prefer more promising places in East Asia for large-scale ventures.

This does not negate Japan as a source of capital, as evidenced by the agreement on an investment of $3 billion for 1169 enterprises in China during the first nine months of 1990, of which $2.17 billion was firmly committed.[6] This represented an increase of 30 percent over the same period in 1989, suggesting both the negative impact of the June events and the positive improvement in the

6. *China Daily*, 2 Jan. 1991, in *FBIS—Chi*, 3 Jan. 1991, p. 3.

investment environment resulting from new legislation. Moreover, the double-digit growth of the special economic zones and the 14 cities with special privileges for joint ventures augurs well for continued expansion in this area.

During the last decade, Chinese officials ritualistically berated their Japanese counterparts for the low level and the type of investment, arguing that it should equal the level of trade and be long-term in anticipation of China's potential market. Eventually, this line faded as Tokyo's inability to direct private enterprise sank in and Chinese officials faced up to the problems inhibiting all foreign investment, whether Japanese or other. Ultimately, the degree to which Japanese private capital is available for mainland modernization will depend on the stability of the Beijing regime, its economic reforms, and the relative returns compared with other countries.

One major complaint voiced against Japanese investment behavior has been over the constraints imposed on technology transfer. To the extent that such transfer has been blocked or impeded by Coordinating Committee for Export Controls restrictions aimed at Communist countries, this complaint should fade in time as restrictions disappear with détente between Washington and Moscow. Chinese accusations of Japanese concern over eventual competition curbing technology transfer, however, are well based and are likely to remain a nettlesome, if minor, aspect of economic relations.

POLITICAL COUNTERCURRENTS

Taken in isolation, the economic interaction between China and Japan should provide a solid basis for bonding the two neighbors, "separated by only a narrow strip of water," as proponents of Sino-Japanese friendship ritualistically repeat. Friction is an inevitable part of such interaction, if only as a bargaining tactic. But the twenty-year record since the reestablishment of relations in 1972 shows the degree to which political prejudices and perceptions have repeatedly countered economic compatibility.

Indeed, by the tenth anniversary of the 1978 Sino-Japanese Treaty of Peace and Friendship, the cumulation of Chinese grievances and Japanese responses had brought the relationship to a genuine crisis. Intemperate accusations by Deng Xiaoping in 1987 had provoked a vice-minister of foreign affairs in Tokyo to suggest that Deng was getting senile, the resulting furor forcing the vice-minister's retirement.[7] Then, just when both sides had succeeded in toning down the dispute, the Beijing massacre forced relations even further downward. With poetic license, a prominent Japanese politician summarized the erratic political pattern, "Notwithstanding the windstorms, rainstorms, and other impediments we have encountered on our way, and notwithstanding the landslides we have sometimes run into in

7. For details, see Whiting, *China Eyes Japan*, pp. 157 ff.

our joint effort to scale the huge mountain of Japanese-Chinese friendship, we have always aimed for the peak."[8]

The particular details of individual issues take on importance only within the larger frame of reference within which the Chinese leadership, and to a remarkable extent the Chinese people, view Japan and the Japanese. That frame of reference is fifty years of expansionism and aggression, underscored by the eight-year invasion of 1937-45. "Remembering the past provides a guide to the future," a standard maxim in Chinese writings about Japan, serves to focus old memories and new consciousness on the invasion, with the Nanjing massacre of December 1937 conveying the sharpest image of Japanese brutality. That atrocity, wherein perhaps 300,000 Chinese soldiers and civilians died during six weeks of uncontrolled rape, plunder, and slaughter, has become the touchstone of nationalism on both sides.

Thus, in the fall of 1990, Shintara Ishihara, Tokyo's former minister of transport and coauthor of the celebrated *Japan That Can Say No*, declared in an American magazine interview that the Nanjing massacre "is a lie fabricated by the Chinese." *Renmin ribao*'s rebuttal vividly described how "Japanese invading troops began burning, killing, raping and looting for six weeks. Wherever they went, mountains and rivers were dyed with blood and the sun and

moon turned pale."[9] Lesser levels of reaction follow when Japanese scholars challenge the accuracy of the Chinese casualty count or when Japanese high school textbooks dismiss the event as an "incident" occasioned by "turmoil" or "civilian resistance." The issue won renewed attention in February 1991 with the discovery of a 190-page document in the German archives detailing the massacre on the basis of eyewitness reports at the time. *Liaowang*, a mainline Beijing journal, reprinted the entire report, including graphic accounts of gang rape and killing.[10]

Thus it is no wonder that the Yasukuni Shrine honoring all the fallen Japanese soldiers of history became the focal point of Chinese anger and protests in 1985 when Prime Minister Yasuhiro Nakasone visited it on the fortieth anniversary of the war's end. University students staged anti-Japanese demonstrations in a dozen cities, most prominently in Beijing, inter alia attacking the "second invasion" in allusion to

8. Hideo Dan, in Xinhua Domestic Service, 6 Sept. 1990, in *FBIS—Chi*, 10 Sept. 1990, p. 10.

9. Dong Ming, "Lies Cannot Cover up the Bloodstained Facts," *Renmin ribao*, 19 Oct. 1990, in *FBIS—Chi*, 22 Oct. 1990, pp. 9-10.

10. The Chinese report on the German archives quoted an eyewitness report that "about 20,000 Chinese women were known to be raped and tens of thousands of others killed." A summary account claimed that more than 30,000 corpses floated on the Yangtze River as late as 4 March 1938. These estimates allegedly coincided with findings of the Far Eastern international military tribunal that estimated that "190,000 Chinese were killed or buried alive en masse in addition to 150,000 killed individually." Xinhua in English, 10 Feb. 1991, summarizing a dispatch in *Liaowang* [Outlook], 10 Feb. 1991, in *FBIS—Chi*, 11 Feb. 1991, pp. 15-16.

Tokyo's economic preeminence following its earlier military ascendancy. Although Nakasone subsequently apologized to China along with the other East Asian countries where similar protests emerged, the damage was done. Moreover, continued annual pilgrimages to the Yasukuni Shrine by other cabinet members, albeit unofficial, repeatedly enflamed feelings elsewhere.

In contrast with the continued resurgence of resentment engendered by recalling past aggression, Chinese statements after Tiananmen and its foreign repercussions emphasized appreciation for Tokyo's help in political rehabilitation as well as economic modernization. The change of tone resulted from the lower level of Japanese criticism over the massacre compared with that voiced by Australia, France, Britain, and the United States. This was followed by Tokyo's pressing the Group of Seven at Houston in July 1990 to lift sanctions, exemplified by Japan's reopening the loan window. By 1991, Prime Minister Toshiki Kaifu was ready to visit China, moving ahead of his Western counterparts in restoring exchanges at the highest level. Sino-Japanese discussions reportedly included a historically unprecedented visit by the newly installed Japanese emperor as a prospective celebrant in Beijing for the commemoration of the twentieth anniversary of resumed relations in 1992.

Chinese treatment of the Japanese defense posture and prospects also changed radically from the pre-Tiananmen years. Previously, as might be expected, the sharpest tone of concern had ritualistically come from the military newspaper, *Liberation Army Daily*, portraying budget increases and weapons acquisition in ominous terms. But its detailed analysis of the new five-year program for the Self-Defense Forces (SDF) adopted in December 1990 specifically identified the anticipated air capability "to retaliate against air attacks" and to provide "air defense over important areas." Likewise, naval growth was "to strengthen defense of the surrounding waters" while ground-force improvements were "to stop the enemy from landing." Meanwhile, "logistics takes up the biggest proportion in the budget . . . in order to strengthen the rear line." To be sure, the analysis closed with the standard assertions of Japan's "relentlessly and vigorously" carrying out "its massive arms expansion," despite the world's moving toward détente. But the enumeration of specific weapons systems and their functions belied serious concern while informing the reader far better than had the earlier analyses.[11]

Likewise, the opportunity to voice alarm over Kaifu's various abortive efforts to participate in the multinational coalition against Iraq in 1990-91 was virtually bypassed, except for immediate reaction to proposals for SDF involvement in noncombat roles. Instead, Kaifu was shown to face "double pressures both at home and abroad" that juxtaposed demands from Congress and requests from Bush for "the maximum contribution possible" against resistance from the Ministry of Finance, public

11. Xi Zhihao, "Japan's New Five-Year Arms Expansion Plan," *Jiefangjun bao*, 28 Jan. 1991, in *FBIS—Chi*, 11 Feb. 1991, pp. 16-17.

demonstrations, and opposition parties.[12] Japanese public opinion polls were spelled out, showing an overwhelming majority to be opposed to sending SDF forces overseas in any capacity.[13] Later, a smaller majority opposed using SDF transport planes to ferry Vietnamese refugees out of the Persian Gulf area, and a near majority was against any financial support for the war. Again, as in the military analysis, the final tone was negative, citing conservative pressure to reinterpret the antiwar constitution so as to permit sending troops abroad and noting that the result of such a reinterpretation could only be apprehension among the citizens.[14] But including the poll results provided a more balanced understanding than Chinese readers had received previously.

Another area of exploitable anxiety in China and East Asia is Japan's nuclear weapons future. Contrary to the line of unspecified concern and negative innuendo manifest in pre-Tiananmen media materials, a prominent world-affairs journal bluntly concluded, "We believe Japan will not make such a bad decision" as to develop nuclear weapons. In addition to asserting that Japan's "nationals have always detested atomic war" because of firsthand experience, the au-

thor spelled out that country's vulnerabilities to nuclear retaliation: "a narrow island country . . . void of strategic depth . . . only a very brief warning period against missiles . . . a high density of factories and population." He even calculated the consequences of conventional warheads hitting any of Japan's forty nuclear-energy reactors. Obvious as these points might be, they had gone unmentioned in earlier public analyses.[15]

None of these articles omit the cautionary caveats that once constituted the only line. All cite the steady increase in Japanese defense spending, usually noting that it ranks third in the world without specifying the order of magnitude separating it from the top two superpowers. The caution is justified insofar as it is objectively impossible to predict Japan's military posture ten years hence. Subjectively, however, there is resistance to redefining Japan in wholly favorable terms, resistance that probably varies in intensity within the Chinese leadership, which is similarly divided on other questions of domestic as well as foreign policy. That division cautions editors and writers not to go too far on this sensitive matter, guidance in foreign policy analysis always being close at hand.

This guidance became manifest in late 1990 when a minor tempest threatened relations as a result of conflicting claims to the Senkaku Islands, known in Chinese as Diaoyutai. These uninhabited rocky out-

12. Wang Huimin and Liu Jiangyon, "Japan's Countermeasure for the Gulf War," *Liaowang*, 28 Jan. 1991, in *FBIS—Chi*, 8 Feb. 1991, pp. 7-8.

13. Beijing Xinhua Domestic Service, 10 Nov. 1990, in *FBIS—Chi*, 15 Nov. 1990, p. 14, reported 78 percent opposed and 21 percent in favor.

14. Beijing Domestic Service, 9 Feb. 1991, in *FBIS—Chi*, 11 Feb. 1991, pp. 17-18.

15. Zhou Jihua, "The Trend of Japanese Defense Policy," *Shijie zhishi*, 16 Jan. 1991, in *FBIS—Chi*, 1 Mar. 1991, pp. 16-19.

croppings roughly 100 miles northeast of Taiwan, although claimed by
Beijing and Taipei, have been administered by Tokyo since Washington
handed them over together with Oki-
nawa in the early 1970s. In 1978,
more than 100 mainland fishing boats
sailed around them with signs claiming ownership, but the two sides
agreed to shelve the dispute in favor
of agreement on the Treaty of Peace
and Friendship. The issue had no
immediate importance, but its long-
range significance lay in the islands'
link to the offshore continental shelf
that is believed to have vast oil reserves under the East China Sea.

In September 1990 a right-wing
Japanese group won recognition from
Tokyo that a lighthouse it had built
on one island could be illuminated as
an official beacon. Reports in Taiwan
prompted an official expression of
concern there on 13 October together
with demonstrations mounted in Taipei and Hong Kong. When a Taiwanese group attempted one week later
to place a symbolic sporting-event
torch on the islands, it was repulsed
by a Japanese Maritime Safety
Agency patrol boat and a helicopter.
This triggered a stronger protest
movement in Taiwan and Hong Kong.

From the very outset, however,
Beijing walked a careful line. Authorities reportedly refused permission to
university students, teachers, and
staff who had applied through channels to demonstrate against Japan on
20 October.[16] On 18 October Beijing's
Foreign Ministry spokesman called
on Tokyo to block the lighthouse as a

violation of Chinese sovereignty, reit-
erating this position at his next
weekly press conference.[17] Not until
27 October did Vice Foreign Minister
Qi Huaiyuan belatedly expand on the
protest in "an urgent appointment"
with the Japanese ambassador. Qi
asserted China's "indisputable sovereignty" but recalled that the two
sides had agreed in 1972 to "shelve
the dispute" until a later date. After
protesting both the lighthouse and
the warships blocking Taiwanese
boats, he proposed that the two sides
consult on "shelving the sovereignty,
jointly developing the resources in
the waters around the Diaoyu Islands, and opening the local fishing
resources to the outside world."[18]

The incident coincided in time
with two contrasting developments
pertinent to Sino-Japanese relations.
On one hand, Prime Minister Kaifu
was endeavoring to send SDF personnel to the gulf crisis. On the other
hand, Premier Li Peng was virtually
begging for Japan to expedite resumption of loans. Rather than beat
the media drums over the islands and
link them with the SDF-Gulf proposals as evidence of Japanese militarism or allow anti-Japanese student
demonstrations, the Chinese leadership chose to limit its response to
official protests supplemented with
cooperative proposals. It blocked efforts by National People's Congress
delegates from Hong Kong to have
the issue debated and to force ministerial action on sovereignty. It imposed a news blackout on mainland

16. *Cheng ming* (Hong Kong), 1 Nov. 1990,
in *FBIS—Chi*, 2 Nov. 1990, p. 7.

17. Xinhua in English, 25 Oct. 1990, in
FBIS—Chi, 25 Oct. 1990, p. 1.

18. *Renmin ribao*, overseas ed., 29 Oct.
1990, p. 1, in *FBIS—Chi*, 29 Oct. 1990, pp. 8-9.

media reporting of demonstrations elsewhere and restricted harsh commentary to the Communist press in Hong Kong as necessitated by the local popular reaction.[19] The loans proved forthcoming, but handbills reportedly circulated clandestinely in Beijing were headlined, "We Want the Diaoyu Islands, Not Yen!"[20]

FUTURE PROSPECTS

Developments in 1990-91 juxtaposed the contending economic and political factors that affect Sino-Japanese relations. Beijing's need for Japanese capital, trade, and technology coincided with concern over Tokyo's effort to participate in the gulf war and renewal of the long-dormant Diaoyutai dispute. The two sides successfully placed economics ahead of politics, avoiding acrimonious public exchanges while accelerating high-level visits suspended after Tiananmen.

Nevertheless, behind the professions of harmony, discordant sounds could be heard in both countries. Debate in Tokyo over various gulf war proposals revealed a strong effort to go beyond financial contributions and devise some material involvement for the SDF. This was carefully monitored in Beijing and noted with due concern. Chinese analyses of Japan's expanding role in international affairs depicted it at a crossroads, moving from economic power

to either military or political power. Each trip by Kaifu to the Middle East, South Asia, and Southeast Asia evoked the same query couched in implicitly negative terms: where is Japan heading?[21]

No less an authority than President Yang Shangkun linked the gulf question with the bilateral issue in warning a Japan-China Friendship Association delegation from Tokyo that, should the Diet approve the dispatch of SDF troops overseas, a deep repugnance would develop among the Chinese people. Yang explained that the Chinese will never be able to forget their suffering from previous Japanese aggression and they are anxious that those events will be repeated. He then expressed fear that the territorial dispute might flare up again between the two countries.[22]

The general and the specific issues were linked by more than timing. Japan's interest in the gulf stems from dependence on Middle Eastern oil for nearly 40 percent of its oil imports, which, in turn, provide the major source of energy. As I have noted, the disputed islands are important because ownership offers one basis for claiming access to the continental shelf with projected—but unproven—oil deposits. In due course, both China and Japan will want these deposits to be explored and, if proven economic, exploited. So far, their competing claims have kept for-

19. The long and staunchly nationalistic commentaries in *Ta kung pao* and *Wen wei po* stood in stark contrast to the virtual silence in the mainland press, all presumably with official guidance.

20. *Cheng ming* (Hong Kong), 1 Nov. 1990, in *FBIS—Chi*, 5 Nov. 1990, pp. 7-9.

21. For a summation of the crossroads theory, see Zhang Mengyi, "Chinese and Foreign Scholars Discuss Japan's Development Trend," *Liaowang*, overseas ed., 12 Nov. 1990, in *FBIS—Chi*, 29 Nov. 1990. pp. 9-10.

22. Kyodo in English, 26 Oct. 1990, in *FBIS—Chi*, 26 Oct. 1990, p. 19.

eign oil companies away, and neither country has pressed the matter. But mainland supply is unlikely to keep up with demand, much less continue to serve export needs to earn foreign exchange for technology imports. At some point the dispute may fall from the shelf if it is not taken off and settled by mutual agreement earlier.

Meanwhile, Japan's expanding responsibility in world affairs, urged on it by the United States and by its own newly internationalistic leadership, may include participation in U.N. peacekeeping activity. That in turn will arouse Chinese protests. At a less explicit level, Japan's growing economic ascendancy in the Asia-Pacific region compared with China's peripheral role will increase concern in Beijing. This concern may be mollified somewhat if China is admitted as a full member of the various Pacific cooperation fora that have emerged over the past decade. But this would require Chinese economic reforms to go much further than they are likely to in the near future.

Thus much will depend on how the post-Deng succession evolves. Should economics first, politics second, be the new leadership's prioritization, Sino-Japanese relations will weather whatever storms may arise from nationalism on either side, evidenced in the post-Tiananmen interaction. Hard bargaining will occur as in all such situations, with Tokyo's hand being forced to loosen technology transfer and lower barriers to the domestic market. Beijing will seek to reduce its dependency by diversifying its sources of capital and foreign exchange. But Japan will re-

main prominent in China's economic modernization.

Should a different leadership follow the death of Deng, with politics contending with economics for priority, the relationship will be far more parlous. Each instance of expanded Japanese presence in world affairs will be looked at askance and each nationalistic provocation at home will be reacted to with rebuke. The inevitable upgrading of Japan's military defenses will outpace China's, causing further concern; the exception will be in the nuclear area, which Tokyo has foresworn. As each side extends its air and sea capability, the question of East China Sea ownership and exploitation will become more sensitive. Nationalism is not likely to fade on either side; on the contrary, it is likely to grow in order to bolster the dubious legitimacy of Chinese Communist rule and as a prideful consequence of an expanded Japanese role abroad.

Thus the key question will be how China accommodates to the challenge of asymmetrical interdependence and the primacy of Japan in the Asia-Pacific region. There are psychological and cultural factors in this challenge that go well beyond the question of foreign policy. Nor are they entirely under the command of a leadership in Beijing, as evidenced by the nationwide anti-Japanese demonstrations by university students in 1985. What happens in Japan will be known, if imperfectly, in China regardless of how manipulated the media may be. Aspirations of economic advancement can be frustrated, with a foreign target becoming a scapegoat for releasing anger that otherwise might target the Chinese regime. Japan is a convenient target under the circumstances.

Conventional rhetoric exchanged between officials from both sides claims that good relations between China and Japan are essential for peace and stability in the Asia-Pacific region. Rhetoric aside, relations need not be good, but they cannot be bad if the region is to continue its recent phenomenal economic growth. Seen in this perspective, the islands dispute pinpoints the real challenge for Beijing. Having achieved successive détentes with Washington and Moscow, it cannot do the same with Tokyo so long as a territorial conflict lies on the horizon. During his triumphal tour of Japan in 1978, Deng Xiaoping proclaimed that "perhaps the next generation can handle this matter better." We may soon know if he was right.

ANNALS, *AAPSS,* 519, January 1992

China and Post-Cambodia Southeast Asia: Coping with Success

By ROBERT S. ROSS

ABSTRACT: Throughout the 1980s China's Asia policy aimed to roll back Vietnamese expansionism in Cambodia. Due to the complementarity of Beijing's objective with the interests of the non-Communist Southeast Asian states, it was relatively easy for Beijing to develop cooperative relations with these states. Yet the very success of Chinese diplomacy in the 1980s has undermined Beijing's ability to maintain its regional influence in the 1990s. Now that the strategic aspects of the Cambodia issue have been resolved, the region is concentrating on economic issues, yet China has little economic influence in Southeast Asia and is thus likely to be excluded from the most significant regional negotiations. In this context, China's military capabilities could assume heightened salience, stimulating increased suspicions of Chinese intentions and thus further undermining Beijing's effort to foster a peaceful environment in which to modernize its economy in preparation for the more competitive twenty-first century.

Robert Ross received his Ph.D. in political science from Columbia University. Before joining the Political Science Department at Boston College, he taught at Columbia University and the University of Washington. He is the author of various works on U.S.-China relations and Chinese security policy in Asia, including The Indochina Tangle: China's Vietnam Policy, 1975-1979. *He is currently completing a book on U.S.-China relations since 1971.*

THE Soviet-Vietnamese alliance and the Vietnamese occupation of Cambodia polarized Southeast Asia throughout the 1980s. China opposed the Vietnamese occupation of Cambodia and was the strategic focus of the regional coalition resisting the Soviet-Vietnamese alliance. In this era of heightened threat perception, it was not difficult for Chinese diplomats to devise successful policy. An unyielding hard line against Moscow and Hanoi satisfied Chinese requirements vis-à-vis its adversaries while the strategic imperative encouraged Beijing's regional allies to develop cooperative relations with China. The diplomacy was relatively simple, but it was also successful. By 1989, China had accomplished its strategic objectives in Indochina.

But having won the contest over Indochina, Beijing must now adjust to the challenges of victory. Although it can take satisfaction from current trends in Indochina, Southeast Asia is no longer polarized by security concerns and China's contribution to regional security has diminished. Moreover, the Southeast Asian agenda has shifted from strategic to economic interests that afford Beijing little opportunity to contribute to regional objectives but that play to Japanese strengths. Thus, despite having won in Cambodia, China faces an uncertain future in the post-Cambodia era.

CHINA AND THE COALITION
AGAINST SOVIET-VIETNAMESE
COOPERATION

After failing to prevent Soviet-Vietnamese cooperation in Indochina in the late 1970s, in the 1980s China

successfully rolled back Vietnamese and Soviet influence on its southern periphery by inflicting high costs on their efforts to sustain the status quo. Simultaneously, Beijing focused attention on the members of the Association of Southeast Asian Nations (ASEAN)—Thailand, Malaysia, Singapore, Brunei, Indonesia, and the Philippines—seeking aid in punishing Vietnamese and Soviet expansionism. And while Beijing cooperated with the ASEAN states, it consolidated bilateral relations with these countries. Because China was the crucial component of the anti-Vietnamese coalition, the ASEAN states needed Chinese cooperation, and they tailored their China policies accordingly.

*Rolling back Soviet-
Vietnamese expansion*

On 23 October 1991, representatives of the warring Cambodian factions signed in Paris the Agreement on a Comprehensive Political Settlement of the Cambodian Conflict, formalizing a cease-fire between the parties and the basis for ending the thirteen-year war in Cambodia. The agreement establishes the domestic and international responsibilities of the Supreme National Council (SNC), a coalition group composed of representatives from all the contending groups and led by Prince Norodom Sihanouk. It also calls for a 1993 United Nations-sponsored election in Cambodia to choose the Cambodian leadership that will ultimately replace the SNC.[1] On this basis, representatives

1. See *Agreement on a Comprehensive Political Settlement of the Cambodian Conflict,* especially Section III.

of all of the resistance factions will return to Phnom Penh to work with the Vietnam-supported leadership within the SNC. Although sporadic, low-level fighting may well continue to occur for the foreseeable future, the agreement offers a realistic possibility to establish peace in Cambodia and signifies the end of the conflict among the outside powers, including Vietnam and China, over influence in Cambodia. China has been clearly pleased with the course of events. It hosted key meetings of the Cambodian protagonists, and it warmly welcomed the final agreement.

But in the most important respects, China achieved its strategic objectives in Indochina over two years ago. Diminished Soviet influence in Vietnam was China's major objective, and it held Sino-Soviet détente hostage to Soviet concessions on Indochina. By 1988, the combination of Chinese policy and Soviet domestic difficulties compelled Moscow to apply military and political pressure on Hanoi to withdraw from Cambodia. The most dramatic step was Moscow's failure to support Vietnam during its March 1988 naval clash with China. Moscow's security commitment to Hanoi further deteriorated as it drew down its naval presence in Cam Ranh Bay. It also significantly cut back its economic assistance to Vietnam, undermining Hanoi's ability to wage war in Cambodia, prepare for war against China, and develop its economy.

China not only sought Soviet retrenchment from Vietnam to reduce Soviet encirclement but aimed to promote a Vietnamese withdrawal from Cambodia with a corresponding increase of Chinese influence in a balkanized Indochina—Beijing's second strategic objective. Hanoi could tolerate civil war in Cambodia and a large Chinese military presence on the Sino-Vietnamese border as long as Moscow guaranteed Vietnamese security and paid the bills. But in the context of diminished Soviet military and political presence in Vietnam and reduced Soviet economic aid, Vietnam faced Chinese power in strategic isolation and was compelled to accommodate China's demands. These developments culminated in Hanoi's withdrawal of nearly all of its troops from Cambodia by September 1989.[2]

But for the last two years following the Vietnamese withdrawal from Cambodia, Beijing continued to support the Khmer Rouge, seeking the formal dissolution of the Vietnamese-installed "puppet" Phnom Penh leadership and the transfer of sovereignty to the SNC. This demand reflected China's insistence that Vietnam gain nothing from its 1978 invasion, not even the possession of legal sovereignty by its Phnom Penh allies. China was inflexible, and it was prepared to resist compromise and support the Khmer Rouge indefinitely. The Comprehensive Political Settlement reflects considerable Chinese success. The Phnom Penh government has been legally dissolved and the SNC is recognized as the "unique legitimate body and source of authority in which . . . the sovereignty, independence and unity of Cambodia are

2. This analysis is based on the author's current research project on the role of Cambodia in the politics of Sino-Soviet détente.

enshrined." It will represent Cambodia in the United Nations and in other international organizations. The status of the former Phnom Penh government has been reduced to mere "administrative agencies, bodies and offices." Moreover, the role of the United Nations in Cambodia during the transition period also meets Chinese demands. Not only will it supervise the elections, but it will also assume responsibility for administering key government services, including foreign affairs, defense, finance, public security, and information, thus depriving the Hun Sen leadership of many of the advantages of incumbency. Finally, the agreement does not criticize the odious policies of the Khmer Rouge during the 1975-78 period. On the contrary, it legitimates full Khmer Rouge participation in the new Cambodian government.

China-ASEAN cooperation

As with the situation with China's bilateral Soviet policy, Beijing formulated policy toward the ASEAN countries in the context of Soviet-Vietnamese cooperation. But whereas the Soviet Union was China's adversary, China and the ASEAN states were strategic partners and Chinese interests benefited from the necessity for cooperation.

ASEAN's contribution to the anti-Vietnam coalition primarily consisted of its global diplomacy aimed at imposing on Hanoi and Phnom Penh diplomatic and economic isolation. Given the high standing of the ASEAN states among both developed and developing countries and their relative low interest in Vietnam as compared to China, they played a vital role in undermining Vietnam's economic ability to sustain the war in Cambodia. Thus China benefited immensely from their participation in the anti-Vietnamese coalition.

China's bilateral relations with the separate ASEAN states also benefited from their opposition to the Vietnamese occupation of Cambodia. In the context of strategic cooperation with China, the ASEAN states sought consolidated relations with China. This trend is clear in Sino-Thai relations. Central to Sino-Thai relations has been the common interest in resisting the Vietnamese takeover. Although China's main focus was the Soviet presence on its southern border and Thailand's focus was the Vietnamese military presence on the Thai border, in practice they coordinated their policies to maximize the diplomatic and military pressure on Vietnam.

After Vietnam occupied Cambodia in 1978, Bangkok permitted the Chinese-supported Khmer Rouge and the other anti-Phnom Penh forces to use its territory and it permitted China to transport military goods across its territory to the resistance forces. In return, China replaced the United States as Thailand's primary security partner, offsetting the threat of Vietnamese power, which had now arrived on the Thai border. The deployment of 300,000 Chinese troops on the Vietnamese border and the possibility that Beijing would teach Hanoi a second lesson provided Thailand with sufficient security to resist Vietnam's occupation of Cambodia.

For China, the relationship with Thailand has been more than a convenient partnership against Vietnamese power, however. Beijing sought a long-term strategic relationship with Bangkok to assure China an ongoing voice in affairs on its southern periphery. Central to this effort has been the development of Sino-Thai military relations. Since the early 1980s, Chinese and Thai senior officers have frequently visited each other's countries to consult on mutual concerns. Most recently, Chinese Minister of Defense Qin Jiwei and the commander of the Chinese air force, General Wang Hai, visited Bangkok, and the commander of the Thai Navy Admiral Praphat Kritsanachan visited Beijing. Lower-level exchanges have also occurred. In 1990, a Chinese naval training vessel visited Thailand.[3]

Beijing and Bangkok have also developed an arms-sales relationship. Although Chinese weaponry may be far from the latest in technological capability, it is often well suited to Thai requirements of maintaining domestic stability in its outer regions and along the coastline. Moreover, Beijing has offered such weaponry on friendship terms, far below the international market price. Since 1987, when the two sides opened discussions on arms sales, China has sold Thailand tanks, artillery, and armored personnel carriers. Most recently, China has completed con-

struction on the first of six guided-missile escort vessels it has agreed to build for Thailand.[4]

China has also moved to develop economic relations with Thailand. Sino-Thai trade has expanded and Thai investment in China has increased. Most important, China has become the largest purchaser of Thai rice, at times buying it despite a sufficient domestic supply.

Faced with a perceived intolerable security threat, Bangkok developed a strategic relationship with Beijing as Hanoi's principal adversary. This same strategic complementarity promoted Chinese interest in the other ASEAN states. China particularly benefited from Singapore's intense opposition to the Vietnamese occupation of Cambodia; Chinese and Singapore positions on a political settlement of the civil war are indistinguishable. Hence, despite the absence of Sino-Singapore diplomatic relations prior to late 1990, close political relations developed. Lee Kuan Yew visited Beijing numerous times, and Chinese leaders frequently reciprocated. Singapore has also developed the most extensive economic ties with China of any Southeast Asian country. Central to Singapore's calculation has been the importance of China in the anti-Vietnamese coalition. Indeed, Singapore has pursued good relations with Beijing de-

---

3. Xinhua, 5 Dec. 1990, in Foreign Broadcast Information Service, *FBIS Daily Report—China* (hereafter cited as *FBIS—Chi*), 6 Dec. 1990, p. 5; *Zhong Hua ribao* (Bangkok), 11 Dec. 1990, in *FBIS—Chi*, 13 Dec. 1990, p. 19.

4. *Wen wei po* (Hong Kong), 26 June 1990, in *FBIS—Chi*, 6 July 1990, p. 14; *Zhong Hua ribao* (Bangkok), 11 Dec. 1990, in *FBIS—Chi*, 13 Dec. 1990, p. 19; *Far Eastern Economic Review* (hereafter *FEER*), 8 Dec. 1988; *South China Morning Post*, 19 Nov. 1988, in *FBIS—Chi*, 21 Nov. 1988, p. 34.

spite its reluctance to offend Jakarta, which remained suspicious of Chinese ambitions.

China's relationship with Indonesia has also benefited from the imperative of anti-Vietnamese cooperation. Although Jakarta has consistently perceived China as a challenge to Indonesian regional leadership and has been relatively sympathetic to Vietnamese objectives concerning China, it has soft-pedaled its suspicions in the interest of ASEAN unity. To minimize intra-ASEAN friction, Jakarta has had to acknowledge Thailand's strategic dilemma, the necessity for Vietnam to withdraw completely from Cambodia, and the corresponding importance of cooperation with Beijing. This has compelled Jakarta to adopt a more adversarial position toward Vietnam than might have otherwise been the case. Moreover, it has countenanced developing Sino-Singapore relations, and it moved to develop limited economic ties with Beijing.

Thailand, Singapore, and Indonesia are the ASEAN states most involved in the Cambodian conflict. Nonetheless, China's relationship with all of the ASEAN states has reflected this general trend. In the strategic context of Chinese opposition to both Soviet and Vietnamese power in Southeast Asia as well as of U.S.-China cooperation, there has been a natural tendency for all of the ASEAN states to develop good relations with China. Simply put, the Soviet-Vietnamese advance into Cambodia, while undermining Chinese security vis-à-vis the Soviet Union, enabled China to consolidate relations with the ASEAN states.

DEALING WITH SUCCESS: CHINA AND SOUTHEAST ASIA AFTER CAMBODIA

In the post-Cambodia era, Chinese leaders will make policy in the absence of a Soviet threat on China's southern border. This is surely a major improvement over the era of Soviet "encirclement," and it creates opportunities for advancing Chinese interests. But in the absence of Soviet and Vietnamese expansionism, the ASEAN states no longer need close cooperation with China. Moreover, although China has eliminated many of its traditional diplomatic liabilities in Southeast Asia, in the aftermath of the Cold War the ASEAN states will increasingly focus on economic matters. China will have difficulty adjusting to these developments and may face insurmountable obstacles to maintaining even the status quo.

Emerging Chinese authority in Indochina

In the wake of the Soviet retreat from Indochina, no other state can offset China's considerable power on its periphery. Having first helped to oust the United States and then the Soviet Union from Indochina, for the foreseeable future China will be the dominant military power in the region. This trend was largely responsible for Vietnam's decision to withdraw from Cambodia, and it will determine future developments in Chinese relations with all of the Indochinese states. Not only will China seek improved relations now that it is dealing from strength, but the Indochinese states will have little alternative other than to accommodate themselves to Chinese power.

Hanoi had long sought improved Sino-Vietnamese relations while it occupied Cambodia, but Chinese leaders resisted for fear of encouraging Vietnamese intransigence and undermining the anti-Vietnamese international coalition. Now, however, Sino-Vietnamese détente is taking place on Chinese terms. With increasing Vietnamese strategic isolation and the withdrawal from Cambodia, Beijing is prepared to be flexible. One of the first signs of this changing posture was the curtailment of Chinese military incursions into Vietnamese territory that had required Hanoi to maintain a high state of military preparedness. China also agreed to open the border to trade between local residents. Then, shortly after Vietnam's January 1989 announcement that it would withdraw its troops from Cambodia by September 1989, the Chinese Foreign Ministry received a Vietnamese Foreign Ministry official for the first time since 1978.[5] In late 1990, when Hanoi appeared to have made significant concessions on a Cambodian political settlement, Chinese leaders hosted a Sino-Vietnamese summit in southwest China. Reflecting its recognition of China's developing regional authority, by early 1991 Hanoi had sent six delegations to Beijing while China had sent only one delegation to Hanoi.

China's relationship with Laos has also improved in recent years. Vietnam's preoccupation with domestic economic problems, its troop withdrawal from Laos in 1988, and its lack of Soviet strategic support meant that Vientiane had both the occasion and the need to improve relations with Beijing. Likewise, Beijing, for the first time since the 1970s, saw the opportunity to establish a presence in Laos. In these circumstances, China and Laos began economic exchange along the border and then improved political relations. In October 1989, Chinese leaders welcomed Lao Party Secretary Kaysone Phomivane to Beijing for the first Sino-Lao summit since the 1970s, and in December 1990, Li Peng paid a reciprocal visit to Vientiane. In 1990, the two sides also signed an interim border agreement calling for a joint aerial survey of the boundary. Furthermore, in an apparent contemporary strategic equivalent of Sino-Lao road building in northern Laos in the 1970s, during the 1990s the two sides will cooperate in the development of an airfield in northern Laos.[6]

Sino-Cambodian relations suggest a similar trend. In the aftermath of retrenched Vietnamese power and Hanoi's diminished ability to contribute to Phnom Penh's economic or strategic security, Phnom Penh has the need and opportunity to pursue Cambodia's traditional diplomatic practice of developing cooperative relations with both Beijing and Hanoi. In the current strategic circumstances, only good relations with Beijing can bring peace to Cambodia and permit political stability, regard-

5. See the critical commentary, "A Step Forward," in *Renmin ribao*, 12 Jan. 1989, in *FBIS—Chi*, 12 Jan. 1989, p. 9.

6. Xinhua, 25 Aug. 1990, in *FBIS—Chi*, 27 Aug. 1990, p. 9; Xinhua, 1 Aug. 1990, in *FBIS—Chi*, 2 Aug. 1990, pp. 4-5.

less of the composition of the Cambodian leadership. Hun Sen's willingness to hold the SNC meeting in Beijing under de facto Chinese auspices indicates that this trend may have already begun. Similarly, recent Chinese diplomacy reflects Beijing's confidence in its regional authority and a corresponding willingness to work even with the Vietnamese-installed "puppets" within a coalition leadership. China not only welcomed the SNC, including Hun Sen, to Beijing in July 1991 but also invited Hun Sen to pay a formal three-day official visit to China after the meeting, thus essentially normalizing relations with the Phnom Penh government.

Toward reduced friction in China-ASEAN relations

Thus, in the aftermath of its victory over Soviet-Vietnamese cooperation in Cambodia, Beijing looks forward to the benefits of being the dominant military power in a balkanized Indochina. Nevertheless, the end of China's struggle for secure southern borders will undermine its ability to maintain cooperative relationships with the ASEAN states. In the post-Cambodia era, China is simply less important to the ASEAN states, and they will make policy with less regard for Chinese interests and with less attention to their bilateral relationship with China.

Chinese leaders believe that as the Cold War continues to recede, economic diplomacy will gradually become a dominant form of competition in Southeast Asia. But they also argue that this is a transition era

leading to a more uncertain and complex multipolar regional order in which more intense strategic competition between the great powers is likely and in which the economic and technological bases of power, developed during the contemporary period, will assume increased military significance. To best prepare for such future uncertainties, China must partake in the current political and economic competition. Failure to participate will merely cede regional influence to China's rivals.

Chinese leaders are concerned that as economic diplomacy assumes heightened salience in Southeast Asia, Japanese economic penetration of the region will increase, yielding Tokyo critical political influence. Because of China's deep suspicion of Japanese ambitions and its assumption that Japanese political and economic power will almost inevitably lead to military power, Beijing views this prospect with significant apprehension. One commentator argued that as an "economic superpower," Japan is "vigorously pursuing 'superpower diplomacy', increasing its political influence in the Asia-Pacific region." Another analyst reflected that whereas the U.S. military and economic position in the region is "on the decline," Japan's "economic strength is gaining dramatically," resulting in "enormous political and economic influence on the ASEAN countries." At minimum, Chinese leaders are asking if in the 1990s, Japan, as an "economic superpower," will pursue "economic hegemonism."[7]

7. Wan Guang, "Evolution of the Postwar Asia-Pacific Pattern and Its Prospects in the 1990s," *Liaowang*, overseas ed., 13 Aug. 1990,

In many respects, China enters this post-Cambodia period in a good position. Primarily due to developments within the ASEAN states, the issues of Chinese ties to the illegal Communist parties and the ethnic Chinese in Southeast Asia no longer significantly obstruct relations with the ASEAN states.

Since the 1970s, China has distanced itself from the region's illegal Communist movements so that its relations with these parties would not interfere in official relations. But the major factor leading to the declining relevance of these Communist parties is the host governments' enhanced stability and legitimacy. This trend is particularly clear in Malaysia. Beijing's relationship with the Malay Communist Party (MCP) in the 1950s and 1960s continued to arouse concern in Kuala Lumpur through the 1980s. Then economic development and Thai-Malaysian border cooperation compelled the MCP leadership to concede defeat. In December 1989, the MCP agreed to destroy its weapons, "respect" the laws of Malaysia, and "participate" in

in *FBIS—Chi*, 24 Aug. 1990, pp. 2-3; Lin Xiao, "Shake off the Influence of the Cold War— ASEAN Members Adjust Their Foreign Policies," *Shijie zhishi*, 1 Nov. 1989, in Joint Publications Research Service (hereafter JPRS), *China Report No. 90-012*, 15 Feb. 1990, pp. 4-5; Tao Bingwei, "On the Asia-Pacific Situation in the 1990s," *Guoji wenti yanjiu*, no. 1, Jan. 1990, in *FBIS—Chi*, 14 May 1990, p. 16. Also see, for example, Tian Zhongqing, "The Pattern of International Relationships in the Asia Pacific Region in the 1990s," *Guoji zhanwang*, 8 Feb. 1990, JPRS, *China Report No. 90-040*, 29 May 1990, pp. 6-9. For an in-depth analysis of this problem, see Allen S. Whiting, *China Eyes Japan* (Berkeley: University of California Press, 1989).

economic development. Moreover, the Voice of Malayan Democracy, one of China's last ties to the MCP, ceased operation in January 1990.[8]

Malaysia may be the most dramatic example of the elimination of the diplomatic significance of the illegal Communist parties, but the same trend is evident in Sino-Indonesian relations. China's ties with the Communist Party of Indonesia (CPI) and the CPI's involvement in President Sukarno's anti-military plot in 1965 continued to create suspicion of Chinese intentions in Indonesia into the 1980s. Yet, by the late 1980s, Jakarta had gained sufficient confidence in its domestic security that it no longer feared CPI subversion, regardless of the Party's relationship to Beijing. To reestablish diplomatic relations with Beijing, Jakarta waited 25 years after the break, and nearly 15 years after both the emergence of a moderate Chinese leadership and the opening of relations with China by Malaysia, Thailand, and the Philippines. This reflected the depth of the leadership's concern for stability as well as Jakarta's concern for Beijing's regional aspirations and Suharto's personal reluctance to break established policy.

This trend in the declining importance of the illegal Communist parties is mirrored by the diminished importance of the region's ethnic Chinese.[9] For many years Southeast Asian governments feared that Beijing could manipulate their Chinese

8. Foreign Broadcast Information Service, *Trends*, 18 Jan. 1990, p. 36.

9. I am grateful to Evelyn Colbert for this insight.

populations to undermine security. Although actual Chinese leverage may have been minimal, Beijing worked assiduously to eliminate such suspicions.[10] But similar to the trend concerning illegal Communist parties, the primary source of change was the domestic situation within the ASEAN states.

Beijing's threat through ethnic Chinese appeared strongest in Singapore, a predominantly Chinese state. In Indonesia and Malaysia, ethnic Chinese are in a minority but are a prosperous and economically influential sector of society. Therefore, they are politically suspect and the focus of potentially destabilizing racism. The economic success of the ASEAN states and historical circumstances, however, have done much to alleviate leadership concerns. First, the fruits of modernization have spread throughout the population, gradually minimizing this source of racial tension and the economic influence of the Chinese minority while lessening the attractiveness of the Chinese mainland for Chinese abroad. Second, it has been nearly fifty years since Chinese emigration to Southeast Asia ended. The number of Chinese who were either born in China or whose parents were born there is rapidly diminishing. This trend affects citizenship issues insofar as the majority of Chinese in Southeast Asia now have no claim to Chinese citizenship. This points to the gradual assimilation of ethnic Chinese as their educational and economic outlook is becoming predominantly shaped by the indigenous culture.

The first state to evidence reduced concern over Beijing's manipulation was Singapore, despite its Chinese majority. As the earliest ASEAN state to develop its economy, Singapore has pursued improved relations with Beijing since the early 1980s. It now has the most extensive economic ties with China of any ASEAN state. A similar trend is apparent with Indonesia and Malaysia. In 1990, Jakarta normalized relations, formalized trade, and restored direct air service with China. This reflected Indonesian confidence that expanded trade, political relations, and contact would neither enable Beijing to manipulate the Chinese minority to the regime's disadvantage nor significantly undermine the assimilation of ethnic Chinese.[11] Kuala Lumpur is even further advanced in this direction. Thirteen Sino-Malaysian joint-ventures in China are worth $500 million, while Kuala Lumpur has approved seven such joint-ventures for Malaysia. Moreover, in August 1990 it lifted restrictions on Malaysians wishing to visit China, an important step, given traditional concerns.[12]

These developments have reduced the diplomatic friction between China and the ASEAN states. They also permitted China to normalize relations with Indonesia and Singapore. Indonesia, as the largest and most influ-

---

10. For a discussion of China and Southeast Asia's ethnic Chinese, see Robert S. Ross, "China and the Ethnic Chinese: Political Liability/Economic Asset," in *ASEAN and China: An Evolving Relationship*, ed. Joyce K. Kallgren, Noordin Sopiee, and Soedjati Djiwandono (Berkeley: University of California, Institute for East Asian Studies, 1988).

11. *FEER*, 14 Feb. 1991, p. 55.

12. Ibid., p. 55; Xinhua, 10 Dec. 1990, in *FBIS—Chi*, 11 Dec. 1990, pp. 17-18.

ential of the non-Communist Southeast Asian nations, was a target of Chinese diplomacy throughout the 1970s and 1980s. Beijing promoted cooperative relations, and bilateral trade already reached nearly $800 million in 1989.[13] But Indonesia's reluctance to develop ties with China inhibited its neighbors from doing so. Thus Singapore insisted that it would not establish diplomatic relations with China until Indonesia did. Malaysia, Brunei, and, to a lesser extent, the Philippines, also considered Indonesian suspicion of China in making policy.

Thus Jakarta's normalization of relations was a major contribution to China's regional objectives. President Suharto maintained that it was time to look toward the future rather than dwell on past conflicts and suspicions. He insisted that "it would be unjust and unrealistic if we, who are living in the present . . . should constantly bear the burden inherited from history" and expressed his "hope" that the two countries would "see the reestablishment of the interrupted bonds of friendship and the restoration of positive cooperation."[14] Shortly thereafter, Singapore established diplomatic relations with Beijing. Then, during his December 1990 visit to Kuala Lumpur, Chinese Premier Li Peng heard Malaysian Prime Minister Mahathir affirm that the restoration of diplomatic relations with Indonesia and the establishment of diplomatic relations with Singapore prove that "ASEAN recog-

nizes the role that the PRC can play in affecting the prosperity and stability" of the region.[15] With good reason, a symposium of Chinese international relations experts held by one of Beijing's leading foreign policy institutes concluded that the "major progress" in China's Southeast Asia diplomacy is "an important link" in its efforts "to strive for a benign international environment."[16]

China and the economic diplomacy and security of Southeast Asia

Thus China enters the post-Cambodia era in an improved position. Two traditional liabilities in developing ties with ASEAN states—ethnic Chinese minorities and illegal Communist parties—are becoming less salient. In addition, Sino-Indonesian relations on a new footing promise enhanced bilateral cooperation and greater Chinese access throughout the region.

But having cleared the agenda of earlier issues, China must adjust to new ones. Indeed, for the most part, recent advances merely removed impediments to Chinese policy. Beijing has yet to show that it has the ability to compete in the post-Cambodia era

13. *Renmin ribao*, 2 July 1990, in *FBIS—Chi*, 5 July 1990, pp. 20-21.
14. Xinhua, 7 Aug. 1990, in *FBIS—Chi*, 8 Aug. 1990, pp. 5-6.

15. Xinhua, 10 Dec. 1990, in *FBIS—Chi*, 11 Dec. 1990, pp. 17-18.
16. *Renmin ribao*, 28 Dec. 1990, in *FBIS—Chi*, 7 Jan. 1991, pp. 3-6. The institution was the State Council's Center for International Studies. Also note that normalization of relations with Singapore and Indonesia had the immediate benefit of helping China offset the damage to its relations with the advanced industrial economies caused by the June 1989 Beijing massacre.

as economic policy instruments assume greater prominence. In this respect, the major obstacle to China's participation in the diplomacy of Southeast Asia is its own level of development and its nonmarket economic system.

In the past there was little complementarity between China and the developing countries of Southeast Asia and thus little basis for Chinese economic involvement in the region. In the future, as the ASEAN economies progress, there will be even less basis for cooperation. Chinese analysts correctly note that the impetus for regional cooperation will be the problems associated with competition between developed countries, particularly trade friction.[17] In these circumstances, there will be little incentive for the developed nations to include China in their cooperative ventures. Chinese analysts also recognize, however, that political competition in Southeast Asia will increasingly depend on economic capabilities and China must promote its interests through regional economic diplomacy. They forecast continued growth on the part of all the ASEAN states. In the context of an increased need for cooperation to minimize and resolve competition-based disputes, they stress that international economic institutions will assume growing importance. As one senior analyst pointed out, "In view of the bilateral and multilateral cooperation that is so obviously helpful to everyone's eco-

nomic development, the prospects for economic trade cooperation in the region during the nineties are even broader."[18]

In such circumstances, China may well be excluded from the major diplomatic trends in Southeast Asia. Beijing recognizes that it cannot depend on economic capability to give it a voice and it is therefore reduced to demanding participation in regional institutions. Wang Shu, former director of the Foreign Ministry's Institute of International Studies, reflected this attitude when he defensively asserted that "all countries, large or small, strong or weak, poor or rich, should be equal in economic cooperation in the Pacific region." He remarked that "reaching a consensus is of great significance," that "all countries should consult with one another patiently," and that it would be "inadvisable to force hasty conclusions, still less bully others by dint of their strength." Wang concluded with the observation that China "has always maintained a positive attitude toward economic cooperation in the Pacific" and the warning that "cooperation of this kind will still be incomplete without the participation of China."[19] Despite Wang's insistence that regional cooperation include both the rich and the "poor" (read: China), the reality is that the demand for cooperation comes from the complexities of development and China remains a developing country. Moreover, the ongoing difficulties that ASEAN business firms face in dealing with the

17. See, for example, Tao, "On the Asia-Pacific Situation in the 1990s"; Wang Shu, "On Some Issues Concerning Cooperation in the Pacific Region," *Liaowang*, overseas ed., 30 July 1990, in *FBIS—Chi*, 14 Aug. 1990, pp. 2-4.

18. Tao, "On the Asia-Pacific Situation in the 1990s."

19. Wang, "On Some Issues Concerning Economic Cooperation."

nonmarket economy will continue to obstruct economic interaction for the foreseeable future.[20]

Indeed, economic weakness will likely lead to a reduction of China's influence on its southern periphery. With the war in Cambodia drawing to a close, Thailand can look forward to economic superiority vis-à-vis the Indochinese countries and feel less dependent on Chinese goodwill. At the same time, Tokyo's influence in Bangkok continues to grow as Japanese investment plays an increasingly crucial role in Thai development. In this context, Bangkok's offer to conduct joint naval exercises with Japan must be disconcerting to Chinese leaders, despite the improbability that Japan would even consider naval operations more than 1000 miles beyond the home islands.[21] Similarly, Japanese business firms have been anxious to enter the Vietnamese market, prompting one Chinese analyst to warn of Tokyo's "pronounced interest there." Moreover, despite the U.S.-led trade embargo against Vietnam, Tokyo already has extensive trade with Hanoi, and, now that the war in Cambodia is drawing to a close, economic relations should rapidly improve.[22]

If Beijing expects to participate in the emerging Southeast Asian economic order and provide some balance to Japanese influence in the region, it must reform its own economy. Only reform will both stimulate economic growth and remove the institutional obstacles to developing regional business interest in China. For political reasons, the industrialized Asian countries may meet Beijing's demands that China be admitted to such organizations as Asia-Pacific Economic Cooperation. Chinese participation in such formal institutions will not yield Beijing the political benefits it seeks, however. As Chinese analysts note, the economic disparities in Asia will undermine the effectiveness of regionwide cooperative institutions, and substantial diplomacy will take place in smaller fora comprised of states at similar levels of development.[23] This will exclude China from participating in cooperative measures involving Japan and the ASEAN states.

Thus China's role in Southeast Asia will be determined by the ability of the leadership to reform China's economic system and pro-

20. For a discussion of the problems of non-complementarity and China's nonmarket system, see Chia Siow-yue, "China's Economic Relations with the ASEAN Countries," in *ASEAN and China*, ed. Kallgren, Sopiee, and Djiwandono. For an extensive discussion of Chinese economic relations with the ASEAN countries, see Chia Siow-yue and Cheng Bifan, eds., *ASEAN-China Economic Relations: Trends and Patterns* (Singapore: Institute of Southeast Asian Studies, 1987).

21. On economic relations, see *FEER*, 13 Sept. 1990; on the Thai offer, see ibid., 24 May 1990.

22. Tian, "Pattern of International Relationships," pp. 6-9; Xinhua, 31 July 1991, in *FBIS—Chi*, 1 Aug. 1991, pp. 18-19.

23. See, for example, Shi Min, "Looking Ahead to the Political and Economic Situation for the Asia-Pacific Region during the 1990s," *Liaowang* overseas ed., 29 Jan. 1990, JPRS, *China Report No. 90-028*, 18 Apr. 1990, pp. 1-4. For a discussion of China's interest in joining Asia-Pacific Economic Cooperation and the obstacles to its admittance, see *FEER*, 8 Aug. 1990, pp. 9-10.

mote economic growth. In the aftermath of the Beijing massacre, the ongoing succession crisis and political immobility make this prospect very uncertain. The danger is that, lacking the economic instruments to compete in an increasingly complex world, China will rely on its blunt but nonetheless potentially destabilizing military capabilities to establish its regional presence. Indeed, there is the possibility that China's reliance on military instruments will converge with the territorial dispute over the Spratly Islands, thereby further alienating China from the ASEAN states.

In addition to China, the Philippines, Malaysia, Vietnam, and Taiwan claim the Spratly Islands. During the 1970s and 1980s, China and the ASEAN countries finessed this conflict in the interest of their larger mutual objective of cooperation against the Soviet-Vietnamese alliance. In the post-Cambodia era, however, the necessity for strategic cooperation has diminished and the salience of the territorial dispute has increased. Moreover, now that the ASEAN economies are more developed and their technological abilities have advanced, interest in mining the ocean floor in the vicinity of these islands has increased. Thus, in recent years, the territorial conflict has assumed increased importance in relations between China and the region.

China's approach to this issue is to remain inflexible on its sovereignty claim while promoting joint economic ventures with the other claimants. In August 1990, Li Peng reaffirmed Beijing's interest in joint exploitation and indicated that "after Sino-Vietnamese relations are normalized" in the aftermath of a settlement in Cambodia, China would welcome Vietnamese participation. China has also welcomed Indonesia's effort to organize a regional forum of all claimants, including Vietnam, on the condition that the agenda exclude political issues and focus, for example, on economic concerns. Thus, in July 1991, it sent an unofficial delegation to Bandung to participate in a meeting on the South China Sea.[24]

Nevertheless, Beijing's economic overtures can only go so far toward ameliorating regional suspicions over Chinese territorial claims. Beijing's growing military capability gives it the unique ability to defend and pursue its claims that extend to islands immediately off the shore of Malaysia. In March 1988, Chinese forces easily overwhelmed Vietnamese units to take possession of several Spratly islands. Since then, Beijing has constructed a helicopter landing facility there and a small port capable of receiving small patrol vessels. Small army detachments, some equipped with artillery, have conducted landing exercises on the islands.[25] Moreover, in January 1991, Beijing announced that after three years of training it was formally in-

24. *FEER*, 30 Aug. 1990, p. 11; ibid., 10 Jan. 1991, p. 11; Xinhua, 26 July 1991, in *FBIS—Chi*, 29 July 1991, p. 11.

25. *Jane's Defence Weekly*, 9 June 1990, p. 1156. Also see, for example, Guangdong Provincial Service, 8 Mar. 1989, in *FBIS—Chi*, 9 Mar. 1989, p. 35; Zhongguo Xinwen She, 29 Sept. 1989, in *FBIS—Chi*, 4 Oct. 1989, pp. 27-28; Xinhua, 9 Mar. 1990, in *FBIS—Chi*, 9 Mar. 1990, p. 6; *Dagong bao* (Hong Kong), 14 Mar. 1990, in *FBIS—Chi*, 14 Mar. 1990. pp. 6-7.

corporating the "first ship-based air-craft unit" into its navy, apparently outfitting flat-top vessels to serve as aircraft carriers for helicopters.[26] While these vessels are technologically primitive and have very limited power projection, they expand Beijing's ability to attack enemy vessels in coastal waters, particularly in the vicinity of the disputed Spratlys.

China's military use of the Spratly Islands and the determined expansion of its blue-water naval capability have enhanced its regionwide military reach. It is the burden of Chinese diplomacy to offset the resulting regional apprehensions. Yet China's economic liabilities will undermine the efficacy of its diplomacy, regardless of its cooperative intentions. Thus the sovereignty dispute and naval buildup will continue to arouse apprehension on the part of the ASEAN states, further undermining China's ability to promote cooperative relations with them.

26. *Renmin ribao*, overseas ed., 9 Jan. 1991, in *FBIS—Chi*, 16 Jan. 1991, p. 46; Zhongguo Tongxun She, 10 Jan. 1991, in *FBIS—Chi*, 10 Jan. 1991, pp. 36-37.

CONCLUSION

As a military power in an era of heightened tension, China played a vital role in promoting strategic cooperation. Geography dictates that military capabilities will still matter in Indochina and that Beijing will develop a major role in shaping political relations on its southern border. But in the rest of Southeast Asia, the agenda will focus on economic development and on the corresponding necessity for economic diplomacy. Although China's inherent strength suggests that Southeast Asian nations will avoid conflict, economic capability will determine the relative influence of nations. China has yet to earn a seat at the table, not to mention a vital regional role. In post-Cambodia Southeast Asia, China's future will be determined by Beijing's ability to develop the Chinese economy and thus enhance its ability to participate in the economic diplomacy of Southeast Asia. But in the context of ongoing succession politics and conflict over economic policy, the course of China's development and thus of its role in Southeast Asia remains, at best, uncertain.

ANNALS, *AAPSS*, **519**, January 1992

China and South Asia

By JOHN W. GARVER

ABSTRACT: Sino-Soviet rapprochement and a reevaluation of India's China policy by Rajiv Gandhi in 1987 have produced the most cordial Sino-Indian relations in over thirty years. Both Beijing and New Delhi desire still further improvements in bilateral relations but have been stymied by a paucity of parallel interests and by continuing fundamental conflicts over the territorial issue and China's role in South Asia. Zhou Enlai's 1960 proposal that China accept Indian claims in the eastern Himalayas while India accept China's claims in the region southeast of the Karakoram Pass no longer stands. Beijing now calls for Indian concessions in the east in exchange for Chinese concessions in the west. China also views military relations between itself and South Asian countries as legitimate relations well within the purview of the Five Principles of Peaceful Coexistence. To New Delhi, they constitute unacceptable threats to Indian security. Because of these continuing fundamental tensions and rivalries, China's entente cordiale with Pakistan remains important to Beijing.

John W. Garver is associate professor in the School of International Affairs at Georgia Institute of Technology. His most recent book is Sino-Soviet Relations, 1937-1945: The Diplomacy of Chinese Nationalism *(1988). A survey of Chinese foreign relations will be published by Prentice-Hall in 1992. His current research interests include Chinese relations with South Asia and the impact of German and European unification on China.*

NOTE: The author spent five months in 1990 in Beijing and Islamabad studying China's relations with South Asia under the auspices of the U.S. National Academy of Sciences' Committee on Scholarly Communications with the People's Republic of China and the American Institute of Pakistan Studies. A Library Travel Grant from the Center for Chinese Studies at the University of Michigan also supported this study.

CHINA'S foreign policy decision makers place South Asia in the middle range of importance. For potential challenges to national security, foreign inputs essential to economic development, and broad diplomatic objectives that enhance China's international position, the United States, the Soviet Union, and Japan receive top priority. Latin America, the Middle East, and Africa impinge only indirectly on security, make only marginal contributions to China's economic development, and are at the outer limits of China's ability to project its power, and hence they receive lowest priority.

At the top of the list of Chinese concerns within South Asia are its relations with India, which are currently the best they have been since the 1950s. The improvement traces back to a series of policy decisions made by New Delhi in mid-1987. Prompted by a border confrontation that took the two countries to the brink of war in 1986-87, Prime Minister Rajiv Gandhi personally investigated the relationship and concluded that changes in the level and method of bilateral discussions were in order. Specifically, he decided that talks should be raised from the vice-ministerial to the ministerial, or even prime-ministerial, level. Gandhi also decided to accept China's 1980 proposal that the two countries improve relations in a series of areas, ultimately achieving a normalization of relations, even while continuing to disagree on the complex territorial issue. While not ruling out certain improvements, from 1980 to 1987 New Delhi had insisted that the full normalization of relations could come

only after real progress was made toward the resolution of the territorial issue. In 1987, this approach was quietly dropped.[1]

These adjustments in Indian policy were communicated to China's Vice Foreign Minister Liu Shuqing during the eighth round of bilateral talks in November 1987. They were formally conveyed by Prime Minister Gandhi during his visit to Beijing in December 1988, the first such visit since 1954 and the first summit meeting since Zhou Enlai's ill-fated mission to India in 1960.[2]

A major factor underlying the shift in Indian policy was Sino-Soviet rapprochement. After assuming office in March 1985, Mikhail Gorbachev rapidly reoriented Soviet policy from opposition to improved Sino-Indian relations and support for New Delhi against Beijing, to encouragement of better ties and disengagement from Sino-Indian disputes. This created difficulties for New Delhi. If Sino-Indian relations remained poor, with a higher risk of confrontation, it could no longer count on Soviet support. This was painfully evident in late

1. Regarding the 1987 shifts in Indian policy, see Sujit Dutta, "Sino-Indian Relations: Some Issues," *Strategic Analysis* (New Delhi), 11(11):1239-64 (Feb. 1988); *Far Eastern Economic Review*, 9 Apr. 1987, pp. 39-40; ibid., 7 May 1987, pp. 33-34.

2. The joint communiqué signed at the conclusion of Gandhi's visit is in Beijing Xinhua in English, 23 Dec. 1988, in Foreign Broadcast Information Service, *FBIS Daily Report—China* (hereafter *FBIS—Chi*), 23 Dec. 1988, pp. 10-13. Regarding the visit more generally, see Wang Hongwei, "Chenggong de er fu you chengguo de fangwen" [A successful visit with plenty of results], *Nanya janjiu* [South Asian research] (Beijing), 1989, no. 2, (35), pp. 78-80.

1986, when Moscow took a neutral position in the face of the escalating border confrontation.[3] Thus the Sino-Soviet rapprochement greatly reduced the value of the 1971 Soviet-Indian Treaty of Friendship, which had been a key element of India's China policy. This prompted New Delhi to rethink that policy.

Gandhi's visit to Beijing opened the door to a succession of high-level exchanges. In October 1989, Vice Premier Wu Xueqian paid a week-long visit to New Delhi to discuss bilateral and regional issues; Wu was the first high-ranking Chinese official to visit India since Foreign Minister and Deputy Premier Huang Hua in 1981. The most substantive portion of Wu's visit probably had to do with Nepal, about which I shall say more later. The symbolic import was perhaps even more significant, indicating that both sides were determined to continue the momentum established by the Gandhi-Deng Xiaoping summit.[4]

Foreign Minister Qian Qichen was the next caller, stopping for three days in March 1990 on his way back from a tour of the Middle East. Qian's visit represented a modest Chinese sacrifice of diplomatic protocol for the sake of sustained momentum in Sino-Indian relations. Late in 1989, it was decided that Indian Minister of External Affairs I. K. Gujral would visit China early in April, since the last high-level exchange had been Wu Xueqian's visit to India. Toward the end of December, however, New Delhi informed Beijing that preoccupations with regional affairs prevented Gujral from making the scheduled trip. Beijing then dropped its concern for protocol and solicited an invitation for Qian to visit New Delhi.[5]

Qian's discussions with Gujral were China's first high-level contact with the National Front government that took office after India's November 1989 general elections. Each side emerged from the talks reassured of the desire of the other to continue developing better relations. Qian made a significant concession on Kashmir, and Gujral promised to try to improve India's relations with its neighbors.

One of the major obstacles to improved relations is the paucity of parallel interests. To get around this, broad international issues such as disarmament, the environment, and the New International Economic Order have entered the agenda. This also recalls Chinese proposals of the early 1980s and, earlier, Zhou Enlai's strategy of uniting with India in the 1950s on the Korean War, decolonization, and peace.[6] The current hope is

3. Gorbachev announced the new approach to Sino-Indian relations in his July 1986 Vladivostok speech. Moscow Television Service in Russian, 28 July 1986, in Foreign Broadcast Information Service, FBIS Daily Report—Soviet Union, 29 July 1986, pp. R1-R20. Regarding Soviet policy toward Sino-Indian relations in the immediate pre-Gorbachev period, see Robert Horn, "The Soviet Union and Sino-Indian Relations," Orbis, 26(4):889-906 (Winter 1983).

4. Regarding Wu's visit, see Asian Recorder, 1-7 Jan. 1990, pp. 20938-39; Beijing Xinhua in English, 13 Oct. 1989, in FBIS—Chi, 16 Oct. 1989, p. 7.

5. Far Eastern Economic Review, 15 Mar. 1990, p. 9

6. A fascinating piece providing some insight into the probable origins of this strategy

TABLE 1

SINO-INDIAN CULTURAL EXCHANGES

	1979	1980	1981	1982	1983	1984	1985	1986	1987	1988	1989	1990*
Number of delegations[†]	7	8	13	17	18	17	14	8	5	18	16	20

SOURCES: Compiled from indexes for Foreign Broadcast Information Service, FBIS Daily Report—China, published by Newsbank.

*First 11 months.

[†]Includes delegations of all sorts, excluding exhibitions or activities involving only diplomats resident in-country.

that wider consultation will increase mutual trust and help produce a political climate in which the territorial issue can ultimately be settled.

Beijing and New Delhi have tried to expand trade and economic cooperation but without much success. In 1989, China enjoyed a surplus of $97 million in a total two-way trade with India of $271 million, the latter figure representing only 0.257 percent of China's total trade of $105.3 billion. One of the specific results of Gandhi's 1988 visit was the establishment of a ministerial-level joint committee on economic, scientific, and technological cooperation that met first in New Delhi in September 1989. The two economies, however, are largely competitive rather than complementary. Neither produces much of what the other wants, and both look to the West and Japan for modern technology, machinery, and equipment. Since early 1990, efforts have shifted

is Bei Moueng, "Cong 50 niandai de Zhong Yin quanxi kan Zhou Enlai zongli dui jianli zhanhou guoji zhengzhi xin zhixu de lishixing gongxian" [Viewing Premier Zhou Enlai's historic contribution to founding a postwar new international political order from the standpoint of Sino-Indian relations in the 1950s], Waijio Xueyuan xuebao [Journal of Foreign Affairs College], 1990, no. 1, pp. 6-12.

from trade to joint ventures, investment, and other types of economic cooperation. But here, too, little has resulted. Indian businessmen find few incentives to invest despite Chinese requests.

Cultural exchanges support a steady flow of dance and music groups, athletes, scholars, writers, journalists, and artists. Nonetheless, despite a new exchange program agreed to during Gandhi's visit, the level has remained fairly steady since 1981 (see Table 1). The sharp drop in 1986 and 1987 was due to the border confrontation during that period.

THE TERRITORIAL CONFLICT

Against the somewhat ethereal character of efforts at bilateral cooperation, the problems in Sino-Indian relations are very specific and fundamental: (1) the territorial conflict and (2) China's relations with India's South Asian neighbors.

The territorial conflict remains stalemated. I use the term "territorial conflict" advisedly. Both sides have occasionally attempted to minimize the issue by calling it a boundary conflict. What is involved, however, is not the delimitation or demarcation of a boundary agreed upon in principle—a boundary conflict—but disagreement about fundamental principles involving the disposition of large pieces of land—a territorial conflict. For example, in the eastern sector of the Himalayas, it is not a question of whether the Himalayan crestline runs along this or that ridge but of whether the southern slope of the Himalayan mountains lies in China or India. The bilateral talks that rotated between capitals and that met eight times from December 1981 through November 1987 were replaced during Gandhi's visit by a "joint working group on the border," the first session of which met in Beijing in June and July 1989. The second session was in August and September 1990. The change was cosmetic. The officials handling the negotiations remained largely unchanged. Discussions also remain at the level of general principles. According to diplomatic sources in Beijing, neither side includes cartographers or military specialists, as required for serious delimitation.

Zhou Enlai's famous—but unofficial—offer broached in 1960, whereby China would accept Indian claims in the eastern sector in exchange for Indian acceptance of Chinese claims in Aksai Chin, no longer stands. China still advocates the principle of "mutual compromise," but, since 1986, it has changed its position on who should compromise where. It now insists that the crux of the territorial dispute lies in the eastern sector, where India must make some concessions. China, for its part, is prepared to make a few concessions in the western sector. The Indian side was apparently rather shocked when it realized that Zhou Enlai's presumed offer no longer stood. When pressed on the issue in November 1987, the Chinese side maintained that there was nothing in the record to show that Zhou had made the offer imputed to him by Indian and foreign observers. "Premier Zhou was only talking about ideas, not specific proposals," Liu Shuqing said.[7] Deng Xiaoping had repeated Zhou's 1960 offer on 21 June 1980 in a discussion with Indian journalists, but, again, the proposal was not made formally. Deng's suggestion was not repeated within the context of the talks with the Indian foreign secretary under way in Beijing at the time of Deng's discussion with the Indian journalists.[8]

There are two plausible explanations of this shift in the Chinese approach. The first is that it is a bargaining ploy to disabuse the Indians of their belief that China implicitly accepts the McMahon line and, therefore, is not really giving up anything by accepting Indian claims in this sector. This attitude was exemplified by Minister of External Affairs P. V. Narasimha Rao when he addressed the Lok Sabha in July 1980 regarding Zhou's offer which had been reiterated by Deng the previous month: "The Government of India has never accepted the premise on which it is based, namely that the Chinese side is making a concession in the eastern sector by the giving up of territory which they allege is illegally incorporated into India. Nevertheless, we

7. *Statesman*, 7 June 1986, p. 2; Dutta, "Sino-Indian Relations," pp. 1252-53.

8. *Keesing's Record of Contemporary Events*, 27(43):31153 (1981).

welcome the prospect of the eastern sector being settled without any particular difficulty."[9] In order to puncture this notion, Beijing had to make New Delhi understand that China was quite serious about its claims in the eastern sector. Only then could there be a quid pro quo.

The second explanation of China's shift is that its leaders have rethought the strategic and economic implications of the southern slope of the eastern Himalayas and have begun preparing the basis for the eventual recovery of that "lost territory." According to some prominent Chinese South Asian analysts at the Chinese Academy of Social Sciences, the region is rich in minerals and hydroelectric potential and suitable for agriculture. China's 1.1 billion people cannot afford to abandon this rich tract of land, which was bequeathed to them by their ancestors and brazenly and illegally occupied by the Indian expansionists.

Of course, these two explanations are not necessarily mutually exclusive. It could be that people with both points of view converged to endorse scuttling Zhou's putative 1960 offer.

The unresolved territorial issue remains a fundamental source of instability in Sino-Indian relations. In early 1987, the two countries came to the brink of war when both sides began asserting military control over a remote but strategically located canyon that had been unoccupied since the 1962 war. Each side believed that the other was attempting to impose its will unilaterally, refused to back down, rushed reinforce-

ments to the region, and began diplomatic preparations for possible conflict. Tensions were eventually defused—in large part by the mid-1987 changes in Indian China policy outlined earlier—but the danger of a flare-up remains. The demilitarized buffer zone that separated frontline positions from 1962 to 1985 disappeared during the 1986-87 confrontation, at least in many sensitive areas. During Gandhi's December 1988 visit, the two sides agreed to thin out forces on the border, but the frontline positions remain very close, in some places as close as 10 meters. Communications have been established between local commanders in an effort to avert clashes of patrols and to resolve problems that arise, but the situation remains rife with the danger of miscalculation. Because of this, neither side can rule out the possibility of war even if one imputes the best of intentions to the other. And there are many leaders on both sides who instead impute the most aggressive intentions.

SINO-SRI LANKAN
RELATIONS AND INDIA

Beijing believes that as sovereign independent nations, China and its South Asian neighbors have the just, legitimate right to establish such relations as they see fit. Whether China and Nepal, Sri Lanka, Bangladesh, or Pakistan wish any particular relations is exclusively for them to decide. For India to attempt to dictate or limit those relations is unacceptable. The way Chinese officials and spokesmen formulate this view is that China will continue to develop

9. Ibid.

friendly relations with all the countries in South Asia on the basis of the Five Principles of Peaceful Coexistence. This theme is constantly reiterated in visits to South Asian capitals.

New Delhi views things differently. From its perspective, India's security requires the exclusion of hostile extraregional powers, such as China, from areas adjacent to its borders. India has a legitimate right to defend itself, and this right includes the exclusion of military relations or overly close political relations between China and India's neighbors. If Beijing attempts to establish such a presence in these countries, New Delhi reserves the right to take counteraction to preempt or terminate such threatening advances.

From Beijing's perspective, this attitude is hegemonic. Although Chinese media and spokesmen no longer publicly use that term to characterize Indian actions, privately and in internal publications, it is used, albeit without the polemical stridency of the 1970s. Public criticism of India's efforts to limit China's relations with South Asian countries is low-keyed and oblique, largely because the leadership realizes that direct criticism will fan anti-China sentiments in India. Moreover, it would probably be counterproductive, confirming Indian suspicions and prompting more assertive actions. Nonetheless, Beijing is still critical of what it takes to be India's violations of the Five Principles of Peaceful Coexistence in this regard. In their "frank" and "sincere" private discussions of "regional issues" with Indian representatives, Chinese diplomats convey their objections, or so I was told by well-informed Chinese sources in Beijing.

China's assertion of its right to multidimensional relations with its South Asian neighbors is tempered by a pragmatic realization that if it asserts those rights too vigorously, relations with India will suffer. Throughout the 1980s Beijing understood that, to some degree, it had to choose between thicker relations with the smaller countries of South Asia and better relations with India. Twice in the past several years Beijing has been forced to make this choice, with respect to Sri Lanka and Nepal. In both cases, it chose in favor of Indian ties.

In the late 1970s and early 1980s New Delhi, then under Indira Gandhi, objected to the increasingly close political and diplomatic relations between Beijing and Colombo. New Delhi opposed President Junius R. Jayewardene's initiation of a military relationship with the United States. His growing relations with China and his advocacy of China-backed and Pakistan-backed positions in international forums such as the Non-Aligned Movement further exacerbated Indian apprehensions. Mrs. Gandhi and her advisers saw Colombo drifting toward the Beijing-Islamabad axis with U.S. encouragement and support. They countered this development by, on one hand, granting sanctuary in Tamil Nadu to Sri Lankan Tamil separatists and, on the other hand, mediating between those groups and Colombo.

Chinese support for Colombo was fairly strong in 1984-85 as the Tamil insurgency in Sri Lanka escalated and Indo-Lankan relations deteriorated. Beijing may have perceived its relations with Colombo within the normal gamut of state-to-state relations rather than as support for Sri Lanka. But in the context of the escalating Indo-Lankan conflict, Beijing's words and actions gave Colombo important help. In May 1984, President Jayewardene visited China for talks with President Li Xiannian. In his welcoming banquet speech, Li stressed the Five Principles of Peaceful Coexistence. If those principles were respected, countries with different social systems, such as China and Sri Lanka, could be good friends and neighbors. "But if they are violated, even countries with similar social systems [such as India and Sri Lanka] may come to confrontation." Li also lauded Sri Lanka's nonaligned foreign policy and promised, "The Chinese government and people . . . firmly support its just struggle to safeguard its independence, sovereignty, and territorial integrity."[10]

Beijing's most dramatic support for Sri Lanka came in November 1985, when a 3000-ton guided-missile destroyer and a supply ship, headed by the commander of China's Eastern Fleet, called at Colombo for a "friendly visit." This was only the second call to a foreign port by the Chinese navy; the first came the previous week, when the ships had visited Karachi. This visit occurred in the context of mounting Indo-Lankan tension in the 22-mile-wide Palk Strait, where the Sri Lankan navy tried to stanch the illicit flow of men and weapons from Tamil Nadu. In January, for example, Indian coast guard vessels had seized a Sri Lankan naval patrol boat for interfering with the activities of Indian fishing vessels. It is likely that the connection between the Chinese port call and deteriorating Indo-Lankan relations was spurious. Nonetheless, it heartened the embattled Sri Lankan government, antagonized India, and involved China more deeply in the Indo-Lankan dispute.

Shortly thereafter, Beijing decided to disengage militarily from Sri Lanka. When President Li visited Colombo in March 1986 as part of a five-nation tour, he made verbal declarations similar to those of 1984. In private, however, Li reportedly voiced preference for a political solution to the island's ethnic problems, revealing China's decision to stop supplying arms to the Sri Lankan government.[11] A tally of Sino-Lankan military interactions confirms this disengagement. From 1981 through 1985 at least one annual high-level military exchange occurred between China and Sri Lanka (see Table 2). From 1986 through 1990 there were none.

China continued to maintain normal high-level political contact and to give Sri Lanka low-keyed political support, even as the confrontation escalated in the spring of 1987 after Colombo rejected New Delhi's advice to search for a political solution and instead opted for a military solution to Tamil separatism. *Renmin ribao*'s

10. Beijing Xinhua in English, 21 May 1984, in *FBIS—Chi*, 23 May 1984, p. F5.

11. *Far Eastern Economic Review*, 17 Apr. 1986; Subramanyam Swamy, "Superpower Game in Sri Lanka," *Outlook*, 16-30 June 1986, p. 48.

TABLE 2
CHINESE-LANKAN MILITARY EXCHANGES, 1981-90

1981	June	Sri Lankan army commander to People's Republic of China (PRC)
1982	June	Sri Lankan air force commander to PRC
1983	April	Sri Lankan naval commander to PRC
1984	July	PRC air force commander to Sri Lanka
1985	July	Sri Lankan head of armed forces to PRC
	November	PRC naval squadron visit to Colombo
1986-89		None
1990*		None

SOURCES: Compiled from *FBIS—Chi* indexes published by Newsbank.
*First 11 months.

coverage of events was factual but obliquely signaled criticism of India and sympathy for Sri Lanka. A commonly used technique, for example, was to report Colombo's protests of various Indian actions, but not New Delhi's justifications.[12]

In July 1987, Colombo finally capitulated to New Delhi. It agreed to the introduction of the Indian Peace Keeping Force (IPKF) to maintain civil order, and the two countries exchanged letters spelling out Sri Lanka's security obligations to India. Beijing did not react. It could not very well complain since the Sri Lankan government had itself agreed to India's terms. Beijing's argument was, after all, that countries should be free to handle their own affairs and foreign relations as they see fit. Privately, however, China's leaders were very critical of India's actions. One internal study by the Chinese Academy of Social Sciences, for example, argued that India intervened in Sri Lanka's internal affairs and forced Colombo to sign the various agreements so as to "control" Sri

Lanka and achieve "regional hegemony" in South Asia. "India has continually dreamed of establishing its regional hegemony," the article said. "It carved up Pakistan and created Bangladesh. It annexed Sikkim. It has purchased aircraft carriers. It has done everything to accomplish this objective."[13] But such views were not expressed openly.

China continued to give Sri Lanka low-keyed political support in the conflict over the withdrawal of the IPKF during 1989. For example, a Xinhua dispatch from Colombo in September noted that the two governments were still deadlocked over the issue, with New Delhi demanding the prior devolution of power to the provinces and Colombo "sticking to its demands for the benefit of its sovereignty and territorial integrity." When Sri Lankan Foreign Minister D. B. Wijetunge visited Beijing in April 1989 as his government was preparing to launch its campaign for withdrawal of the IPKF, Prime Min-

12. See *Renmin ribao* [People's daily], 6 May 1987; ibid., 6 June 1987; ibid., 15 June 1987.

13. Zhen Ru, "Si Yin hexieyi yi qi yinxiang" [The Sri Lankan-Indian peace agreement and its influences], *Nanya yu Dongnanya ziliao*, [Materials on South and Southeast Asia] (Chinese Academy of Social Sciences), 1989, no. 28.

ister Li Peng lauded Sino-Lankan friendship and promised to continue to develop relations in the political, economic, and cultural fields. There were the usual statements about the Five Principles of Peaceful Coexistence, but endorsements of Sri Lanka's struggle to protect its sovereignty and territorial integrity were absent.[14]

SINO-NEPALESE RELATIONS AND INDIA

The case of Nepal involved an even more direct clash of Chinese and Indian interests. In March 1988, the North China Industrial Corporation (NORINCO) agreed to sell some $20 million worth of light arms, ammunition, boots and uniforms, and 16 antiaircraft guns to Nepal. The process through which China made this decision is still unclear. It is safe to assume that purely commercial motives governed NORINCO's decision. It is unclear, however, whether NORINCO's decision had higher-level clearance, perhaps by the foreign affairs Small Group of the Central Committee. I have analyzed this problem at length elsewhere and conclude that NORINCO probably did not have higher clearance.[15] Nonetheless, once the issue erupted, Beijing defended it. From its perspective, military relations are part of normal state-to-state relations. A sovereign independent country such

as Nepal has the right to acquire such materials as it deems necessary for its defense, and China has the right to sell such materials. Moreover, the materials sold to Nepal could not in any way be construed as constituting a threat to India, or so Beijing argued.

Again, New Delhi viewed things differently. From New Delhi's perspective, this was an effort to alter the military status quo in the central Himalayas. Those mountains constitute India's northern strategic defense barrier, which China must not breech. The arms sale was the beginning of a process that, if allowed to continue, might lead to just such a result. Moreover, Kathmandu was obligated by the terms of the 1950 Indo-Nepali Treaty of Peace and Friendship, letters exchanged at the time of that treaty, and a further set of letters exchanged in 1965 to purchase arms only from India or from third countries only with India's permission—at least this was New Delhi's interpretation of those documents.[16]

Kathmandu refused to heed India's warnings not to go through with the purchase—India apparently learned of the planned sale as early as December 1987. Nepal also refused to give post hoc guarantees that there would be no further purchases of arms from China and that the weapons already purchased would not be used against India. New Delhi struck hard. It refused to extend the trade and transit treaties that had

14. Beijing Xinhua in English, 30 Apr. 1989, in *FBIS—Chi*, 2 May 1989; Colombo Lankapuvath in English, 2 May 1989, in ibid., 3 May 1989.

15. John W. Garver, "Chinese-Indian Rivalry in Nepal: The Clash over Chinese Arms Sales," *Asian Survey*, in press.

16. The text of the 1950 treaty and ancillary letters is in Raj Kumar Jha, *The Himalayan Kingdoms in Indian Foreign Policy* (Ranchi, Bihar: Maitryee, 1986), pp. 347-50. The gist of the 1965 letters is presented in *Asian Recorder*, 27 Aug.-2 Sept. 1989, pp. 20740-42.

expired in March 1988. When those treaties finally lapsed—after two six-month extensions—in March 1989, it closed down 13 of 15 border-crossing points and instituted a series of other economic sanctions against Nepal. These dealt a severe blow to Nepal's economy.

According to Chinese and Western sources in Beijing, China had quietly told Nepal in late 1988 and early 1989 not to expect it to provide an economic alternative to India, saying geographic and financial constraints on China were too great to permit that. Nonetheless, when the Indian blow fell, Beijing gave modest economic support. In the first months of the blockade, Chinese aircraft ferried some 300 tons of gasoline and kerosene into Kathmandu. By early May, tank-trucks and lorries were delivering fuel and food via the Lhasa-Kathmandu road. China reportedly charged above world-market prices for the oil to compensate for high transportation costs. Several delegations traveled between Lhasa and Kathmandu in an effort to expand trade, and additional passes, mostly mule paths, were opened for local trade. China conspicuously continued with its several aid projects in Nepal, sending State Councillor Chen Junsheng to commission a new sugar plant in Lubimbi in January 1990. A deputy minister of the Ministry of Foreign Economic Relations and Trade (MOFERT) was a member of Chen's delegation. MOFERT head Zheng Tuobin also accompanied Premier Li Peng to Kathmandu in November 1989. During the latter visit, China gave Nepal $13.6 million for new economic projects.

China also gave low-keyed political support. Shortly after the Indian blockade began, a Chinese foreign ministry spokesman expressed concern about the "serious difficulties facing the Nepalese people" and called on Nepal and India to "iron out their differences . . . and resume their normal trade at an early date."[17] He also maintained that landlocked countries were entitled to transit through neighboring countries. China criticized India's actions, albeit obliquely. A Beijing Review article in July 1989, for example, reported, "The key [to the India-Nepal dispute] is that India wants its security interests to take priority in its relations with Nepal, while Nepal persists in keeping relations with India on the basis of mutual respect for sovereignty, equality, and mutual benefit."[18]

China's highest-profile support came in the form of Premier Li Peng's visit in November. Li's tour of Pakistan, Nepal, and Bangladesh that month served multiple domestic and international purposes. Most important for the present inquiry were a wish to demonstrate a continuing determination to remain involved in South Asia and a desire to reassure China's friends in that region that better Sino-Indian relations would not reduce China's ties with them. Thus Li reassured his hosts in Kathmandu, "It has always been China's steadfast policy to develop good-neighbourly and friendly relations

17. Beijing Xinhua in English, 13 Apr. 1989, FBIS—Chi, 13 Apr. 1989, p. 1.

18. Ren Yujun, "Will Nepal-India Relations Improve?" Beijing Review, 24-30 July 1989, pp. 15-16.

with every country in South Asia. No matter what happens in the international situation, China will always support Nepal and other South Asian countries in their efforts to safeguard independence and sovereignty."[19] Li also implied criticism of India, telling a press conference in Kathmandu that China was "concerned" about the situation in South Asia where "some factors" gave rise to "instability." In this regard, China believed that "all countries, big or small, should be treated equally. Problems and disputes should be handled according to the Five Principles of Peaceful Coexistence without resorting to force or other means." Referring specifically to the Indian-Nepal confrontation, Li said that "as a major country in South Asia," India should be "more magnanimous and generous" in handling issues with Nepal.[20]

The victory of the democratic movement in Nepal in April 1990 and the acceptance of India's terms by the new Nepali Congress Party-led government in June represented a major blow to Chinese influence there. In the joint communiqué signed in New Delhi by Indian Prime Minister V. P. Singh and Nepali Prime Minister Krishna Prasad Bhattarai on 10 June, the latter pledged to have "prior consultations with a view to reaching mutual agreement on such defense-related matters which in the view of either country could pose a threat to its security."[21]

19. FBIS—Chi, 20 Nov. 1989, pp. 20-21.
20. Tokyo Koydo in English, 21 Nov. 1989, in FBIS—Chi, 21 Nov. 1989, p. 12.
21. Link (New Delhi), 24 June 1990, p. 6.

Since China's military relationship with Nepal was a major reason for India's economic throttling of Nepal, it is somewhat surprising that Beijing's response was as mild as it was. There seem to be two main reasons for the restraint. One was the desire to sustain the momentum in Sino-Indian relations resulting from Rajiv Gandhi's December 1988 visit. Having invested a decade of diplomatic energy in Sino-Indian rapprochement, Beijing was loath to risk that still-fragile relationship by upholding too forcefully the right to conduct relations with Nepal as it and Kathmandu saw fit. Second, China's domestic upheaval in 1989 and the deterioration of Sino-Western relations after Beijing's bloody repression of that upheaval constrained China's ability to challenge India. Having responded to Western sanctions by stressing its relations with the Third World, Beijing hardly wanted to risk deterioration of relations with India.

China's concerns regarding the nature of India's relations with other South Asian countries were on the agenda of Wu Xueqian's October 1989 and Qian Qichen's March 1990 discussions in New Delhi. These countries were China's close neighbors, Wu said during his public comments. China was endeavoring to develop relations with them on the basis of the Five Principles of Peaceful Coexistence. Regarding relations between India and its neighbors, " 'China sincerely hopes that the South Asian countries will handle their mutual relations in accordance with the Five Principles of Peaceful Coexistence and strengthen their cooperation in a spirit of equality and mutual benefit,'" according to Wu.[22] During his visit, Qian said, "There exists a time-honored friendship between the Chinese people and the peoples of South Asia" and "the improvement and development of Sino-Indian relations will by no means adversely affect the existing friendly relations between China and other South Asian countries."[23] Qian also praised the intentions of the new Indian government to improve its relations with its neighbors. China was "concerned," he said, about stability, peace, and development in the region and hoped that the South Asian countries would "coexist peacefully, treat each other in a friendly manner, and solve each other's [sic] problems through friendly consultations on the basis of the Five Principles of Peaceful Coexistence."[24] Stripped of diplomatic ambiguity, the statements by Wu and Qian meant that China intended to continue developing relations with its South Asian neighbors and hoped India would not resort to coercive measures to prevent this.

THE SINO-PAKISTANI ENTENTE

China's entente cordiale with Pakistan remains extremely important to Beijing. Indeed, its importance may have increased as India has asserted its influence over Sri Lanka and Nepal in recent years. Close relations with Pakistan provide China

22. Beijing Xinhua in English, 13 Oct. 1989, in *FBIS—Chi*, 16 Oct. 1989, p. 7; *Asian Recorder*, 1-7 Jan. 1990, p. 20939.

23. *Asian Recorder*, 30 Apr.-6 May 1990, p. 2126.

24. Xinhua, New Delhi, 23 Mar. 1990.

with literal and metaphorical access to the Middle East and the Islamic world. The Karachi airport is the foreign airport most frequented by Chinese aircraft, often refueling en route to Europe, Africa, the Middle East, South Asia, and even the Americas. Politically, close relations with Pakistan, a Muslim country in good standing with the Islamic world, allows Islamabad to use its good offices to facilitate ties between China and other anti-Communist Islamic countries. For example, Pakistan played a role in the establishment of ties between China and revolutionary Iran in the early 1980s. More recently, Pakistan helped ease the way for the normalization of Chinese-Saudi Arabian ties. Islamabad also helps China burnish its image as an Islamic country, facilitating the journey of Chinese hajji to Mecca and providing scholarships for Chinese Muslims to study at the International Islamic University in Islamabad.

Pakistan also provides China with important political support on a wide range of issues. In the aftermath of the massacre of 4 June 1989, when China's relations with many countries suffered, Islamabad stood by Beijing. Within three weeks, Foreign Secretary Humayun Khan arrived in Beijing for "annual consultations." During Khan's visit, Beijing's ambassador to Islamabad, Tian Ding, declared that China appreciated Pakistan's support in its hour of need. "We shall never forget it," he said.[25] Other Pakistani delegations followed in quick succession. During China's fortieth National Day cele-

25. *Muslim* (Islamabad), 24 June 1989.

brations on 1 October 1989, boycotted by most Western countries, Pakistan was represented by a parliamentary delegation led by the speaker of the National Assembly. Li Peng's visit to Islamabad in November 1989 also demonstrated Pakistan's support for Beijing at this particularly difficult juncture; Pakistan was the first country to receive one of China's top leaders following the Beijing massacre. In Islamabad, Li Peng expressed his gratitude for Pakistan's support: "Prosperity makes friends and adversity tries them . . . At a time when China is suffering some temporary difficulties, we see clearly who are our true friends and who are not."[26] Early in May 1990, it was announced that President Ghulam Ishaq Khan was to be the guest of honor and the only foreign head of state at the Eleventh Asian Games, held in Beijing. Beijing devoted considerable money and energy to these games to demonstrate to the Chinese people that their government and country were not international pariahs.

Mutually beneficial cooperation in the development of modern weapons systems is another component of the entente. The two countries are cooperating in the production of F-7P fighter aircraft at Pakistan's Kamra aeronautical complex. The F-7P involves fitting U.S. General Electric F404 engines and U.S.-designed avionics and fire-control systems in an updated airframe of a MiG-21. This fighter was first deployed by the Pakistani air force in November 1989 and is slated to become Pakistan's main ground-support fighter.[27] They are also working together in the development of a new Main Battle Tank. In June 1990, NORINCO and Pakistan's defense ministry concluded an agreement providing for collaborative efforts to develop a state-of-the-art Main Battle Tank for use in the twenty-first century; the tank is to have increased mobility, lethality, and survivability.[28] Some analysts believe that Pakistan is becoming an important channel for Chinese acquisition of sophisticated military-related technology denied to China by the United States since the 4 June massacre.

The primary and oldest rationale for China's entente with Pakistan also remains active: sustaining Pakistan's power in order to prevent India from concentrating its might against China. Given the reality of Indo-Pakistani suspicion and hostility, a strong Pakistan means that India must keep the bulk of its armed forces deployed on its western borders. Indian defense planners also tend to believe, rightly or wrongly, that in the event of an all-out war between India and China, Pakistan would join on China's side. Thus India must keep guard in the west while dealing with any northern challenge. Were India able to dissolve this two-front threat by subordinating Pakistan, its position against China would be much stronger.

26. *Renmin ribao*, 15 Nov. 1989, p. 4, in *FBIS—Chi*, 21 Nov. 1989, p. 6.

27. Regarding the F-7P collaboration, see *Asian Recorder*, 24-31 Dec. 1989, p. 20934; Aabha Dixit, "Enduring Sino-Pak Relations: The Military Dimension," *Strategic Analysis* (New Delhi), 12(9):988-89 (Dec. 1989); *Nation* (Lahore), 24 Nov. 1989.

28. *Frontier Post*, (Peshawar), 10 June 1990.

Members of China's elite differ in their estimates of India's intentions. But even those who maintain that New Delhi is not fundamentally hostile and that Beijing should be ready to solve the territorial dispute on the basis of minor adjustments insist nonetheless on a position of strength for China. One of the verities of Chinese estimates of India, crossing the entire spectrum of Chinese strategic thinking, is that strength and firmness are necessary to make New Delhi act soberly. Moderate analysts believe it is possible for India and China to agree on an acceptable and mutually beneficial modus vivendi, but that this cannot be achieved by relaxing vigilance or retreating before threats. The modifications of India's China policy following Beijing's firm approach during the 1986-87 border confrontation provided proof of this proposition. Therefore a strong Pakistan friendly to China remains extremely useful. Viewed from a different perspective, if India were to achieve dominance of the vast area between the Hindu Kush and the Mekong River, Mauritius and the Strait of Malacca—which is how some Indian leaders define the natural and historical limits of India's sphere of influence—the potential Indian threat to China would be much greater. If China is to prevent this dominance, Pakistan is perhaps its last and best bet. This is especially true after China's defeat in Nepal and India's victory in Sri Lanka.

Thus Pakistan remains a major recipient of Chinese largess. Between 1956 and 1989 China supplied it with roughly $1.75 billion in soft loans and grants.[29] The most recent installments were a $10 million soft loan extended during Li Peng's November 1989 visit and another $10 million, 30-year loan extended during Defense Minister Qin Qiwu's visit to Pakistan in February 1990. This continuing assistance comes at a time when China has sharply reduced its assistance to other countries.

THE NUCLEAR FACTOR

Nuclear rivalry constitutes an important dimension of the China-India-Pakistan triangle. Indian analysts are often jealous and apprehensive about the world's third-largest nuclear arsenal, which their neighbor to the north possesses. They believe that China's nuclear status is one reason Beijing enjoys greater international status and is taken more seriously by the superpowers than New Delhi. They also fear that China might use nuclear weapons to redress a defeat inflicted by India's superior conventional forces in a war arising from the territorial dispute.[30] China has repeatedly pledged that it would never be the first to use nuclear weapons, implicitly ruling out the use of such weapons against nonnuclear India. Indian analysts tend to discount such pledges. They feel that nuclear weapons would be used

29. Author's discussion with informed Chinese diplomats. The dollar amount was obtained by dividing the renminbi amount, 3 billion yuan, by the 1981 exchange rate.

30. R. R. Subramaniam, "China and India: Conflicting Strategic Perspectives," *Strategic Analysis*, 123(3):233-42 (June 1988); K. Subrahamanyam, "National Security Doctrine for India," ibid., 12(11):1135-46 (Feb. 1990).

THE ANNALS OF THE AMERICAN ACADEMY

in extreme situations where all bets would be off. China's leaders would do whatever they felt necessary to prevail.[31]

To date, such considerations have not been sufficient to persuade India's leaders to build nuclear weapons. Since test-exploding a nuclear device in 1974, India has abstained from producing weapons, although it has continued weapons-related research and has fabricated various bomb components. Two factors underlie India's acceptance of nuclear inferiority vis-à-vis China: (1) the enormous cost of nuclear weapons and the drag they would constitute on India's economic development, and (2) Pakistan. Given the large sums that India has spent on conventional armaments, the latter factor is probably the more important. Were India to go nuclear, Pakistan would follow in short order and a nuclear arms race would result. Aside from this diversion of economic resources, this arms race would vastly increase the destructiveness of a "fourth round" between India and Pakistan. It might also diminish the clear superiority of conventional forces that India has enjoyed over Pakistan since the early 1970s.

Following India's 1974 nuclear test, Pakistan adopted a two-track response to this incipient nuclear threat. On one hand, Islamabad called for a nonnuclear zone in South Asia. On the other hand, it launched a covert nuclear weapons program. China supported both moves. It promptly endorsed the notion of the nuclear-free zone.[32] This stand has been routinely repeated while India has just as routinely rejected it, since it would institutionalize India's nuclear inferiority to China. From the Indian perspective, nuclear arms control and disarmament cannot be considered solely in a South Asian context. China's large nuclear arsenal must also enter the picture.

Pakistan's covert nuclear program centered on construction of a gaseous-uranium-enrichment facility at Kahuta, southeast of Islamabad. This is its only significant source of fissionable material and is reportedly able to produce enough weapons-grade uranium for one to three bombs per year. It was, in part, Pakistani resumption in early 1990 of production of weapons-grade uranium, suspended in the early 1980s, that led the Bush administration not to certify Pakistan's nonnuclear status in October 1990.[33] Foreign assistance for the construction of this facility came primarily from Western firms motivated by commercial concerns.[34]

It is significant that China, which has had gaseous-uranium technology since the late 1960s, did not provide the equipment to build the Kahuta

31. Author's discussions with Indian and U.S. diplomats in Beijing.

32. See Ch'iao Kuan-hua's speech to the 29th session of the United Nations General Assembly, in *Peking Review*, 11 Oct. 1974, pp. 9-16.

33. *Washington Post*, 20 Nov. 1990.

34. U.S., Congress, Senate, Committee on Foreign Relations, *Nuclear Proliferation in South Asia: Containing the Threat*, 100th Cong., 2d sess., Aug. 1988, pp. 4-5; U.S., Congress, Senate, Committee on Governmental Affairs, Subcommittee on Energy, Nuclear Proliferation, and Federal Services, *Nuclear Proliferation: The Situation in Pakistan and India* (hearing), 96th Cong., 1st sess., 1 May 1979, pp. 6, 10.

plant. Yet China has supported the program in other ways. A September 1986 agreement provided Chinese assistance to Pakistan's nuclear energy effort. Under this program, Beijing sold two mini research reactors to Pakistan in November 1989 and February 1990. Also in November 1989, China agreed to sell a 300-megawatt pressurized water nuclear power plant. In August 1990, China agreed to export uranium fuel to Pakistan.[35] While directed primarily toward peaceful uses of nuclear power, all of these moves will have spin-offs for Pakistan's nuclear arms program.

China's support for Pakistan's nuclear effort is rooted in a desire to grant the wishes of an old and valued ally on an issue that Pakistan's leaders deem essential to their vital national interest. More fundamentally, Beijing wants to see Pakistan remain outside India's orbit. As noted earlier, China's overriding strategic interest is to keep Pakistan independent, powerful, and confident enough to present India with a standing two-front threat. In this regard, China's policy may be influenced by its own earlier experience deterring first the United States and then the Soviet Union. China's leaders believe that possession of nuclear weapons was one factor deterring attack by the vastly superior superpowers, and they may have concluded that nuclear weapons are Pakistan's best long-term guarantee of independence from Indian hegemony.

But from India's perspective, Beijing's actions cast grave doubts on Chinese professions of friendship. China's tacit support of Pakistan's nuclear weapons program is tantamount to arming India's enemy. In this regard, it is perhaps significant that in early 1990, India began assisting Vietnam's nuclear research.[36]

SINO-INDIAN RAPPROCHEMENT AND THE SINO-PAKISTAN ENTENTE

Some analysts have argued that with Sino-Indian rapprochement the Sino-Pakistan entente "may become a residual partnership, sustained more by the habits of political ritual than by strategic necessity."[37] China's military disengagement from Sri Lanka circa 1986 and its low-keyed reaction to India's subordination of Nepal in 1989-90 tend to substantiate this hypothesis. It remains to be seen whether Beijing will take a similarly detached approach in the event of an Indo-Pakistan confrontation. What is clear, however, is that Beijing is pursuing two substantially contradictory objectives—maintaining its entente cordiale with Pakistan and improving relations with India—and must make adjustments in pursuit of this balancing act.

The clearest example of balancing came during the Indo-Pakistan confrontation over Kashmir in early 1990. As that crisis escalated, Islamabad pushed its friends, including China, for statements of support,

35. Beijing Xinhua in English, 17 Nov. 1989, in *FBIS—Chi*, 20 Nov. 1989, p. 9; Hong Kong, Zhongguo tongxun she in English, 22 Aug. 1990, in ibid., 23 Aug. 1990, p. 13.

36. *Renmin ribao*, 18 Apr. 1990, p. 4.

37. Steven I. Levine, "China and South Asia," *Strategic Analysis*, 12(10):117 (Jan. 1989).

hoping to build, in this fashion, international pressure on New Delhi to reopen the Kashmir issue. When the crisis erupted, China's position traced back to statements by Deng Xiaoping and Huang Hua in 1980, when China was just beginning its push for better relations with India: Kashmir was a bilateral conflict that would be solved peacefully in accord with the Simla accords of 1972 and the relevant U.N. resolution. In 1980, this formulation represented an important shift away from the "firm support for the just struggle of the Kashmiri people for self-determination" that had typified Chinese pronouncements from 1964 to 1978.[38] Yet it still represented a noticeable tilt toward Pakistan, since mere mention of the U.N. resolutions was anathema to New Delhi and constituted an implicit endorsement of the plebiscite called for by those resolutions. Thus when Prime Minister Benazir Bhutto's special emissary, Iqbal Akhund, called on Chinese leaders in February 1990 to solicit support, Li Peng stated that the Kashmir issue should be resolved peacefully via friendly negotiations "in accord with the relevant U.N. resolutions and accords reached by both countries." Qian Qichen used a similar formulation on the occasion of Akhund's visit.[39]

India was very unhappy with what it took to be China's help for Pakistan's efforts to internationalize the Kashmir issue in violation of the Simla agreement. New Delhi maintains that the Simla agreement supersedes the earlier U.N. resolutions, which are now obsolete and irrelevant. Thus, when Qian Qichen arrived for talks with I. K. Gujral in March 1990, the Indian side argued that talk of U.N. resolutions was tantamount to raising the plebiscite issue and that both U.N. resolutions and plebiscite had been rejected by India.[40] Qian acquiesced, telling reporters that the Kashmir issue should be resolved "via mutual peaceful consultations on the basis of the Five Principles of Peaceful Coexistence"; he did not mention the U.N. resolutions.[41] His only nod to Islamabad came in noting that the issue "has been discussed by the United Nations."[42] Subsequent Chinese pronouncements on Kashmir cited bilateral negotiations and failed to mention the United Nations or its resolutions. A high-ranking Indian diplomat in Beijing told me that New Delhi was satisfied with China's approach. Unlike in the past, China had not sided with Pakistan, he said.

Clearly, Beijing values the recent and still-fragile rapprochement with India and is willing to adjust its relations with other South Asian countries to avoid unnecessary friction with New Delhi. It would probably be wrong to conclude, however, that China has made, or is likely to make, a conscious decision to concede South

38. See Naveed Ahmad, "Sino-Pakistan Relations, 1971-1981," *Pakistan Horizon* (Karachi), 34(3):73 (1981).

39. Beijing Xinhua Hong Kong Service in Chinese, 15 Feb. 1990, in *FBIS—Chi*, 15 Feb. 1990, p. 6; Beijing Xinhua in English, 16 Feb. 1990, in ibid., 16 Feb. 1990, p. 4.

40. *Times of India* (New Delhi), 22 Mar. 1990.

41. Beijing Xinhua in English, 22 Mar. 1990, in *FBIS—Chi*, 23 Mar. 1990, p. 4.

42. Xinhua, New Delhi, 23 Mar. 1990.

Asia as an Indian sphere of influence. Such a move would spell the virtual end to Chinese aspirations of being the leading Asian power and would greatly weaken China's position against Indian power. What is more likely is that there will be continual maneuvering between China and India for power and influence in South Asia, but with both sides attempting to keep this rivalry from taking the two countries back to the era of open confrontation.

ANNALS, *AAPSS*, **519**, January 1992

China and the
Middle East since Tiananmen

By YITZHAK SHICHOR

ABSTRACT: By the late 1980s, the Middle East had become a solid base of operations for China's foreign policy in political, economic, and military terms. Put to the test of the Tiananmen massacre, the reliability of this base remained unshaken while China was trying to break through the Western-imposed isolation, paving the way for an eventual international rehabilitation. This was made possible following Iraq's violent annexation of Kuwait. China used the Persian Gulf crisis to restore its position as a great power whose cooperation is essential for settling outstanding regional problems all over the world. Consequently, China's strained relations with the West in general and the United States in particular have been gradually improving. At the same time, by insisting on a peaceful solution to the crisis, China has managed to maintain its image as the true representative of the Third World, having easy access to all parties concerned, friends and foes alike.

Yitzhak Shichor is dean of students and senior lecturer in political science and East Asian studies at the Hebrew University of Jerusalem. Formerly executive director of the Harry S Truman Research Institute for the Advancement of Peace, he holds a Ph.D. from the London School of Economics and Political Science and has written extensively on Beijing's relations with the Middle East and the international aspects of its defense modernization.

BY the eve of the Tiananmen incident, the Middle East had assumed increased importance for Beijing's foreign policy in three intertwined spheres. Politically, it had provided the People's Republic of China (PRC) with ample opportunities to take an active part in settling outstanding regional problems and thereby play a greater role in international politics. Economically, the Middle East had swallowed a significant slice of China's export of civilian goods and labor, while providing funds for investment and loans, thereby helping reduce the recurrent deficit in the Chinese balance of payments. Militarily, Middle Eastern governments had become the largest customers for Chinese arms and military equipment. Returns from these sales, in the form of unprecedented amounts of precious hard currency, accessibility to advanced technologies and intelligence, and experience gained under battlefield conditions, have been extensively used in the PRC's defense modernization.

After three decades of self-imposed isolation and reluctance to involve themselves in Middle Eastern affairs, China's leaders finally decided to take initial steps, not only in words but also in deeds, to start climbing the ladder as an upcoming great power. By the late 1980s, the PRC had apparently become a legitimate and respectable participant in the everlasting game of Middle Eastern politics. Achieved laboriously since the early 1980s, the impressive Chinese accomplishments in the Middle East could have been eroded following the Tiananmen incident in the late 1980s.

Indeed, China's hitherto respectable position in international affairs suffered a painful blow as a result of its brutal suppression of the Tiananmen demonstrations. Led by Washington, most of the Western governments immediately imposed sanctions on China, including an embargo on the transfer of arms and military technology, the exchange of visits and delegations, and a suspension of many economic transactions such as impending large-scale loans, private and governmental investments, and negotiations on various economic agreements. Much of the regular diplomatic activity had also come to a virtual standstill. In June 1989, the PRC appeared to be more isolated from the international community than at any time in the post-Mao period.

Yet by early 1991, a year and a half later, China was once again taking part in international politics, playing a role that could not be ignored. Many of the Western-imposed sanctions had been lifted and the exchange of high-level visits resumed. Most of this change should be attributed to Middle Eastern developments, namely, Iraq's invasion and annexation of Kuwait in early August 1990—but not all of it. In fact, it was immediately after Tiananmen that the Chinese themselves began to prepare the ground for an eventual comeback by taking measures to offset and break the isolation imposed on them.

PAVING THE WAY

While much of this isolation resulted from Western policies and reactions, China's relations with the

Third World were not particularly affected. To make sure that these relations would continue and, furthermore, improve, the PRC immediately launched a counteroffensive. Directed toward the Third World in general, these efforts concentrated specifically on the Middle East, which became "the most important link in China's overall diplomatic plan."[1]

Policies

Beijing's increased attention to the Middle East has been based not only on the specific characteristics of this region and their implications for the PRC but also on general considerations. Most important among these has been a revised attitude toward the Third World. The PRC's post-Mao reforms had necessarily been associated with the Western countries as the principal source of technology, capital, know-how, and equipment. The Third World has very little to offer in these respects, and consequently its position on China's foreign policy priority list had been inevitably downgraded.

Yet, following the suppression of the Tiananmen demonstrations, the Third World suddenly became more meaningful for the conservatively inclined Chinese leaders. On one hand, the outbursts of hostile reaction against Beijing proved to them that, while the West could by no means be trusted, the Third World remained

1. For example, Hsia Lu, "China Plays 'Middle East Card,'" Ming pao (Hong Kong), 14 May 1990, p. 8. For background, see Yitzhak Shichor, The Middle East in China's Foreign Policy 1949-1977 (London: Cambridge University Press, 1979).

more dependable. On the other hand, the restoration of some traditional socialist, even Maoist ideological values by these leaders could not but legitimize a reorientation toward the Third World based on the common and time-honored distrust of the West.

As part of this reorientation, Middle Eastern countries are especially attractive to the PRC. One reason is that they include some of the richest less developed countries in the world. Having huge oil reserves, these countries could provide the Chinese with an alternative source of investments and foreign exchange and thereby offset at least some of the consequences of the West's sanctions. For another, the Middle East had become one of the most important markets for Chinese goods and labor services, as well as arms, spare parts, and ammunition.

No less important, the Chinese must have realized that greater involvement could be easier and more profitable in the Middle East than in any other region. As proven earlier, when the Chinese had tried to avoid joining an arms embargo on Iran and Iraq, regional problems and conflicts could no longer be settled without China's participation. Therefore, by concentrating their activities on the Middle East, the Chinese would not merely break the imposed isolation but pave the ground for an eventual comeback.

Implementation

Within days of the Tiananmen crackdown, PRC ambassadors in Middle Eastern capitals met local leaders to explain the so-called recent developments in China and to reaffirm Beijing's commitment to continue its reform, open-door policy, and friendly and cooperative relations with other countries. Within weeks, distinguished emissaries were sent to the Middle East to underscore this policy. The first was the PRC foreign minister, Qian Qichen. Starting 15 September 1989, he visited Jordan, Egypt, Syria, Tunisia, and, after participating in the U.N. General Assembly session in New York, Iran. It was his first visit to the Middle East since becoming foreign minister in April 1988.

Even more important was President Yang Shangkun's visit to four Middle East states—Egypt, the United Arab Emirates, Kuwait, and Oman—in the latter half of December 1989. The importance of his visit cannot be overestimated. Making the trip within four years of his predecessor's visit to Egypt, Yang had become one of the strongest power brokers in Chinese politics, both before and, even more so, after the military suppression of the Tiananmen demonstrations. Significantly, this was his first visit to the Middle East as well as his first foreign trip since the suppression.

Two months later, Foreign Minister Qian was again in the Middle East, this time visiting Iraq, the Arab Republic of Yemen, the People's Democratic Republic of Yemen, Bahrain, and Qatar. Seypidin Aze, vice chairman of the Standing Committee of the National People's Congress, visited Turkey in April 1990. Wan Li, chairman of the National People's Congress, led an official goodwill mission to Iraq and Iran in May, while

Han Xu, former Chinese ambassador to Washington and now president of the Chinese People's Association for Friendship with Foreign Countries, was visiting Libya. General Qin Jiwei, state councillor and minister of defense, headed a military delegation to Egypt and Jordan in June. In July, Qian returned to visit Saudi Arabia, Cyprus, Morocco, and Algeria.

This list of visitors, by no means exhaustive, nevertheless represents a concentrated and unusual Chinese effort to preserve and promote Sino-Middle Eastern relations. The effort paid off.

MIDDLE EASTERN RESPONSE

PRC achievements in the Middle East since Tiananmen could not have been the result of unilateral effort. It was the positive response of the Middle Eastern governments, immediately after the massacre, that enabled the PRC to break the international isolation and lay the foundation for an eventual come back.

The evidence

Unlike many other leaders, none of the major Middle Eastern leaders openly criticized the Chinese. While not approving of the massacre, these leaders expressed understanding, even "complete" understanding, of measures undertaken by Beijing. Hoping that the situation in China would return to normal, they insisted that no one had the right to interfere in China's internal affairs and underscored the need to respect other countries' sovereignty. Moreover, they undertook to continue to develop their friendly and cooperative relations with the PRC, indicating their satisfaction with the "stable situation prevailing in China."[2]

Consequently, while other foreign, mostly Western, leaders deliberately withheld visits to the PRC, Middle Eastern leaders resumed such visits before the end of 1989. In October, one of the first major figures to arrive in China was Yasir Arafat, chairman of the Palestine Liberation Organization (PLO). Given the full red carpet treatment as "president of the State of Palestine," Arafat was quoted by Xinhua (New China News Agency) as saying, "We felt anxious when turmoil occurred in Beijing and were glad when China quelled the anti-government riot and controlled the situation."[3] Denied by PLO authorities, these remarks were nevertheless repeated by the Chinese. Other visitors included United Arab Emirates President Sheikh Zayid Bin Sultan al-Nuhayan, who came to the PRC for the first time, and Egyptian President Hosni Mubarak, both arriving in May; the Syrian vice president, in June; the foreign ministers of Bahrain and Tunisia and the PLO's "foreign minister," Faruq Qaddumi, in July 1990.

These and other visits reflected the attitudes of most, if not all, Middle Eastern governments, including the two that still did not have full diplomatic relations with the PRC at the time of the Tiananmen demonstrations. One was Israel. Eager for diplomatic relations with the Chinese, it practically dismissed the Tiananmen massacre with a rather perfunctory and low-level Foreign Ministry statement. Furthermore, the unofficial Sino-Israeli dialogue that had gathered momentum by the mid-1980s not only proceeded undisturbed but made headway. While he was visiting the Middle East in September 1989, Foreign Minister Qian indirectly justified the Sino-Israeli consultations, "within the UN context," as a part of the efforts by the Security Council members toward reaching a peaceful settlement to the Arab-Israeli conflict.[4]

Indeed, shortly afterward, Qian held a publicized meeting with Moshe Arens, the Israeli foreign minister, in New York. Following the meeting, Israel was informed that it could now send its representatives to establish a permanent mission in Beijing within the framework of an academic center. This development was later confirmed by President Yang Shangkun, during his visit to Egypt in December 1989. He added that the PRC might consider establishing diplomatic relations with Israel if Israel would change its "hardline stand" and would contribute to the peace efforts.[5]

2. Remarks by King Hussein of Jordan, Xinhua, 17 Sept. 1989 in Foreign Broadcast Information Service, *FBIS Daily Report—China* (hereafter *FBIS—Chi*), 18 Sept. 1989, p. 18.

3. Xinhua, 4 Oct. 1989, in Foreign Broadcast Information Service, *FBIS Daily Report—Near East and South Asia* (hereafter *FBIS—NES*), 6 Oct. 1989, pp. 4-5.

4. Xinhua, 19 Sept. 1989, in *FBIS—Chi*, 19 Sept. 1989, pp. 11-13.

5. Middle East News Agency, 19 Dec. 1989, in *FBIS—NES*, 21 Dec. 1989, p. 7. See also Xinhua, 20 Dec. 1989, in *FBIS—Chi*, 22 Dec. 1989, p. 6. For background on Sino-Israeli

Yang's statement was the highest-level, as well as the mildest, ever made on the issue of Sino-Israeli relations. It ignored those preconditions set by Beijing in the past, namely, a complete Israeli withdrawal from all occupied territories, including Jerusalem, and the establishment of an independent Palestinian state. This change probably reflected the realization of China's leaders that, to play a role in Middle Eastern affairs, they need access to all parties; it perhaps also reflected their appreciation of Israel's continued positive interest in the PRC despite Tiananmen. In early 1990, the Israeli Academic Center was set up in Beijing. In June, a year after Tiananmen, it was officially and publicly opened and in early 1991 it was further upgraded, after the Chinese had allowed Israel to send a veteran Foreign Ministry ambassador to join the mission as well as to expand its staff.[6]

The other government whose relations with the PRC were upgraded was Saudi Arabia. Since the late 1970s, the PRC had launched successive offensives employing diplomatic, economic, religious, and military means to win official Saudi recognition. Unofficial Sino-Saudi relations were pushed forward with the establishment of commercial representative offices in March and April 1989. These were being organized at the time of the Tiananmen incident. With a rare exception, there was no Saudi criticism of the massacre.[7]

Furthermore, the development of Sino-Saudi relations hardly suffered.

---

relations, see Gerald Segal, "China and Israel: Pragmatic Politics," *SAIS Review* (Summer-Fall 1987); Yossi Melman and Ruth Sinai, "Israeli-Chinese Relations and Their Prospects," *Asian Survey*, 27:4 (Apr. 1987); Yitzhak Shichor, *Small Crack in the Great Wall: The Prospects for Sino-Israeli Relations*, Research Report no. 5 (London: Institute of Jewish Affairs, 1987); Julian M. Sobin, "The China-Israel Connection: New Motivations for Rapprochement," *Fletcher Forum of World Affairs*, 15:1 (Winter 1991).

6. In October 1990, Qian told the Israeli foreign minister that the establishment of official diplomatic relations could be possible only along with the development of peace in the Middle East. The gulf war, which exposed, on one hand, the deep splits in the Arab world and, on the other hand, Israel's restraint in the face of missile attacks, has led to a considerable improvement in Sino-Israeli relations. In

an interview held in early March, Deng Xiaoping reportedly said that diplomatic relations might be established before the end of the year. Later that month the director-general of the Israeli Foreign Ministry visited the PRC. Aware that, with the end of the gulf war, the Arab-Israeli conflict would top the international agenda, China welcomed the preparations for a regional peace conference. Once it starts, the establishment of Sino-Israeli diplomatic relations could be expected. See "Qian Qichen Speaks on China's Relations with South Korea, Israel, and the Vatican," *Zhongguo xinwen she*, 7 Oct. 1990, in *FBIS—Chi*, 9 Oct. 1990, p. 2; Chen Chieh-hung, "Deng Xiaoping's Talk on China's Diplomatic Line," *Ching pao* (Hong Kong), 10 June 1991, pp. 30-31, in *FBIS—Chi*, 6 June 1991, p. 3.

7. One Saudi article, conveniently published in London, placed the responsibility for the bloodshed squarely on PRC leaders Deng Xiaoping and Prime Minister Li Peng, calling it "the most criminal massacre of the 20th Century." Nadim Nasir, "Majzarat Peking, nihayat 'asr Mao" [The Beijing massacre: End of the Mao era], *Al-Majallah*, 14-20 June 1989, no. 488, pp. 22-26. For background, see Yitzhak Shichor, *East Wind over Arabia: Origins and Implications of the Sino-Saudi Missile Deal*, China Research Monograph no. 35 (Berkeley: University of California, Institute of East Asian Studies, Center for Chinese Studies, 1989).

Riyadh's commercial representative—in fact, a Foreign Ministry official—presented his credentials in late August to the PRC's foreign minister. Within less than a year, in July 1990, Prince Bandar bin Sultan, Saudi Arabia's ambassador to Washington, who had orchestrated the acquisition, exposed in 1988, of DF-3 (or CSS-2) intermediate-range ballistic missiles from China, arrived in Beijing with King Fahd's agreement to establish diplomatic relations. This was done a few days later, by Qian in Riyadh. The Tiananmen massacre was completely ignored, as were the reports, circulated since April, of Muslim unrest in Xinjiang.[8]

The rationale

This leniency toward China has been determined by cultural and political orientations as well as by international considerations. Respect for human rights and democratic values has never been uppermost in the minds of Middle Eastern autocrats. Brutal suppression of opposition has not been uncommon; in fact, it has been accepted as an indication of a strong and stable government. Accordingly, the Tiananmen crackdown was considered an internal affair in which no one should interfere. It was also regarded as a necessary and understandable measure, taken legitimately by a sovereign government that felt threatened. One can

assume that most Middle Eastern regimes sympathized with and preferred to deal with the more conservative Chinese leaders than with the reformists.

In addition, the international context influenced reactions. To begin with, at a time when traditional allies such as the Soviet Union and Eastern Europe were gradually and systematically falling apart, China, especially after Tiananmen, proved itself an island of stability in a sea of foreboding change. Middle Eastern government and national liberation movements could no longer expect the same political, economic, and military support provided them by the European socialist countries headed by Moscow. Although Beijing's support has been much less impressive in terms of quality as well as quantity, the Chinese have acquired the image of being more dependable.

Evidently the motives behind the hasty Western response against China have been seen by the Arabs as suspect. Their alignment with China has reflected not only the shared memories of harsh colonial rule but, more specifically, a protest against what they regarded as Western indifference to the suppression of the Palestinians under Israeli occupation. It was this positive Middle Eastern response to the Chinese overtures following the Tiananmen massacre that laid the foundation for China's rehabilitation.

8. For a summary, see Wu Su-li, "The 'Jihad' Bloodbath in Xinjiang," *Kai fang* (Hong Kong), 15 May 1990, no. 5, pp. 13-14, in *FBIS—Chi*, 21 May 1990, pp. 57-59. See also *South China Morning Post* (Hong Kong), 13 Apr. 1990; *Hong Kong Standard*, 13 Apr. 1990.

CHINA'S COMEBACK

Within a year of Tiananmen, the Chinese managed to rebuild and improve their base of operations in the

Middle East and, no less important, their bruised international image. By the summer of 1990, China had been searching for a way to restore that image. The opportunity was provided by Iraq's invasion of Kuwait on 2 August 1990, skillfully manipulated by Beijing to its own advantage.

After an initial hesitation, the PRC regarded Iraq's invasion of Kuwait as a violation of the U.N. Charter and of the norms of international relations and therefore as absolutely unacceptable. This attitude was based on two main principles: "First, China resolutely opposes the Iraqi invasion and annexation of Kuwait and second, China maintains that every effort should be made to seek a peaceful solution to the Gulf crisis."[9]

These two principles reflected a double-edged policy. On one hand, the PRC actively joined the consultations within the U.N. Security Council and supported its resolution, beginning with Resolution 660, that approved the use of all means—economic, political, diplomatic, and military without specifying the use of force—to make the Iraqis withdraw from Kuwait and to restore its independence and sovereignty.

On the other hand, China all along supported efforts to work out a peaceful solution within the Arab world and, following its traditional policies, without external, least of all Western, intervention. It was this attitude that determined China's abstention from voting on U.N. Security Council

Resolution 678, which sanctioned the use of military operations against Iraq. While unable to vote in favor of such a resolution, neither could China use its veto power and vote against it, a step that would have led to a further deterioration in Sino-Western and especially Sino-American relations.[10]

China and the West: Rehabilitation

By using this double-edged policy, China managed to regain its voice in world affairs. The gulf crisis proved that it is impossible to reach an understanding on the settlement of major international problems without PRC participation, a message China has been trying to transmit particularly to the West ever since Tiananmen, if not before.

With Saddam Hussein stigmatized as the bad guy by the Western powers, the PRC suddenly became more respectable. This was demonstrated in September when Foreign Minister Qian held a series of meetings in the United Nations, inconceivable a year earlier, with Western foreign ministers, including Secretary of State James Baker. This was their first official meeting since Tiananmen. The Iraqi annexation of Kuwait also provided some people in the U.S. administration with the ex-

9. Qian Qichen, "The Changing World Situation and China's Foreign Affairs," *Qiushi*, 16 Dec. 1990, no. 24, pp. 8-11, in *FBIS—Chi*, 4 Jan. 1991, pp. 1-4.

10. "Crisis Brings China Back into the Fold," *South China Sunday Morning Post* (Hong Kong), 2 Dec. 1990; "Another Embodiment of the Independent Foreign Policy of Peace," *Wen wei po* (Hong Kong), 1 Dec. 1990, in *FBIS—Chi*, 3 Dec. 1990, p. 1. For China's official position, see *Beijing Review*, 10-16 Dec. 1990, p. 4.

cuse to rehabilitate U.S.-PRC relations that they had apparently been seeking for some time. When Qian visited Cairo in November 1990 in search of a settlement to the crisis, he met Baker again.[11]

Later that month, Qian held an unusual working meeting with Soviet Foreign Minister Eduard Shevardnadze in Urumqi "to exchange views on the current situation in the Gulf and brief each other on matters of common concern."[12] Such a high-level discussion of Middle Eastern issues has been uncommon in Sino-Soviet relations. Similar discussions recurred throughout the crisis.

Following these meetings and China's decision to abstain on rather than veto the U.S.-sponsored Security Council Resolution 678, Qian was officially invited to Washington in early December for the first time since the summer of 1989. In addition to Secretary Baker, he met with a number of congressmen as well as with President George Bush. Obviously, the U.S. ban on high-level official contacts had been lifted. Earlier, in October, the 12 nations of the European Community—including France, whose reaction to Tiananmen had been the most severe—had decided to lift virtually all their sanc-

tions on the PRC, except for certain arms sales.[13]

China and the Third World: Consolidation

Associated with the gulf crisis, these developments opened the door for China's return as a player in the game of international politics. While regaining its position as a world power, the PRC also managed to consolidate its identity as a Third World nation and as a representative of Third World interests, both inside and outside the United Nations. The role played by the Chinese during the crisis clearly demonstrated this intention.[14]

Within three weeks of Iraq's invasion, Middle Eastern pilgrims began arriving in Beijing for consultation and support. They included representative of all regional parties to the conflict. First came members of the

13. China welcomed this decision. Xinhua, 23 Oct. 1990, in FBIS—Chi, 24 Oct. 1990, p. 1. Later, in 1991, President Bush managed to regain for the PRC its most-favored-nation status, despite strong opposition in Congress. *International Herald Tribune*, 25 July 1991. In July, China participated in a U.S.-sponsored conference of the world's major powers on the subject of curbing arms sales to the Middle East.

14. Samuel S. Kim, *The Third World in Chinese World Policy*, World Order Studies Program, Occasional Paper no. 19 (Princeton, NJ: Princeton University, Woodrow Wilson School of Public and International Affairs, Center for International Studies, Jan. 1989); Lillian Craig Harris and Robert L. Worden, eds., *China and the Third World: Champion or Challenger?* (Dover, MA: Auburn House, 1986). See also Yitzhak Shichor, "China and the Role of the United Nations in the Middle East: Revised Policy," *Asian Survey*, 32:3 (Mar. 1991).

11. During both meetings, they held discussions not only on the gulf and other international issues but also on bilateral relations. Xinhua, 29 Sept. 1990, in *FBIS—Chi*, 1 Oct. 1990, pp. 6-7; ibid., 6 Nov. 1990, in *FBIS—Chi*, 7 Nov. 1990, p. 2.

12. *Beijing Review*, 3-9 Dec. 1990, p. 6. See also "Chinese and Soviet Foreign Ministers Hold Talks in Xinjiang," *Hsin wan pao* (Hong Kong), 23 Nov. 1990, p. 1, in *FBIS—Chi*, 23 Nov. 1990, p. 7.

anti-Iraqi coalition, such as the foreign ministers of Kuwait, Saudi Arabia, and Egypt as well as, on their first visit, the emir of Kuwait and his entourage; then came officials from Iraq itself, including First Deputy Prime Minister Taha Yasin Ramadan; and finally came representatives from neutral states including Jordan's deputy prime minister and foreign minister, Iran's defense minister, and Hoseyn Musavi, former Iranian prime minister and adviser to the president.

The Chinese, however, were not content with merely the role of passive hosts to Middle Eastern dignitaries. In a more vigorous diplomatic effort, Foreign Minister Qian visited Turkey in early September and then Egypt, Saudi Arabia, Jordan, and Iraq in early November. Among the foreign ministers of the permanent Security Council members, he was the only one who could shuttle between all four capitals, including Baghdad.

The stated purpose of his visits was to explore with the leaders of those countries the possibility of a peaceful settlement of the crisis. Yet he was careful enough to add, "I have not brought any specific proposal, nor am I going to be a mediator."[15] These PRC efforts were welcomed by all parties concerned. Even the emir of Kuwait expressed understanding of China's abstention from the vote on Security Council Resolution 678, a resolution that he and his Western and Middle Eastern allies had firmly supported.[16]

This understanding shows that the PRC succeeded not only in maintaining its image as a Third World global power but also in preserving good relations with both friends and foes in the Middle East. Already manifest throughout the Iran-Iraq war, this Chinese attribute is also shaped by common economic and military interests.

ECONOMIC INTERESTS

Until the late 1970s, foreign economic relations had not played an important role in PRC international activities and certainly not in the Middle East. There, economic relations had been limited in quantity and quality to trade and aid and had been determined, at least partly, by strategic, political, and ideological considerations.

Most of these constraints have been removed since the death of Mao Zedong. As overall modernization assumed top priority, foreign economic relations became indispensable. The dramatic expansion of such relations is clearly reflected in China's economic transactions with the Middle East.

Before Tiananmen

Though its share in the value of overall Chinese foreign trade has not increased substantially, the Middle

---

15. Xinhua, 6 Nov. 1990, in *FBIS—Chi*, 6 Nov. 1990, p. 7. See also Shih Chun-yu, "Not Making Any Proposals, Not Serving as Mediator," *Ta kung pao* (Hong Kong), 7 Nov. 1990, in *FBIS—Chi*, 7 Nov. 1990, pp. 1-2.

16. Xinhua, 27 Dec. 1990, in *FBIS—Chi*, 27 Dec. 1990, p. 18. To further consolidate China's position in the Middle East, Prime Minister Li Peng visited Egypt, Jordan, Saudi Arabia, and Syria, in July 1991.

East has become an extremely important market for Chinese exports and, furthermore, a valuable source of foreign trade surplus. The huge and steady difference between the high level of exports and the low level of imports that reached more than $12 billion in the years 1983-88—a yearly average of more than $2 billion—helped the Chinese reduce their balance-of-payments deficit, especially since the mid-1980s.[17]

For similar purposes, economic aid to the Middle East, which in Mao's time had been modest and motivated more by ideological and political considerations than by economic ones, has been further curtailed since the late 1970s. Instead, the Chinese initiated a new international economic activity, motivated by purely economic considerations: labor exports and construction services.

By June 1989, more than seventy corporations and companies had been set up by the Chinese government, some provinces, and a number of cities to engage in these new activities. Within the decade, these organizations were awarded contracts valued at more than $10 billion, mostly in the Middle East, with Iraq taking the lead. In addition to the earnings in foreign exchange, crucial for China's balance of payments, these activities helped to ease unemployment problems in China as well as exposing tens of thousands of Chinese workers and managers to advanced foreign technologies.

Finally, the Middle East has also contributed to China's economy as a source of investment and loans, something Mao had not allowed. From 1982 to 1989, the Kuwait Fund for Arab Economic Development (KFAED) alone provided China with $310 million in soft loans for the construction of 13 projects.[18] Although the flow of Middle Eastern capital to China has been much smaller than the flow of funds from other sources, it can by no means be ignored. To sum up, on the eve of Tiananmen, the Chinese considered their economic relations with the Middle East important, profitable, and promising.

After Tiananmen

There is no evidence that these relations were disrupted by Tiananmen. Within a month, a series of normal Sino-Middle Eastern economic exchanges took place. These, and others that followed in the next months, included visits and delegations, discussions, and the signing of numerous trade and economic cooperation agreements in industry, science and technology, and related areas.

Trade provides a good example, as shown by comparison of the 12 months from June 1989 to May 1990 with the previous 12 months. Whereas the value of Chinese imports from the Middle East remained practically the same, Chinese exports increased by more than 10 percent and in particular cases by much more. Exports to Iraq in the first 6

17. Data derived from the International Monetary Fund, *Direction of Trade Statistics* (Washington, DC: International Monetary Fund, various years).

18. Wang Gang, "Friendly Relations between China and Kuwait Develop in an Overall Way," *Renmin ribao*, 28 Dec. 1990, in *FBIS—Chi*, 7 Jan. 1991, pp. 11-12.

months of 1990 were up 35 percent compared to the corresponding period of 1989; Saudi sources claimed a 70 percent increase in imports from the PRC over the same period.

Likewise, whereas loans offered to the Chinese by international organizations and foreign governments were suspended following the massacre, Arab capital continued to flow. In September 1989, for example, Kuwait provided the PRC with a $21 million loan to help finance a cast-iron pipe project in Liaoning province. In October, KFAED offered a loan of $28 million to finance the acquisition of navigation instruments and equipment for the Shenzhen airport. In early February 1990, it was reported that the Xiamen airport was being expanded with a further loan of $20 million from Kuwait. In December 1990, yet another soft loan of $30 million for modernizing an aluminum-foil factory in Chengdu, Sichuan province, was extended by KFAED, now operating from London, after Kuwait itself had been occupied by Iraq.

Purely economic considerations also governed the allocation of construction contracts to PRC companies and corporations operating in the Middle East. Headed by the China State Construction Engineering Corporation, these organizations were awarded additional contracts, mainly in Iraq, Jordan, the two Yemens, and Turkey.[19] These activities, which were hardly affected by Tiananmen, were later seriously disrupted by Iraq's invasion of Kuwait.

Following the invasion, China began evacuating its 10,000 workers from Iraq and Kuwait. Their share in the value of China's labor services had reached 75 percent in the Middle East and 55 percent worldwide! The damage must have been considerable. In an official statement in early November 1990, China admitted that, in implementing the sanctions against Iraq, it suffered a direct economic loss of some U.S.$2 billion in trade, transport, and civil aviation, not including Iraq's financial debt for Chinese labor services and other economic activities.[20]

MILITARY INTERESTS

Throughout the Maoist era, the PRC did not use military sales to promote its relations with the Middle East. This had little to do with the supposedly limited capacity or low quality of China's arms production. In fact, in the 1960s China's conventional military potential was greater and more up to date than it is today. Most Chinese arms were delivered, free of charge, to three buffer countries: North Vietnam, North Korea, and Pakistan. The rest of China's weapons exports, no more than 15 percent, were thinly spread among several Third World countries and national liberation movements, including the PLO but not including Middle Eastern countries. These countries were saturated with arms from the Soviet Union, the United

19. For details on contracts and loans given to China, see weekly issues of *Middle East Economic Digest* (London).

20. Xinhua, 1 Nov. 1990, in *FBIS—Chi*, 1 Nov. 1990, p. 1; *China Daily (Business Weekly)*, 26 Nov. 1990, p. 1. See also "Beijing and the Gulf War," *China News Analysis*, 1 Feb. 1991, no. 1428, p. 4.

States, and their allies. There was simply no room or need for inferior Chinese weapons, particularly when the PRC was being regarded as subversive and extremist. Governed primarily by security and strategic considerations, the PRC's arms transfer policy did not apply to the distant Middle East.[21]

Arms sales in the 1980s

By the late 1970s and early 1980s, however, most if not all of these circumstances had changed considerably. In the PRC, economic development had replaced political and security considerations as the top priority. This called for, among other things, increased exports directed at earning as much foreign exchange as possible. Arms became a legitimate export item. China could now afford to sell weapons because of reduced threat perceptions, the removal of ideological constraints, the underutilized potential of defense industries, and, last but not least, the availability of customers, first and foremost in the Middle East.

The eruption of a series of military confrontations there created a growing demand for weapons, spare parts, and ammunition that traditional suppliers, both Eastern and Western, were unwilling or reluctant to provide. China was quick to step into this vacuum, offering large quantities of cheap weapons that could be easily integrated with existing Middle Eastern arsenals, primarily those based on Soviet military technology.

Indeed, since the late 1970s, about 90 percent of all Chinese arms sales, valued at more than $15 billion, have been channeled to the Middle East, not only to warring Iran and Iraq but also to Egypt, Syria, Libya, and Saudi Arabia. As a result of these arms supplies, the PRC has become the fourth or fifth largest military exporter in the world, with a definite advantage in those weapons—in particular, intermediate-range ballistic missiles—whose proliferation has been limited or banned under international agreements, such as the Intermediate-Range Nuclear Forces Treaty, which China has not signed.

While highly profitable not merely in terms of foreign exchange but also as an indispensable input for defense modernization, arms sales, especially of missiles, caused some friction in U.S.-China relations in 1987 and 1988. Annoyed by what they regarded as "American interference," the Chinese nevertheless assured Washington, rather vaguely, that they would not engage in the sale of missiles, such as the M-9 requested by Syria. Otherwise, China continued its arms transfers to the Middle East.[22]

The end, in August 1988, of the war between Iran and Iraq, the PRC's most important customers, did not immediately affect the flow of Chi-

---

21. Anne Gilks and Gerald Segal, *China and the Arms Trade* (London: Croom Helm, 1985).

22. "China Said to Sell Missiles," *Washington Post*, 30 Mar. 1990; see also "Beijing gets on Washington's Nerve," *International Herald Tribune*, 25 Apr. 1991. For background, see Eden Y. Woon, "Chinese Arms Sales and U.S.-China Military Relations," *Asian Survey*, 29:6 (June 1989); Yitzhak Shichor, "Unfolded Arms: Beijing's Recent Military Sales Offensive," *Pacific Review*, 1:3 (Oct. 1988); idem, "The Middle East," in *Chinese Defence Policy*, ed. Gerald Segal and William T. Tow (London: Macmillan, 1985), pp. 163-278.

nese military exports. Contracts signed long before the cease-fire had yet to be implemented. In the longer run, further contracts could be expected since both states had to rehabilitate their shattered military systems. For the PRC, continued arms sales have been of the utmost importance militarily as well as economically and politically. This endeavor could have been disrupted by the Tiananmen massacre.

From Tiananmen
to the gulf

For obvious reasons, precise information about PRC arms sales is not readily available. Still, although the exchange of military delegations between China and the Middle East was apparently suspended in the first year after Tiananmen, military shipments probably continued. This was implied in December 1989, when high-level U.S. envoys, National Security Adviser Brent Scowcroft and Deputy Secretary of State Lawrence Eagleburger, sought and won more assurances that China would not sell missiles in the Middle East.

In the following months, press and intelligence reports said that Beijing was assisting the Iraqis in the construction of high-speed centrifuges used to produce enriched weapon-grade uranium needed to fuel a nuclear bomb. It was also reported that the PRC not only resumed missile sales to Iran as a part of a $6 billion arms deal but also delivered short-range M-9 missiles to Syria.

Many of these reports, categorically denied by the PRC, were fabricated or exaggerated but probably con-

tained a grain of truth. Whatever the precise details, one thing is obvious: PRC arms sales to the Middle East were not affected by Tiananmen. Actually, in early 1990, the Arab Organization for Satellite Communications, which represents Jordan, Kuwait, Saudi Arabia, Bahrain, Morocco, Syria, and Iraq, chose the PRC's Great Wall Corporation to launch an Arab communications satellite.

In mid-1990, the exchange of military visits between China and the Middle East resumed, in spite of the Western-initiated sanctions. State Councillor and Defense Minister General Qin Jiwei paved the ground by visiting Egypt and Jordan in June to discuss bilateral military cooperation. Shortly after his return, Egypt's Air Defense commander arrived in Beijing to hold talks with People's Liberation Army chief of the General Staff, Chi Haotian and others. Within days the chief of the General Staff of Sudan's armed forces also appeared in Beijing.

These extensive military relations suffered a partial setback as a result of the violent annexation of Kuwait by Iraq. Following the Chinese vote for U.N. Security Council Resolution 660, China stated that "it [would], naturally, not sell arms to Iraq under such circumstances" and that it would respect the embargo.[23] Within two months of the Iraqi invasion, China began to complain about its "tremendous" economic losses. These must have included the loss of income

23. "Arms Shipments Halted to Iraq," *Beijing Review*, 13-19 Aug. 1990, p. 8; "Foreign Ministry Spokesman Says China Will Not Sell Arms to Iraq," *Renmin ribao*, 6 Aug. 1990, in *FBIS—Chi*, 6 Aug. 1990, p. 13.

from arms sales, considered a legitimate economic transaction by China's post-Mao leadership.

At the same time, the gulf crisis provided the Chinese military with precious lessons about war itself and the performance of Chinese- and Soviet-made weapons. Also, Beijing could now explore and expand alternative arms markets, such as Iran, without having to worry about Iraq's reaction. Thus, in October, Iran's minister of defense and armed forces logistics visited the PRC, making the first visit of this kind since the establishment of diplomatic relations between the two countries in 1971. Of course, once the gulf crisis ends, China might hope to resume arms sales to Iraq as well.

PROSPECTS

In the last decade of the twentieth century, Sino-Middle Eastern relations are better than ever before. Both Moscow and, to a lesser degree, Washington now acknowledge China's right to participate in the settlement of regional problems. To do so, the PRC now has the necessary economic, military, and political means, both inside and outside the Middle East. Except for Israel, all Middle Eastern governments—including what is called the State of Palestine—have full diplomatic relations with the PRC, which they regard as their representative in the U.N. Security Council.

Looking ahead, there is little doubt that, whatever the outcome of the power struggle that follows the death of Deng Xiaoping, the PRC will not give up its accomplishments in the Middle East. We can anticipate that the Chinese will seek to participate in the postwar settlement of the gulf imbroglio, as well as in other regional problems, first and foremost the Arab-Israeli conflict. As soon as progress is made in this direction, China is expected to establish full diplomatic relations with Israel.

Yet, a word of caution is required. China's greater involvement in Middle Eastern affairs does not imply greater influence. China remains a developing country, largely dependent on Western economies, technology, and capital. In this sense, its foreign policy is not yet as independent as China would like it to be. The PRC's voting in the U.N. Security Council on the gulf crisis clearly reflects its dilemmas and identity crisis: is it a Third World backward country or is it a great power, a new Middle Kingdom?

The emerging temporary answer is both. While no longer sitting on the fence, the PRC is still trying to eat its cake and have it, too, that is, to maintain good relations with all parties, West as well as East, North as well as South. To resolve this identity crisis, China is working to provide the link between the different worlds and thereby accomplish its real independence.

ANNALS, *AAPSS*, **519**, January 1992

China and Europe

By DAVID SHAMBAUGH

ABSTRACT: Relations between China and Europe have traveled a fluctuant course since 1949. To a significant extent, China's relations with both Eastern and Western Europe have been a function of its broader pattern of relations with the Soviet Union and the United States. Yet, in both cases, independent factors have served to sustain and strain ties. This article examines the course and dynamics of these relationships over the past four decades. Sino-European relations today are businesslike yet fragile—a fragility that the receding Cold War, the collapse of communism in Eastern Europe, and the West European common market of 1992 will all serve to intensify.

David Shambaugh is lecturer in Chinese politics at the School of Oriental and African Studies, University of London, and editor of the China Quarterly. *Previously, he directed the Asia Program at the Woodrow Wilson International Center for Scholars in Washington, D.C. He holds a B.A. in East Asian studies from George Washington University, an M.A., in international relations from the School of Advanced International Studies, Johns Hopkins University, and a Ph.D. in political science from the University of Michigan. His most recent book is* Beautiful Imperialist: China Perceives America, 1972-1990 *(1991).*

EUROPE, both eastern and western, has traditionally held a derivative position in Chinese foreign policy. Since 1949, Sino-European relations have principally derived from China's relations with the two superpowers. Whether as a function of China's postwar two-camp worldview, the Sino-Soviet and Sino-American estrangements, Mao's theory of the three worlds, or Deng Xiaoping's polycentric diplomacy, Europe's position in Chinese foreign policy has largely been determined by Beijing's relations with Washington and Moscow. Relations with European states have not been viewed by China as necessarily worthy pursuits in their own right but have rather been considered as adjuncts to China's relations with the two superpowers.

The historical pattern of interaction between China and Europe, much like that between the United States and China, was an ambivalent one. Europe served as a source of emulation and stimulus to modern China's development, but it was also a source of imperial encroachment and destabilization. The newly triumphant Chinese Communist Party (CCP) carried this ambivalent baggage with them when they came to power in 1949.

Mao Zedong's views of Europe were, however, not so ambivalent. Unlike many of his comrades in arms, Mao did not experience London, Paris, or Lyon as an overseas student. The late Chairman viewed the West European powers through a sinified Leninist lens; World War II had been the result of Europeans' search for expanding spheres of influence and increased profits as much as it had been a fight against fascism. Moreover, Mao perceived Europeans as having built up the Chinese "comprador bourgeoisie" on whom he blamed much of the Kuomintang corruption and national impotence in the face of foreign aggression. In Mao's eyes, the European treaty ports symbolized the fundamental problems that his revolution sought to rectify. Thus, while Sino-European relations had previously passed through phases of emulation, a more sober assessment existed when Mao and the Communist Party came to power.

CHINA AND EUROPE DURING THE 1950s

Despite the antipathy felt by the CCP toward the European powers, several European states were among the first to recognize the new People's Republic of China (PRC). Following the Soviet Union's lead of extending diplomatic recognition the day after the PRC's founding, Bulgaria, Romania, Poland, Hungary, Czechoslovakia, and Yugoslavia followed suit between 2 and 5 October 1949. In January 1950, Norway, Denmark, Finland, and Sweden recognized the PRC. So, too, did the United Kingdom, on 6 January, but this was rejected by the Chinese side, as the United Kingdom maintained unacceptable consular relations with the Nationalist government on Taiwan. China did, however, agree to permit diplomatic ties at the chargé d'affaires' level with the United Kingdom. Other than the Scandinavian states, Britain was the only Western nation with a diplomatic mission in Beijing until de Gaulle recognized China in 1964. China permitted Britain this status largely because of their mutual interest in governing Hong Kong. The Federal Republic of Germany was permitted a resident trade mission beginning in 1955, but Adenauer and other Western leaders otherwise followed the American-led boycott of the PRC until 1972.

Mao's policy of "leaning to one side" meant that during the 1950s China entered into extensive barter trade relationships with the East European members of the Soviet-dominated Council of Mutual Economic Assistance, in which China was granted observer status. East German, Polish, and Czechoslovakian technicians built scores of factories in China during the 1950s. Sino-East European political relations during much of the decade were less positive, however. They were shaped largely by Sino-Soviet relations and Mao's problems with Khrushchev in particular. Beginning with Mao's denunciation of "Yugoslav revisionism" in 1954, changes in Eastern Europe became central issues on the Sino-Soviet agenda. The Chinese denounced Tito for bolting from the socialist community and pursuing ideologically heretical policies. Stalinism continued to cast a long shadow over Beijing despite Stalin's death in 1953.

The year 1956 was a pivotal one in Sino-East European relations. The Polish and Hungarian uprisings brought contradictory responses from Beijing. In the midst of the brief period of liberalization during the Hundred Flowers campaign, the Chi-

nese openly supported Gomulka and his experiments in socialism. The Soviets read this as a challenge to their sphere of influence as Mao was beginning to assert his independence from Moscow. Just as the Hundred Flowers movement gave way to the draconian Anti-Rightist campaign in China, so, too, did the Chinese position on "independent paths to socialism" change. In inner-party documents, the CCP bitterly criticized Khrushchev's invitation to Tito to visit Moscow, although Soviet pressure elicited a public statement to the contrary by Beijing. The Chinese also supported the forcible suppression of the Hungarian uprising. While Mao was intrigued by the reform movement in Hungary, as he was with Gomulka's Poland, he perceived the existence of a united socialist camp to be at risk, and, given the more pressing danger from the imperialist camp, such "splittism" could not be tolerated.

The simmering dispute between the Soviet Union and Albania also drew Mao's interest. Both Tirana and Beijing were shocked by, and opposed to, Khrushchev's secret speech denouncing Stalin. Mao began to see a like-minded ideological ally in Enver Hoxha. Henceforth, one of the more bizarre and utopian relationships in contemporary Chinese foreign policy began to take shape.

CHINA AND
EUROPE IN THE 1960s

The open rupture of Sino-Soviet relations in 1960 had definite follow-on effects for China's ties with Eastern Europe. East European economic technicians and military advisers departed China hastily in the wake of their Soviet counterparts. Party-to-party ties were severed with all except Albania and Romania. Trade dropped off precipitously, although diplomatic relations were maintained. Such a state of affairs endured through the Soviet invasion of Czechoslovakia in 1968. China's only friends in Eastern Europe were Nicolae Ceausescu and Enver Hoxha.

China's relations with Western Europe during the 1960s were also influenced, initially, by the Sino-Soviet split and later in the decade by the extreme radicalism of the Cultural Revolution. Following Beijing's break with Moscow, West European Communist parties became a conundrum for the Chinese. At first, China continued its sharp attacks on West European Communists—particularly the Italian Communist Party[1]—because of their continued allegiance to Moscow and "Khrushchev revisionism." The Chinese even attempted to set up an alternative Communist International, but among European parties only Albania joined. The French, Italian, and Spanish Communist parties continued to pursue their strategy of gaining power through the ballot box, a tactic deemed anathema to the increasingly militant Maoist leadership. Nor did West European Communist parties—with the exception of French students in 1968—show much enthusiasm for Mao's Cultural Revolution. Toward the end of the decade, China and these nonruling parties did begin

to find some common ground when they mutually condemned the Soviet Union's invasion of Czechoslovakia and the proclamation of the Brezhnev Doctrine. Beijing also began to warm to what the Chinese perceived to be more pluralistic tendencies within the Soviet-centered International Communist and Workers Movement.[2]

On the state-to-state level, de Gaulle's diplomatic recognition of China in 1964 was a significant symbolic breakthrough for Beijing, but not much came of it substantively. It did facilitate a modest increase in bilateral trade—as was also the case with West German trade—but a combination of China's internal convulsions and American pressure blocked any significant expansion of commercial or diplomatic ties through the remainder of the decade. U.S. pressure apparently convinced the German chancellor not to follow de Gaulle's lead and recognize Beijing at that time, a move he had contemplated in 1964.

Any potential rapprochement that seemed possible during the first half of the decade quickly disappeared as China lurched leftward into the Great Proletarian Cultural Revolution. Chinese ambassadors were withdrawn from those European countries with whom China had had diplomatic relations, and remaining embassy staff often tried to incite local Maoists. In Beijing, rampaging Red Guards besieged the British mission and, after several days of ten-

1. See "The Differences between Comrade Togliatti and Us," *Peking Review*, 4 Jan. 1963, pp. 1, 4.

2. William E. Griffith, "China and Europe: Weak and Far Away," in *The China Factor*, ed. Richard Solomon (Englewood Cliffs, NJ: Prentice-Hall, 1981), p. 171.

sion, burned it to the ground. Nor were Red Guard activities in the colony of Hong Kong much appreciated by the British government. By the end of the decade, China found itself thoroughly isolated from both Eastern and Western European states. Even Beijing's ties with Tirana had begun to unravel.

CHINA AND EUROPE IN THE 1970s

It was not until after Mao's death and the arrest of the radical Gang of Four in China that a rapprochement process with Eastern Europe began. The first major foreign head of state to visit China in the post-Mao era was Tito, who had long been the pariah of Beijing's radicalism. Mao's anointed successor, Hua Guofeng, warmly welcomed Tito, reopening party ties and establishing a Chinese beachhead for countering Brezhnevite domination of Eastern Europe. Tito was the perfect, if ironic, symbol to signal Beijing's new conception of a polycentric socialist community of nations. The Tito visit in 1977 also signaled an alteration of China's economic development strategy. The experimentation with worker participation in management, a limited role for the private sector, and devolution of economic decision-making power to the republics in Yugoslavia all intrigued reform-minded Chinese economists who were beginning their rehabilitation from Cultural Revolution oblivion.[3] Thereafter, numerous

Chinese study missions were dispatched to Yugoslavia, Hungary, and Romania. In 1978, the then-obscure Communist Party leader of Sichuan province, Zhao Ziyang, led one such delegation. What Zhao witnessed was soon to influence his own maverick reforms as he was catapulted to power in Beijing and put in charge of restructuring the Chinese economy.[4]

While China was intrigued by the economic experimentalism in Eastern Europe and encouraged political distancing from Moscow during the late 1970s, Beijing found other developments more troubling. The Polish crisis, which culminated in 1980-81, petrified the Chinese leadership, particularly newly paramount leader Deng Xiaoping. The rise of independent trade unions had obvious implications for China. Deng therefore welcomed the imposition of martial law and suppression of Solidarity.[5]

While China was intrigued by economic developments in Eastern Europe during the 1970s, but wary of the political example of Solidarity, it also recognized that developing ties with the Balkan states could bring pressure on the Soviet Union's underbelly. Romania and Yugoslavia were the principal targets of this strategy.[6] As China cultivated Tito and

3. See Nina P. Halpern, "Learning from Abroad: Chinese Views of the East European Economic Experience, January 1977-June 1981," *Modern China* (Jan. 1985).

4. See David L. Shambaugh, *The Making of a Premier: Zhao Ziyang's Provincial Career* (Boulder, CO: Westview Press, 1984), chap. 6.

5. See Michael B. Yahuda, "China and Europe: The Significance of a Secondary Relationship," in *Chinese Foreign Policy: Theory and Practice*, ed. Thomas W. Robinson and David Shambaugh (Oxford: Oxford University Press, forthcoming).

6. See D. A. Andelman, "China's Balkan Strategy," *International Security*, Winter 1979-80, pp. 60-79.

Ceausescu, Enver Hoxha was sacrificed. The Albanians had, in fact, been some of the most vocal critics of the Sino-American rapprochement in 1971-72.

The Chinese Balkan strategy also permitted Beijing an opening to the Italian and Spanish Communist parties, as both had, by the mid-1970s, established an anti-Soviet axis of sorts. Italian Communist Party leader Enrico Berlinguer visited China in 1979, and his Spanish counterpart, Carillo, did so a year later, both establishing party-to-party ties.

The 1970s also witnessed the blossoming of full diplomatic relations with the balance of the European states. Following the American opening to China, other West European states moved quickly to establish ties. Great Britain and the Federal Republic of Germany exchanged ambassadors with China in 1972, and the remainder quickly followed suit. The European Community extended recognition to China in 1975, and it conferred preferential trade status on Beijing in 1978. This status and a series of bilateral agreements helped boost the total volume of Sino-West European two-way trade to $5.8 billion by the end of the decade.[7] West Germany surpassed Great Britain as China's largest European trade partner during this period. Accords on scientific and cultural exchange were

7. As cited in Qiu Shiqian, "Sino-West European Economic and Trade Relations in Sustained and Steady Development," *Journal of the Chinese People's Institute of Foreign Affairs*, 1988, no. 9, p. 53. Also see Harsh Kapur, *China and the European Economic Community: The New Connection* (Dordrecht: Martinus Nijhoff, 1986).

also signed, permitting an interflow of scholars and data between China and Western Europe.

As the decade progressed, it became clear that China's leaders perceived Western Europe increasingly in terms of national security. In its effort to deflect Soviet pressure from the tense Sino-Soviet border, China became a vociferous advocate of the North Atlantic Treaty Organization (NATO). In the Chinese conceptualization, Europe belonged to the "second world" and, as such, could be mobilized into a worldwide anti-Soviet united front. Chinese officials chided their European counterparts to spend more on defense, warning that Moscow was "feinting to the east, but would strike to the west." China bristled at any Western moves toward détente with Moscow. Willy Brandt's *Ostpolitik* strategy was condemned in strong terms by Chinese leaders and commentators. The Chinese thereafter began to cultivate the most hawkish elements in West European political circles. Although the growing number of security consultations was really more symbolic than substantive, by the late-1970s China had been labeled by many as the "sixteenth member of NATO."

Such status also afforded China increased access to European defense suppliers. From 1975 to 1980, China dispatched dozens of inspection and shopping missions to NATO member states. People's Liberation Army personnel were shown around important NATO bases and introduced to defense industrialists. The Chinese observed a great deal but bought relatively little. Not unexpectedly, they were primarily interested in NATO's frontier defense planning against a Soviet land invasion, the use of battlefield tactical nuclear weapons, and antitank technology. After much window shopping, China did purchase anti-air and antitank missiles from Italy and West Germany, radars from France, and jet-fighter technologies from Great Britain, but on the whole it made relatively few purchases.

CHINA AND
EUROPE IN THE 1980s

If the 1970s were the decade in which China and Western Europe reestablished contact, it was during the 1980s that relations were fully normalized. All West European heads of state and prime ministers visited China, and several Chinese leaders paid visits to Europe. Diplomatic, commercial, cultural, scientific, and military exchanges all proceeded apace.

From China's perspective, these expanded exchanges were pursued increasingly in their own right rather than as an adjunct to Beijing's anti-Soviet united-front policy. Whereas Western Europe was deemed an ally of China in the antihegemonic struggle of the late-1970s, it was increasingly viewed as a source of technology and capital in the 1980s. This change in perception followed China's reassessment of the global balance of forces.

Beginning in 1980-81 Chinese international affairs specialists began to articulate the view that the U.S. defense buildup had begun to stabilize the balance of power between the superpowers. Moreover, these analysts perceived the emergence of an increasingly multipolar world as the defining characteristic of international relations in the "new era." For China, this meant that close alignment with the United States and NATO was not as necessary to Chinese security as had been the case during the previous decade. The gradual thaw in Sino-Soviet relations further contributed to this perception. Based on this perception of a changed international environment, China was able to proclaim its "independent foreign policy" in 1982.

In this new multipolar world, Chinese analysts thought Europe constituted one pole. As such, Western Europe could act as a counterweight not just against Moscow but against the United States as well.[8] Such an analysis reflected China's desire for the extinction of bipolar international relations and the creation of a world in which regional powers such as China played defining roles. But, in the case of Western Europe, such perceptions seriously underestimated two factors.

First, China overestimated the political unity of Western Europe. Organizations like the European Parliament in Brussels and movement toward the creation of a common market in 1992 no doubt fueled such perceptions, but China's Europeanists repeatedly demonstrated a tendency to inflate the degree of political consultation and shared perspective between West European governments. Chinese analysts and leaders almost invariably spoke of "Europe"

8. Of many such analyses, see Si Kunyang, "The Position and Role of Western Europe in Present World Politics," *Journal of the Chinese People's Institute of Foreign Affairs*, 1988, no. 7, pp. 43-52.

doing this or that, while rarely taking note of divergencies between London, Paris, Bonn, Rome, and other capitals.

The second misperception on China's part was the perception of West European independence from the United States within NATO. There was an underlying assumption prevalent among many of China's Europe specialists that NATO was an organization forced upon Europeans by Americans. This misperception had policy implications as China sought to probe and cultivate anti-American sentiment on the Continent and thus perhaps drive a wedge between Washington and its allies. In the words of the late Huan Xiang, China's leading international affairs specialist and adviser to Deng Xiaoping during his lifetime, "the positions and interests of the allies on the two shores of the Atlantic do not actually have much in common."[9]

Whereas China sought to cultivate the anti-Soviet elements in Europe such as Franz Joseph Strauss during the 1970s, during the 1980s increased efforts were made to woo anti-American and antimilitarist elements. The Chinese press followed the peace movement closely, and the Chinese government began inviting Green Party activists and politicians on all-expense-paid trips to China. China did not exactly reembrace the Baader Meinhof and the Irish Repub-

9. Interview with Huan Xiang, "Pekin et les trois mondes," *Politique international*, Spring 1986, p. 191, as cited in Jean-Pierre Cabestan, "Sino-European Relations," in *Chinese Politics and Foreign Policy Reform*, ed. Gerald Segal (London: Kegan Paul International, 1990), p. 219.

lican Army, groups it had supported in earlier years, but it was clear that a new strategy of cultivating the Left took place during the early 1980s. Proponents of European nationalism and antimilitarism were viewed by Beijing as natural allies in its new strategy to accelerate the world's trend toward multipolarity. Increasingly, Beijing deemed any and all strains in American relations with the Continent as for the better.

By mid-decade China's approach to Western Europe had begun to shift again. China began to adopt a more conciliatory attitude toward U.S.-European relations in general and strategic ties in particular. The catalyst was apparently the pending Intermediate-Range Nuclear Forces Treaty. Soviet SS-20 medium-range ballistic missiles threatened Chinese territory as much as they did Western Europe. Consequently, China began lobbying NATO member governments, especially the United States, to include Soviet SS-20s based east of the Urals in any accord; Japan also undertook its share of lobbying on this issue. Chinese efforts apparently paid off, as these medium-range systems were included in the Intermediate-Range Nuclear Forces Treaty, signed in 1987, and the USSR agreed to dismantle 170-odd SS-20s in the Soviet Far East.

China also began paying more attention to West European businessmen during the 1980s. Perhaps in an attempt to diversify its growing dependence on Japan and North America for technology, China began to increase its trade ties with West Europeans. By 1987, two-way trade totaled $13 billion—more than a doubling since 1980. Of this amount, Chinese imports from Western Europe had grown by 169 percent over the same period. Nonetheless, this amounted to a mere 15 percent of China's total foreign trade, and 1 percent of total European Community trade. Among West European states today, Germany garners the lion's share of trade with China, accounting for nearly 40 percent. By 1990, the United Kingdom had surpassed France and Italy as suppliers of industrial and economic equipment to China, a fact probably reflecting the high cost of power-generation equipment that GEC, a British company, was providing for the Daya Bay nuclear power plant. West European governments have also been somewhat reticent to extend loans to China. But what is most surprising is the abysmal amount of West European direct investment in China. As of 1987, France, Italy, Great Britain, and then-West Germany accounted for only 1.7 percent, or $39 million, of total foreign investment in China. This reluctance has caused Chinese officials to call, more than once, for increased European investment.

Sino-East European relations also expanded during the 1980s. Students from Czechoslovakia, Poland, Hungary, and East Germany returned to China during the 1983-84 academic year, the same year that Soviet students returned for the first time since the 1960 split. China also exchanged visits with many East European heads of state, but party-to-party ties remained frozen—except with Yugoslavia and Romania—until 1986-87. The German Democratic Republic's Honecker and Poland's Jaruzelski visited China during 1986, Bulgaria's Zhivkov and Hungary's Kádár in 1987, and Husák of Czechoslovakia and Romania's Ceausescu during 1988. China's then-Premier Zhao Ziyang reciprocated by visiting five East European states during June 1987. Aside from reestablishing party ties and normalizing state relations, reforms and commerce were the principal items on the agenda of these visits. Both sides sought to learn about each other's reform policies, while the Chinese perceived Eastern-bloc nations to be a good outlet for Chinese-produced consumer durables. East European technicians were also welcomed back to China, to refurbish plants built during the 1950s. In addition, a number of delegations in the military and public security spheres were exchanged during 1986-88. Security exchanges with Romania were particularly active. Only Bulgaria and Czechoslovakia did not send or receive delegations in these sensitive fields during these years.[10]

On balance, China witnessed a flowering of relations with both Eastern and Western Europe during the 1980s. As it was poised to further consolidate these ties, the momentous events of 1989—in both China and Europe—erupted.

CHINA AND EUROPE
AFTER TIANANMEN

The Tiananmen massacre had considerable fallout on Sino-West European relations. Like Americans, Europeans were riveted by the events

10. I am indebted to Alyson J. K. Bailes for bringing this to my attention.

unfolding in Beijing and other cities across China during April and May 1989, only to witness the horrors of the crackdown on 3-4 June. Individual West European governments quickly enacted sanctions that paralleled those of the United States, although cultural exchanges were not officially suspended as was the case for the United States.

At the European Community's summit meeting in Madrid on 27 June 1989, Community leaders discussed what steps to take against China. They agreed to impose tough economic sanctions individually and collectively via the Community, suspend all military contacts and arms sales, withhold all ministerial-level official visits to China and defer those already scheduled, freeze all government-guaranteed loans, and release a sharply worded statement condemning the Beijing bloodbath. Member governments also extended visas for 10,000-odd Chinese students who sought not to return to China under current conditions. These sanctions, though, were never intended to inhibit European businesses from continuing their projects or starting new ones in China.

The French government also gave sanctuary and political asylum to numerous Chinese involved in the democracy movement. Included among these were, of course, several notable dissidents and movement leaders, such as political scientist Yan Jiaqi, playwright Su Xiaokang, student leader Wuer Kaixi, and computer entrepreneur Wan Runnan. The presence of these dissidents in Paris caused severe strain in Sino-French relations, particularly after the

French government permitted them a place in the bicentenary parade on Bastille Day.

Tiananmen also caused particular problems for the British. With 1997 drawing ever closer, the two governments were involved in sensitive negotiations over the content of the Hong Kong Basic Law and other important details related to the handover of the colony to Chinese sovereignty. Tiananmen had a major impact in Hong Kong, bringing hundreds of thousands of demonstrators into the streets for unprecedented demonstrations. The brain drain and general exodus of professionals from Hong Kong had been serious prior to 4 June, but they accelerated sharply thereafter. The British and other Western governments were pressed even harder to formulate immigration plans to absorb those who were voting with their feet. While Australia, Canada, the United States, and some Scandinavian countries offered to accept larger numbers, the ultimate burden fell on London to formulate a credible immigration package that would provide a "right of abode" while still encouraging Hong Kong residents to stay in the territory through 1997.

In December 1989, after months of debate inside and outside the House of Commons, Britain passed a special amendment to the 1981 Nationality Act that promised British passports to 50,000 heads of Hong Kong households, thus to include families, bringing the total figure potentially to as many as 250,000. China's response was to "firmly oppose" the granting of the right of abode for Hong Kong citizens, but there was little Beijing could do about it at the time.

During 1990, however, Beijing noticeably increased its pressure on the Hong Kong government. Zhou Nan, a noted political hard-liner, was assigned to head up Xinhua News Agency in Hong Kong—the de facto PRC government representative—and Lu Ping, another hard-liner, was appointed head of the State Council's Hong Kong and Macao Affairs Office. Premier Li Peng and Vice Premier Wu Xueqian both made tough statements concerning the colony during the year.

At issue is Britain's mandate to govern the colony prior to the handover in 1997. This includes the United Kingdom's ability, via its Hong Kong governor, to make all major financial decisions regarding the colony's future. The Hong Kong government's plan to build a new airport costing $16.3 billion is the most illustrative case in point. The Beijing government opposed the project on the basis that it was not consulted as the plan was being drawn up and that it will bankrupt the colony and leave nothing in its coffers when Beijing takes over. To alleviate the situation, intense negotiations took place throughout 1990 and 1991 before an eleventh-hour agreement was reached in July 1991, permitting the project to proceed while alleviating Chinese fears of depleted Hong Kong financial reserves. Nonetheless, it is clear that Beijing will exercise effective veto power over the Hong Kong government as 1997 nears.

Most of the West European sanctions on China resulting from Tiananmen were lifted during the summer of 1990.[11] Following the Group of Seven summit and U.S. President Bush's indication that the United States "would not oppose" the allies' lifting sanctions, the West European governments moved to slowly reinitiate ministerial contacts and government-backed loans. For the time being, arms sales and military contacts remain frozen, but ministerial and head-of-state visits are resuming.

For China's part, Beijing has been far less vociferous in its condemnation of West European sanctions than of American, although it does blame European sanctions and post-Tiananmen nontariff trade barriers for a sharp reduction in two-way trade for 1990.[12] Nor does Beijing particularly blame West European governments, as it does the United States, for trying to undermine Chinese socialism via the strategy of "peaceful evolution." Sino-West European relations have always reflected a more businesslike and pragmatic pursuit of bilateral interests than the often emotionally charged state of Sino-American relations. One possible reason for this is that Europeans do not exhibit the same missionary complex about remolding China that many Americans do.

Nonetheless, politics—exiled Chinese dissidents in particular—have

11. For further discussion of the European reaction to Tiananmen, see Mary Brown Bullock, "The Effects of Tiananmen on China's International Scientific and Educational Cooperation," in *China's Economic Dilemmas in the 1990s: The Problems of Reforms, Modernization, and Interdependence,* ed. U.S., Cong., Joint Economic Committee, vol. 1 (Washington, DC: Government Printing Office, 1991).

12. Xiao Qu, "Hopes and Hurdles in Sino-EC Ties," *China Daily,* 24 Dec. 1990.

become important items on the Sino-European diplomatic agenda. Beijing has made its displeasure known to the French for the granting of political asylum and for permitting Chinese dissidents to locate the headquarters of the Federation for a Democratic China in Paris. In December 1990, China and Sweden became involved in a rare dispute that resulted in the mutual expulsion of diplomats—the first foreign diplomats to be expelled from China since some Soviets in 1976. The catalyst was a Swedish accusation that Chinese diplomats were monitoring and harassing Chinese students in Sweden, a charge that has been repeated in several West European capitals. During the pro-democracy demonstrations in West European capitals before and after the Tiananmen massacre, Chinese diplomats frequently filmed demonstrators and attempted to intimidate the Chinese students among them. Since Tiananmen, innumerable undercover agents have been sent abroad as students in order to monitor dissident activities and set up party cells in the overseas student community.

Eastern Europe's reaction to the Tiananmen massacre varied. The Polish, Hungarian, and Yugoslavian governments made public statements condemning the use of force but did not impose any kind of sanctions against China. The reactionary regimes of Bulgaria, Czechoslovakia, East Germany, and Romania made their approval known to the Chinese but generally stifled news of the massacre internally.[13]

13. Personal communication from a Sinologist in Czechoslovakia.

Throughout the fall of 1989, as East European Communist regimes were coming under increasing pressure, China dispatched several officials to consult with the governments of East Germany, Bulgaria, and Romania. No doubt these emissaries imparted their recent experience and counsel to their East European comrades. Politburo member Yao Yilin visited Erich Honecker within a fortnight of his overthrow, and there is evidence that Honecker ordered the use of force to suppress demonstrators—what he reportedly called the "Chinese solution"—but that his order was disobeyed by key generals and the Stasi. Politburo member and internal security czar Qiao Shi similarly visited Bucharest to consult with Ceausescu shortly before his overthrow and execution.

The reaction of the post-Tiananmen hard-line Chinese government to the democratic upheavals in Eastern Europe during the fall of 1989 and winter of 1990 was one of shock. As one Communist regime after another was overthrown, the Chinese leadership looked on in horror. While the Chinese government refrained from commenting publicly on these momentous events at the time, internal Communist Party documents blamed Mikhail Gorbachev for permitting them.

The Romanian case had a devastating effect on the Chinese leadership, not only because Ceausescu had been an ally of long standing but particularly because of the defection of parts of the Romanian army and security apparat. Following Ceausescu's execution, China's leaders convened emergency meetings, tightened martial law in Beijing, and placed the army on high alert for fear of a repeat performance in the Chinese capital. Subsequently, an intensive campaign was unleashed inside the People's Liberation Army to indoctrinate soldiers to obey the "absolute leadership" of the Communist Party.[14]

The democratic revolutions in Eastern Europe and the reunification of Germany, not to mention the problems gripping the Soviet Union, have left the Chinese leadership in a paranoid state, isolated in the rapidly shrinking socialist world, and fearful of the future. China has taken pains to maintain state-to-state relations with the new regimes in Eastern Europe, but China's role in the region—indeed, in the world in general—has become more marginalized.

FUTURE PROSPECTS

Sino-European relations during the remainder of the decade will no doubt be shaped in large part by the two momentous processes taking place in Europe today—the democratization of Eastern Europe and the integrative currents in Western Europe associated with the 1992 establishment of a common market. Both processes will make relations with Europe more difficult, rather than easier, for China.

The collapse of communism in Eastern Europe can only continue to serve as a beacon of hope to China's

14. For more on this campaign and post-Tiananmen indoctrination in the People's Liberation Army, see David Shambaugh, "The Soldier and the State in China: The Political Work System in the People's Liberation Army," *China Quarterly* (Sept. 1991).

aspiring democrats and a threatening omen to its hard-line leadership. State-to-state relations with the nations of Eastern Europe are likely to remain correct but hardly cordial. Both sides' pressing need for hard currency will serve to limit trade potential. Should the former Communist countries eventually gain full membership in the European Community—they are now under consideration for associate status—it may help to facilitate East European exports to China but could well restrict imports.

The establishment of the European common market in 1992 will have an uncertain effect on China's relations with the nations of Western Europe. It will undoubtedly facilitate exports and European Community-backed financing for trade and investment in China. But if the fears of protectionism among Common Market countries are realized, then Chinese exports will suffer and the already severe asymmetries in two-way trade will only sharpen. Still, China is likely to continue to look to European firms as suppliers of industrial equipment and technology because of the comparative advantages of European producers but also in order to reduce its dependence on Japanese and American sources.

Politically, if the European Community's Parliament and member countries continue to criticize human rights abuses in China and provide sanctuary for Chinese dissidents and students, the Chinese government will no doubt make its irritation known. Bilateral relationships that to date have been pragmatic and businesslike may increasingly take on a contentious cast similar to that of Sino-American relations.

Finally, the fading of the Cold War in Europe, the dissolution of the Warsaw Pact, and the reunification of Germany will all undoubtedly bear on the future evolution of Sino-European relations. China has, to date, viewed these trends with skepticism. On one hand, China welcomes the emergence of a more peaceful and unified Europe, especially if it begins to constitute a new pole in the international system, because it serves China's primary foreign policy objective of weakening superpower influence in the world. On the other hand, China may find it more difficult to deal with this new democratic and capitalist Europe.

For the nations of Europe, China will remain a distant land with marginal bearing on the lives of Europeans or on the concerns of European statesmen. European insularity and the proclivity to look across the Atlantic rather than toward the Pacific, together with Chinese preoccupation with the superpowers and Japan, will ensure that Sino-European relations remain of secondary importance for both sides.

ANNALS, *AAPSS*, 519, January 1992

China and Africa

By GERALD SEGAL

ABSTRACT: It is hard to make a case that Africa matters very much to China. The 45-odd countries of the continent constitute roughly a quarter of all U.N. members and something like a half of all developing states, but they count for little in the overall scheme of Chinese foreign policy objectives. To be sure, there have been times when China was less involved with the international community and its rhetorical policy of support for African causes appeared to suggest that Africa was important to China. But especially since the late 1970s, when China sought prosperity through greater integration with the states of the global market economy, the rhetoric about Africa has been shown to be unsupported by real initiative. Yet this is not to suggest that it is pointless to review China's African policy, for at least a brief survey can help highlight the priorities of Chinese foreign policy and help separate the reality from the sometimes lofty rhetoric.

Gerald Segal is a senior fellow at the International Institute for Strategic Studies and editor of The Pacific Review.

I T is hard to make a case that Africa matters very much to China. The 45-odd countries of the continent constitute roughly a quarter of all U.N. members and something like a half of all developing states, but they count for little in the overall scheme of Chinese foreign policy objectives. To be sure, there have been times when China was less involved with the international community and its rhetorical policy of support for African causes appeared to suggest that Africa was important to China. But especially since the late 1970s, when China sought prosperity through greater integration with the states of the global market economy, the rhetoric about Africa has been shown to be unsupported by real initiative. Yet this is not to suggest that it is pointless to review China's African policy, for at least a brief survey can help highlight the priorities of Chinese foreign policy and help separate the reality from the sometimes lofty rhetoric.

FROM TRADITION
TO REVOLUTION

It is often noted that China's traditional approach to the outside world was based on its Sinocentric world view. China viewed itself as the center of the universe and saw little purpose in making contact with anyone except its immediate neighbors who sometimes posed military threats to Chinese civilization and who traded goods on China's periphery. As a continental power, China paid little attention to naval power until the coming of Western imperialism forced open China's doors and demonstrated that there were other great civilizations that could impose their will.

Yet there was one great exception to this picture of a smug, parochial China. In the fifteenth century, the Ming dynasty sent naval expeditions as far as the coast of East Africa. Although these voyages were not for the purpose of conquest or even really for trade, they were intended as demonstrations of the greatness of Chinese civilization. In many ways, the expeditions were far more impressive than the European voyages of exploration and conquest that were soon to sweep around the tip of Africa on their way to exploit the riches of the Chinese empire.[1] But the challenge of European civilization was so great that traditional China, like Africa in subsequent centuries, was to be shattered by the experience. When China's Communists were making revolution in Asia in the 1930s, Mao Zedong did consider the similarities between the predicaments of Asians and Africans, but with a traditional Sinocentric hubris. Mao felt more confident that Asians could be successful in liberating themselves, and even more sure that China could set an example for Africans. The conquest of Ethiopia by Italy in 1936 may not have been so different from the Japanese occupation of China, but Sinocentrism was a distorting lens for Chinese leaders.[2]

In truth, China's revolutionaries paid little attention to events in Africa, and there were no significant

1. For the ebb and flow of this story, see Gerald Segal, *Rethinking the Pacific* (Oxford: Oxford University Press, 1990).
2. Philip Snow, *The Star Raft* (London: Weidenfeld & Nicolson, 1988).

contacts between revolutionary movements. By the time the People's Republic of China was established in 1949, it was clear that Africa was not going to assume an important place in Chinese foreign policy priorities. Unlike the more distant Latin America, which had established states, Africa, more than anywhere else in the developing world, was stuck in the age of colonialism. In the 1950s, there were official statements of Chinese support for the aspiration of Africans for liberation, but the main struggles were seen to be taking place in Asia. China certainly seemed far more agitated about such events as the Suez crisis of 1956 or the Lebanon crisis of 1958 than it did about any campaign for national liberation in Africa. This was also a period of relatively close cooperation between Soviet and Chinese foreign policy, and even for the far more powerful Soviet Union, events in Africa were near the bottom of the international agenda. China's only real contacts with the continent in this period was the sending of Chinese Muslims to North Africa, where the bulk of the independent states of the continent were to be found. But overall, if Soviet power could not reach Africa, then China was certainly unlikely to expend scarce resources on distant battles.

Yet as the struggles for national liberation developed in Africa, and China began to drift away from the Soviet foreign policy line, the basis was laid for a more active Chinese approach to Africa. It was not so much that China was intrinsically concerned with the individual struggles in Africa as much as it saw the continent as undergoing a stage in the revolutionary process that China had already endured. China also felt that its revolutionary experience in a poor, peasant country was far more appropriate to African conditions than was the experience of the Soviet Union. As Moscow and Beijing fell out over the extent to which they should support revolutionary causes and the best strategies to be pursued in the developing world, China began to see Africa, as it did Asia, as a testing ground of its principles that were disputed by the Soviet Union.

As the Sino-Soviet split came further into the open in the early 1960s, it was fortuitous for China that the Africans began achieving a degree of national self-determination. Yet it is clear that the Africans, although interested in the Chinese experience, did not see it as anything like a guiding light or an especially appropriate example. African revolutionaries were mostly trained in Europe, often in the country of the governing colonial power, and learned their ideology from European examples. China was certainly in no position to offer material assistance and had no influence on the ruling European powers.

After the split in the Communist world became a public feature of the international balance of power, China embarked on a more open campaign to win its share of support in the developing world. The burnishing of China's credentials as the main revolutionary power depended on winning more support in the developing world than in the Soviet Union, and the fast-breaking struggles in Africa in the early and mid-1960s were especially fertile ground for seeking new friends. In 1963-64, Premier

Zhou Enlai led China's first high-level delegation to Africa. He carried the message that China and Africa shared a common experience and could build a new pattern of what would be later known as South-South cooperation.

In fact, in the next decade China was to reach the peak of its real cooperation with African states. The basis of the policy was the relative isolation of China from the mainstream of the international community of either East or West. As China broke with the Soviet Union, it sought to demonstrate that it was possible to wage a more active struggle against what was called American imperialism. China's own activities were virtually confined to Asia, where it supported revolutionary movements and helped Vietnam take on American power. At home, China's descent into the Cultural Revolution was a demonstration of a kind of revolutionary model, but it also meant that Chinese leaders paid less attention to the outside world.

Few African leaders were attracted to such Chinese radicalism, and many resented the rifts that Beijing tore in the cloth of international revolutionary solidarity. Yet this was also the high point of Chinese material support for revolutionary causes. Nearly every liberation movement received some degree of arms, funds, and training from China. At times, Beijing supported opposing forces, and it often proved adept at shifting with the treacherous winds of African revolution.[3] There was never a great

deal of money involved in the Chinese military aid, but the level of technology and training often proved more suitable than the heavier Soviet assistance did.

Perhaps the most celebrated, and overrated, Chinese aid project was the construction of the Tanzania-Zambia railway during the years 1970-75. In one respect, this was a demonstration that China could provide large-scale aid when other great powers declined to do so. But it was also evidence that China sought to bolster friends engaged in support of revolution in southern Africa. The railway was intended to free the Zambian economy from dependence on the white-ruled states of the region and provide safer bases for guerrillas.[4] By 1971, China had replaced Britain as Tanzania's main trade partner. Other Chinese aid was a way of demonstrating that Europeans, by failing to grow such crops as tobacco in Somalia or sugar in Mali, intentionally impoverished Africans. China's favorable terms for loans and aid and its provision of experts who lived in similar conditions as their hosts were designed to show that China had a more appropriate model and a more sympathetic approach. In the 1960s, China demonstrated a grandiose theatrical style of foreign aid by buying a quarter of Tanzania's tobacco crop after the country was left with a huge surplus.[5] It also bought up African coffee and chocolate, despite an absence of demand in China,

3. See details in Anne Gilks and Gerald Segal, *China and the Arms Trade* (London: Croom Helm, 1985).

4. Martin Bailey, *Freedom Railway* (London: Rex Collings, 1976).

5. Alan Hutchinson, *China's African Revolution* (London: Hutchinson, 1975), p. 199.

in order to ensure more balanced trade.[6]

What was more salient, but far less important, was the high level of rhetorical support from China for African causes. Of course, China was a poor country with a limited military reach and was often absorbed by struggles at home or in Asia. To go by China's public statements alone, it would seem that China was a far more important player in the African struggles of the decade from the mid-1960s. When viewed from the perspective of Africans, however, China was valued for its material aid, but advice was rarely taken on matters of grand strategy. Indeed, as the Cultural Revolution faded in intensity in the early 1970s, it was remarkable how little China stressed its Communist ideals and concentrated on vaguer aspirations for South-South cooperation. By then, most African states had won their independence, and development became the main priority. Struggles were still being waged against white-ruled states in southern Africa, but a worrying number of coups and local conflicts in independent Africa led to the fragmentation and continued impoverishment of the continent.

In the early 1970s China emerged, in part thanks to the African votes in the United Nations, as the most powerful spokesman for developing states. Although Chinese leaders were loath to say so explicitly, they saw their seat on the United Nations Security Council as a demonstration of China's arrival as a great power, and the only one that was itself a

developing state. China's foreign policy rhetoric became more explicitly focused on managing North-South relations and less on revolutionary struggles. In 1974, Deng Xiaoping espoused the Chinese view that there should be new commodity cartels formed by developing states in order to force changes in the international economy. At this stage, China was not yet set on taking part in the international market economy and still entertained hopes of changing the system by means of direct challenges to the developed world such as those used by the Organization of Petroleum Exporting Countries. China's vocal support for a New International Economic Order, access by developed states to resources on the seabed, removal of trade barriers in the richer world, and assistance from the North to restructure the economies of the developing world have all been features of the foreign policy agenda of African states.

Yet, by the mid-1970s, a growing sense had developed in China and Africa that China was simply not very important or effective in supporting its rhetoric. Not surprisingly, China was unable to change the nature of the international market economy, and certainly there was little basis for South-South economic cooperation. But even more worrying was China's self-centered approach to regional conflicts and its inability to do much that was effective in the military realm. Since the open hostilities along the Sino-Soviet frontier in 1969 and the rapid improvement of Sino-American relations in the early 1970s, China's policy in Africa as elsewhere in the developing world

6. Snow, *Star Raft*, chap. 5.

had begun to use anti-Sovietism as the litmus test. States such as Zaire that were strongly anti-Soviet were lavished with praise from Beijing even though they were among the most openly pro-Western and unhelpful to revolutionary causes. China's attitude toward the conflict in the Horn of Africa in the 1970s shifted as the local participants exchanged superpower patrons. China professed to see a sweeping Soviet strategy of expansion in Africa that included naval expansion into the ports of Ethiopia and Somalia. China warned Africans and the West that the Soviets were after strategic minerals and had to be opposed by a coalition of African states no matter what their political color. Concern was expressed about the Soviet Union's strategy in the Indian Ocean, and China seemed to focus more on East Africa than ever before. At one point in the 1970s, China was the only major power with an embassy in the Comoro Islands.[7]

But when it came to the major conflicts of the period, such as the war in Angola in the mid-1970s, China was unable to develop its small-scale guerrilla aid missions when the fighting grew heavier.[8] At one time, China supported two of the anti-Soviet rebel factions of the Popular Movement for the Liberation of Angola and eventually found itself backing the South Africa-supported rebels of the National Union for the Total Independence of Angola. The Chinese rationale was a relatively simple strand of anti-Sovietism, but when the Soviet Union and Cuba stepped up the level of their military aid, China simply lacked the ability to compete. The ignominious retreat, and the subsequent inability to provide major aid in the struggles in Zimbabwe and Mozambique, did serious damage to China's position. When it came to the crunch of struggles in southern Africa, China was a peripheral actor.

Yet this Chinese retreat was not merely a matter of military weakness. By the late 1970s, there were important signs of change in Chinese domestic and foreign policy. Although the anti-Soviet line was to remain a guiding feature at least for a few years into the 1980s, China had begun to reassess its attitude toward the international market economy and saw a new role for developing states. The age of domestic reform in China that began in late 1978 did not always mean that foreign policy was reformed,[9] but in many senses it can be said that China's foreign policy matured in the 1980s and its policy toward Africa was adjusted as a result.

AFRICAN POLICY IN THE AGE OF REFORM

In 1978, all of Africa accounted for less than 1 percent of Chinese trade.

7. Ibid., chap. 6.

8. John Marcum, *The Angolan Revolution* (Cambridge: MIT Press, 1978); Eugene K. Lawson, "China in Ethiopia and Angola," in *Soviet and Chinese Aid to African Nations*, ed. Warren Weinsten and Thomas Henriksen (New York: Praeger, 1980).

9. Gerald Segal, ed., *Chinese Politics and Foreign Policy Reform* (London: Kegan Paul International, 1990).

Although these figures were to fluc-
tuate in subsequent years, the per-
centages remained largely unchanged
in 1989 and roughly a third the level
of trade with the more distant Latin
America. Chinese trade with the 14
million people of Holland was some
30 percent higher than that with
all of Africa. Chinese aid to Africa
had dropped to a total of some $200
million per year. Although China's
public statements suggested that it
still cared about Africa, the reality was much harsher. Africa had
consistently failed to make progress
in terms of modernization and so
lacked the basis to trade with a China
that was interested in greater openness to the international market
economy as a way to modernize the
life of 1.1 billion Chinese. What is
more, as China improved relations
with the Soviet Union in the 1980s,
there was even less rationale for
seeking the support of anti-Soviet
states in Africa.

It was certainly hard to find rem-
nants of China's former position as a
supporter of revolutionary causes in
Africa. On Premier Zhao Ziyang's
major tour of Africa in 1982-83, there
was a very distinct line that the two
superpowers were to blame for the
problems of the region, but the tone
was far less aggressive than during
Zhou's visit a little over two decades
earlier. Certainly, the anti-Soviet line
of the years just previous had clearly
been moderated. China wooed the Africans with backing for their candidate as U.N. secretary-general but
with little else.

The Chinese never risked compli-
cating their position by taking sides
either in the civil war in the Sudan or

in the dispute over ownership of the
Western Sahara. During the long-
running civil war in Chad, China declined to become involved as an arms
supplier and now is a clear supporter
of national-unity politics. A Guangxi
firm won the contract to build Chad's
parliament.[10] As various disputes in
Africa evolved in the 1980s, China
became a consistently cautious supporter of negotiations. As West Africa
was destabilized by the brutal civil
war in Liberia in 1990, China did
little more than express careful concern.[11] Beijing frequently expressed
bland support for the Organization of
African Unity and mediation, as in
the case of the dispute between Senegal and Mauritania.[12] When the parties to the disputes in Namibia and
Angola became ready for compromise
in the late 1980s, China assumed the
lofty position of a United Nations Security Council member whose position was virtually indistinguishable
from that of the Soviet Union. China
supported the massive U.N. operations to monitor the cease-fire and
supervise the elections in Namibia.
China seemed prepared for a similar
approach to the conflict on the Horn
of Africa, although the prospects for
peace seemed far slimmer.[13] On a
visit to East Africa in January 1991,

10. Various Xinhua reports in June 1990,
in British Broadcasting Service, *Summary of
World Broadcasts—Far East* (hereafter *SWB—
FE*) no. 0803, sec. A-5, p. 1; ibid., 17 Nov. 1990,
in *SWB—FE*, no. 0937, sec. A5, p. 1.

11. Xinhua, 27 Aug. 1990, in *SWB—FE*, no.
0856, sec. A5, p. 1.

12. Foreign Minister Qian Qichen on 27
Aug. 1990, in Foreign Broadcast Information
Service, *FBIS Daily Report—China*, 1990,
FBIS-Chi-90-166-12.

13. *Beijing Review*, 6-12 Aug. 1990.

Foreign Minister Qian Qichen spoke in Kenya about the common view toward the United Nations' sanctioned collective security in the Persian Gulf crisis. In his visit to Ethiopia, Qian stayed out of local politics, but his very visit suggested some support for the endangered regime.[14] Essentially, it seemed as if China was anxious to see a reduction of tension so that its friendship would not be tested and fine words would suffice for a policy.

Even on the key question of the future of South Africa, China has been content to take up a posture that requires no action.[15] Persistent rumors of clandestine trading relations with South Africa, especially in diamonds, may have been part of the reason. But, more broadly, China was happy to see South Africa evolve in 1990 toward black majority rule and without a major armed struggle. The apparent differences within the black community reminded China of the earlier disputes between African states and that even during the Nigerian civil war China had refrained from declaring its position. The tentative reforms in South Africa in 1990 were welcomed by China in part because they meant that fewer demands might be made on China to support an anti-Western cause and there would be less need to prop up Front Line States in southern Africa. China showed signs of easing sanctions in line with the gradual reforms in South Africa.[16]

Essentially, China was hoping that few demands would be made upon it by African states, as China had other priorities at home and in Asia. Thus China declined requests from Guinea and Mali to build another railway similar to that between Tanzania and Zambia. China declined a request to build a dam on the borders of Mali and Senegal and, perhaps most striking of all, declined to give any substantial aid to Nigeria, the most populous country on the continent.[17] Chinese aid projects in the late 1980s were derisory. China agreed to construct the People's Palace in Chad, and a tiny loan was granted to the Central African Republic in April 1990. Algeria picked up disaster-relief funds to the grand sum of 1 million yuan, and medicine and medical equipment valued at $30,000 was given to Ethiopia in January 1990. China rescheduled the Congo's debt in November 1990, but no figures were provided on the terms.[18] Long gone were the days of high-profile projects and aid designed to teach the Africans and the world a lesson about Chinese benevolence and the Chinese road to development. Chinese comments on the far stronger French position in Africa raised the usual complaints about unfulfilled promises regarding modernization, but the reality remained that French aid was much higher and

14. Reports on the visit, in *SWB—FE*, no. 0968, sec. A5, pp. 1-2.

15. *Beijing Review*, 16-22 July 1990; ibid., 15-21 Oct. 1990.

16. For a sample of the Chinese view, see

Beijing home service on 9 June 1990, in *SWB—FE*, no. 0788, sec. A5, p. 1, and *Wen wei po* (Hong Kong), 22 Nov. 1990, in *SWB—FE*, no. 0937, sec. A5, p. 1.

17. Snow, *Star Raft*, chap. 6.

18. Details in *China News Analysis* 15 June 1990, no. 1412, and *SWB—FE*, no. 0937, sec. A5, p. 1, for events in Nov. 1990.

African affection for France was much clearer than it was for China.[19]

Not even in the aftermath of the Beijing massacre in June 1989 did China's policy toward Africa change to any substantive extent. To be sure, Captain Blaise Comparoe of Burkina Faso was the first foreign leader to turn up in Beijing after the killing, and he was rewarded with a loan and a children's playground for his country. Congratulations on the success of the operation in Beijing were received from the chairman of the South-West African People's Organization and Algeria's Pan Africanist Congress. Of course, few African states can claim to be liberal democracies, and the record of abuse of human rights on the continent meant that there was little surprise when African states helped block any attempt to raise the matter of Chinese actions in June 1989 at the United Nations. Foreign Minister Qian Qichen set off on a six-nation tour of Africa in the summer of 1989, receiving warm praise on every stop.

But in the developed world, where concern with human rights in China was highest, the speculation that China would turn to the dictators of the developing world and forsake contacts with the developed world simply never materialized. For one thing, there has been regular evidence that Chinese often have deeply ingrained racist attitudes toward Africans, which surface periodically in unrest at Chinese universities. But more important, China needed the developed world for trade and investment, and Beijing guessed—as it

turns out, correctly—that the Western sanctions would gradually be lifted. For all the brutality of the suppression of opposition inside China in 1989, the leadership remained pragmatic about dealing with the outside world. Africa, and the developing world as a whole, was no substitute for decent relations with the developed world.

Indeed, there were signs, at least in the first year after the Beijing massacre, that parts of the developing world, and especially Africa, were wavering in their support for China. Now that China was no longer a major provider of aid and its model of development looked like yet another part of the international market economy, there was little reason for Africans not to be pragmatic about finding friends and funds. Taiwan had a briefly successful surge in buying the diplomatic recognition of several developing states, including Liberia, Lesotho, and Guinea-Bissau.[20] China responded by severing ties with these states, but by late 1990 it had become clear that China had done better out of the recent shift in diplomatic recognitions, picking up the far more valuable Saudi Arabia, Indonesia, and Singapore. It was a sign of the poverty of Africa and the lack of principle in international relations with the continent that the poor African states could be bought by the higher Taiwanese offers of aid.

By the late 1980s, the broad pattern of Chinese relations with Africa had settled down to a state of minimum care. For example, a delegation

19. *Beijing Review*, 9-15 July 1990.

20. On the latter case, see Radio Beijing on 2 June 1990, in *SWB—FE*, no. 0782, sec. A5, p. 1.

from the parliament of the Comoros turned up in Beijing in June 1990 on what was plainly a junket, to be told that China and African states shared many basic approaches. But the Chinese spoke mainly of their current concern, that the West was anxious to subvert the socialist system, while this worry was not really on the agenda of the visitors. The language of shared concerns with modernization and a New International Economic Order was also present but with little evidence that South-South cooperation was being translated into much of value for either state.[21] Qian Qichen and Jiang Zemin had met the foreign minister of Burkina Faso earlier in the month, and the themes at that time also included expressions of worry about the international debt problem.[22]

One of the more notable absences from the run of relations was military exchanges. In China's relations with the Middle East in particular, but also with Latin America, the question of Chinese arms sales and military cooperation had become far more important in the years of pragmatism and domestic reform.[23] But as the Africans had little money to spend on wars and as China was not selling at friendship prices in the age of reform, there was little business to be done. To be sure, some military delegations

did turn up in Beijing, but there was little evidence of major deals being done.[24]

In 1990, after the effects of the ending of the Cold War began to be felt, China also seemed to be acknowledging the limited appeal it might have in Africa. At a time when Africans were growing ever more worried about the focusing of major international lending institutions on Eastern Europe, China knew it was in no position to fill the aid gap. Indeed, China itself was making major demands on these same institutions. The collapse of communism also meant that socialism as an ideology, although never at the forefront of the Chinese appeal to Africa, was even more tarnished than before. China openly acknowledged the inroads that former colonial powers such as France were having in Africa in 1990 due to the increased desire on the part of some African states to take a more positive approach to the international market economy.[25] Certainly the North Africans were especially involved in such shifts, and many also were far more interested in the prospects for integration with Europe after 1992 than in pursuing South-South cooperation. Chinese commentaries tried to build support in Africa by noting that international aid agencies were now demanding far more sweeping domestic changes before major loans could be granted, and the conditions increasingly included a concern with greater democ-

21. Xinhua, 22 and 23 June 1990, in *SWB—FE*, no. 0803, sec. A5, p. 1.

22. Xinhua, 12 and 13 June 1990, in *SWB—FE*, no. 0794, sec. A5, p. 1.

23. Wolfgang Decker, "Latin America: How China Sees the Region," *Pacific Review*, 1989, no. 3; Yitzhak Shichor, "Unfolded Arms: Beijing's Recent Military Sales Offensive," ibid., 1988, no. 3.

24. A delegation came to Beijing from Tanzania in 1990, noted in *SWB—FE*, no. 0782, sec. A5, p. 1.

25. *Beijing Review*, 9-15 July 1990, p. 10.

ratization. Given China's post-1989 sensitivity on such matters, such remarks perhaps said more about Chinese than about African concerns.[26] But with the outbreak of the Persian Gulf war in 1991, there were some signs that China and many African states shared a common unease about the implications of leading Western powers' joining forces with friendly Arab regimes to defeat Iraq. The tone of Chinese and African commentaries suggest a heightened worry with neocolonialism.

To be sure, China continued to try to build bridges on the basis of concern in the developing world over the ending of the Cold War and extent to which the developed world would now see less reason to vie for the friendship of the South. In a meeting with the Zambian prime minister in July 1990, Li Peng was at pains to point out that conflicts still existed in the developing world and that the developed world still bore much of the blame.[27] The language of South-South cooperation had not faded, even in the midst of the crisis in the neighboring Persian Gulf when the Arab world was rent apart.[28] It seemed that much of the rhetoric was the same, despite an obviously changing reality. Of course, without the shared worry about the machinations of the developed world, there would be even less to hold China and Africa together.

26. *People's Daily*, 20 July 1990, in *SWB—FE*, no. 0826, sec. A5, pp. 1-2.
27. Xinhua, 23 and 24 July 1990, in *SWB—FE*, no. 0826, sec. A5, p. 1.
28. Li Peng's meeting with Nyerere on 27 Aug. 1990, in *SWB—FE*, no. 0854, sec. A5, p. 1.

ONLY ONE WAY TO GO

The reality of Chinese policy toward Africa in the 1990s is harsh. Trade and aid are tiny, and neither Chinese nor Africans sense that the other is very important in the overall scheme of their foreign policy. Both sides represent parts of the developing world, although Africans continue to see China as in the developing world while not truly being of it. Yet this is unfair, for China, like other developing states, especially in Asia, has simply chosen to take a more positive approach to the international market economy than many Africans, and parts of China are skilled enough to prosper in that world. That China is an aspiring superpower is perhaps the more important reason for differentiating China from the African states.

As China grows strong, there may be some reason to expect an enhanced Chinese role in African affairs. Events in the Middle East show that China can move from mere rhetoric to being a real force in local politics if it, for example, engages in major arms sales and, as a member of the United Nations Security Council, takes an active role in managing regional security. China's trade with the Middle East has also benefited from the fact that some states of the region are rich but short of manpower. But in Africa, there is little basis for major trade relations. Moreover, two decades of South-South cooperation have shown little progress. The fading of the East-West Cold War may well place greater emphasis on North-South relations, but the crisis in the Persian Gulf suggests that the

South is far more likely to be so divided that it will mean little to talk of North-South relations. Certainly China seems to be still committed to the view that one must work within the international market economy rather than try to confront it from a Southern fortress.

Thus there may be grounds for believing that as China grows strong, it will grow somewhat more important for Africans. But in the Chinese perspective, it seems that while Africa will attract attention from the writers of official policy statements, the continent will remain the least important area for Chinese foreign policy, whether of an expanding or a withdrawing kind.

ANNALS, *AAPSS*, 519, January 1992

China's Relations with Hong Kong and Taiwan

By PARRIS H. CHANG

ABSTRACT: National reunification is one of the Beijing leadership's topmost priorities, and the People's Republic of China (PRC) will take over control of Hong Kong in 1997. In recent years, the PRC has blocked Hong Kong's democratic reform and increasingly meddled in local Hong Kong affairs to strengthen Chinese control. These actions have exacerbated Hong Kong's crisis of confidence, causing a severe brain drain and flight of capital from the colony. In Taiwan, the accession to office in 1988 by President Lee Teng-hui, a native Taiwanese, and the growing democratization of Taiwan's politics and power structure, with calls for Taiwanese independence, are worrisome to Beijing. Hence the PRC authorities are pulling out all stops, including a low-keyed threat of force, to forestall separatism and press the government in Taipei to come to the negotiation table. Years before Hong Kong's reversion to China in 1997, Beijing seems likely to intensify the reunification campaign toward Taiwan. Should the PRC use coercion against Taipei, Beijing and Washington would be on a collision course, because the United States has a strong interest in Taiwan's stability, security, and continuous prosperity.

Parris H. Chang is professor of political science and director of East Asian studies at Pennsylvania State University. Born in Taiwan in 1936, he received his B.A. from National Taiwan University in 1959, his M.A. from the University of Washington in 1963, and his Ph.D. from Columbia University in 1969. He has written Radicals and Radical Ideology in China's Cultural Revolution *(1973),* Power and Policy in China *(1990), and* Elite Conflict in Post-Mao China *(1983) and has contributed to more than a dozen other books.*

I N the minds of Chinese Communist Party (CCP) leaders, Hong Kong, Macao, and Taiwan are Chinese territories and must be reunited with the mainland. In a major policy speech delivered to an assembly of ranking party cadres on 16 January 1980, Chinese leader Deng Xiaoping identified the containment of hegemonism, the reunification of China, and economic modernization as the three top national priorities for the 1980s.[1] Since then, the Chinese leadership has devoted much effort to achieving these three objectives.

With regard to the reunification of China, Beijing has secured the consent of Great Britain to return Hong Kong in 1997, and Portugal will turn Macao over to China in 1999. Although the Chinese leadership has pledged to preserve Hong Kong's capitalist and free-port system, there is a severe crisis of confidence among Hong Kong residents and in the international business community, especially after the Tiananmen massacre, and the capital flight and brain drain from Hong Kong are serious.

While the prospect of Taiwan's reunification with mainland China remains remote, Taiwan-mainland relations have changed significantly and continue to change. The trade, economic ties, communications, and human interactions between the two have expanded enormously since the late 1980s, due to a host of factors, including policy shifts in both Beijing and Taipei.

The CCP leadership is unquestionably pleased by these develop-

1. *Deng Xiaoping's Selected Works, 1975-82* (in Chinese) (Beijing: People's Publishing House, 1983), pp. 203-4.

ments, which Beijing attributes to its peace offensive and skillful "united front" operation. Not a few CCP officials, however, seem quite ambivalent and apprehensive as Taiwan undergoes democratization and Taiwanization in elite composition and power structure. The result could entail independent nationhood. In the past, Beijing has taken various steps, including interference in Taiwan's political process, threat of force, and countermeasures against Taipei's "flexible diplomacy," to stem this tide.

In addition to China's policy toward Hong Kong and Taiwan, this article will also examine the responses of Hong Kong and Taiwan, their interactions with China, and the evolving relations of the three parties.

HONG KONG:
A BORROWED PLACE
ON BORROWED TIME

Britain took Hong Kong from the Manchu dynasty in three stages. Hong Kong Island was ceded by China under the 1842 Treaty of Nanking. A small part of Kowloon opposite the island, plus Stonecutter's Island, were leased to Britain in perpetuity under the 1860 Treaty of Beijing. The New Territories, which includes most of Kowloon Peninsula and constitutes 89 percent of Hong Kong's total land area, was obtained from China under the 1898 convention of Beijing on a 99-year lease, which expires on 1 July 1997.

Both the Communist government and the Nationalist, or Kuomintang (KMT), government on Taiwan held that all these treaties were invalid because they were imposed on China by force and therefore the entire colony should be returned to China. In 1984, after two years of negotiation, China and the United Kingdom announced the Joint Declaration on the Question of Hong Kong, agreeing that the British government would turn the entire Hong Kong territory over to China in 1997. Hong Kong will then become a special administrative region (SAR) of China.[2]

In the agreement, Beijing pledged (1) not to change the prevailing capitalist system and life-style for 50 years, and (2) that the local government will be administered by the people of Hong Kong and will have a high degree of autonomy. A Basic Law that will serve as a constitution for the SAR has been drafted by a committee appointed by China. Hong Kong will have its own executive, legislative, and judicial offices, and Beijing has promised that the current laws can remain unchanged as long as they do not conflict with Chinese law. But China's National People's Congress must approve SAR laws, and its State Council will have the power to nullify them.

The present judicial and legal system will be maintained, but all legal proceedings are to be locally contained, with no appeals available through the higher courts of either China or the United Kingdom. The National People's Congress's Stand-

ing Committee, however, rather than the Hong Kong courts, will have the power to interpret the Basic Law for the SAR after it is enacted. The Hong Kong and Shanghai Banking Corporation and Chartered Banks will continue to issue the Hong Kong dollar, which will remain a freely convertible international currency. The Hong Kong police will maintain law and order, although Beijing has stated that it will dispatch troops to the region to provide security. Hong Kong citizens will continue to enjoy the freedom to travel overseas. An Anglo-Chinese Joint Liaison Group is monitoring the transition period and the transfer of power.

Ever since the agreement was signed, many local residents and foreign investors have questioned whether the People's Republic of China (PRC) will live up to all its pledges. There is doubt that Beijing will be able to long tolerate Hong Kong's free economy, free press, and independent court system or that China will be able to allow the people of Hong Kong rights denied to those on the mainland.[3] Such doubt was reinforced when the Chinese authorities used violence to suppress prodemocracy demonstrators in Tiananmen Square in June 1989.

On the other hand, many people continue to believe that Hong Kong does have a future. For them, Hong Kong has been very important to the Chinese economy, which has received nearly 35 percent of its annual foreign exchange from exports to and through the colony and from invest-

2. For an analysis of Hong Kong SAR laws and governmental structure, see Byron S. Y. Weng, "Taiwan and Hongkong, 1987: A Review," in *China Briefing 1988*, ed. Anthony G. Kane (Boulder, CO: Westview Press, 1988), pp. 134-37.

3. Ross H. Munro, "Who Lost Hong Kong?" *Commentary*, 90(6):34-39 (Dec. 1990).

ments there. Thus Hong Kong's future rests largely on the stability of the Chinese leadership and its continued emphasis on pragmatism and economic modernization. Speaking at a luncheon organized by the Hong Kong General Chamber of Commerce on 21 June 1990, Zhou Nan, director of the Hong Kong branch of Xinhua, or the New China News Agency (NCNA), stated: "A stable and prosperous China not only constitutes the key to the stability and prosperity of Hong Kong, but also is an essential factor in stabilizing the situation in Asia as well as in the world."[4] The crucial question is whether China will be stable and its leadership pragmatic.

PREPARATIONS
FOR TAKEOVER

In May 1985, the Joint Liaison Group was set up to monitor the implementation of the bilateral agreement, to smooth intergovernmental relations during the transition period, and to aid in the transfer of power in 1997. The group is composed of a chief delegate with ambassadorial rank and four additional members from each side. It met in Beijing, London, or Hong Kong alternately, but it set up offices in Hong Kong after 1 July 1988.

The Joint Liaison Group was formed only for liaison purposes and has no vested power. It has dealt mainly with issues concerning Hong Kong's international status, such as membership in the General Agreement on Tariffs and Trade, international rights and duties, ship registration, and passport and visas for

4. *Beijing Review*, 2-8 July 1990, p. 9.

Hong Kong residents. Although the plan did not call for the group to take part in the administration of Hong Kong, the Chinese delegation tends to use it to interfere in the governing of Hong Kong.

Since the group is composed of two delegations actually representing the positions of their respective governments, decisions are usually reached through compromise. It appears that conflicting interests between China and Britain have sometimes hindered the group's efficiency, however. Moreover, Hong Kong residents are not represented, a fact that reinforces local feelings of abandonment to an uncertain fate.

Although legal authority will not shift to Beijing until 1 July 1997, the PRC has lost no time in becoming involved in local affairs. It has set up a shadow government in the colony to strengthen its control apparatus in preparation for taking over Hong Kong's administrative functions. The local branch of Xinhua, the informal but official agent of Beijing, has become increasingly active in the colony. As a result of a reorganization since 1985, the agency has set up 10 departments to coordinate with different sectors in Hong Kong, including administration, research, propaganda, foreign affairs, economics, culture, education, art and sports, and social affairs. During the years 1983-89 the agency was headed by Xu Jiatun, a former first party secretary of Jiangsu province and a former member of the CCP Central Committee. As Beijing's chief spokesman, Xu frequently appeared in public and expressed his government's views through the news media.

Besides its growing formal political influence in Hong Kong, the agency has tried to affect the territory's cultural life. This campaign is intended to make friends and gain influence for China within literary, art, educational, and mass-media circles, as well as to neutralize anti-Communist influences. Before 1989, many critical and even hostile intellectuals, businesspersons, professionals, publishers, and journalists toned down their attacks on China and its Hong Kong policy, indicating that the NCNA had achieved some success in these efforts.

PRC-HONG KONG
RELATIONS SINCE TIANANMEN

On several occasions in the spring and summer of 1989, as many as 1 million Hong Kong residents took to the streets to show their support for the pro-democracy movement in China and to protest the violent crackdown on students and citizens in Beijing. Such massive demonstrations were unprecedented in the history of the colony. Even the CCP-controlled newspapers, especially *Wen wei po*, deviated from the Party line, reported freely on the pro-democracy movement, and expressed strong support for it. These responses reflected the people's acute concern for the future of Hong Kong, which has been seriously jeopardized by the Tiananmen massacre and the perceived British sellout. A rush of applications for emigration is indicative of their loss of confidence in the post-1997 situation.

China's relations with Hong Kong deteriorated badly after Tiananmen.

PRC authorities mounted an intense propaganda barrage against hostile and anti-Communist elements, accusing them of subversion, infiltration, interference in China's internal affairs, and providing shelter to exiled Chinese dissidents. The PRC also took concrete actions. In July 1989, Beijing sacked Li Zisong, the outspoken publisher of *Wen wei po*.[5] Since then, it has quietly eased out pro-reform cadres from the Hong Kong NCNA and other PRC-controlled organizations, replacing them with hard-liners.[6] Those who have been transferred or retired are known to be associates of Xu Jiatun, the reform-minded ex-NCNA director, who defected to the United States in May 1990.[7]

Beijing also put immense pressure on the Hong Kong authorities to disband a number of pro-democracy organizations and to arrest or repatriate Chinese dissidents. Beijing was most critical of the Hong Kong Alliance in Support of the Patriotic Democratic Movement in China, headed by two leading political and civic figures, Szeto Wah and Martin Lee. The alliance played a leading role in fundraising, mobilizing popular support for the democratic movement in China, and providing financial aid to

5. Li, 78, had followed the CCP line for more than forty years before openly rebelling against the CCP leadership during the spring of 1989 in his columns. In protest at Li's dismissal, about thirty of the staff at *Wen wei po* resigned.

6. Ann Scott Tyson, "China Eases Pro-Reform Cadres out of Hong Kong," *Christian Science Monitor*, 7 Jan. 1991, p. 6.

7. In Feb. 1991, Xu was expelled from the CCP and dropped from the Standing Committee of the National People's Congress.

political dissidents smuggled out of China who had organized a democratic movement in exile, in Paris. Unable to force the Hong Kong authorities to disband the alliance, Beijing suspended Szeto and Lee from the Basic Law Drafting Committee in October 1989, so as to intimidate its critics in Hong Kong.

In spite of PRC pledges that Hong Kong could preserve its prevailing capitalist and social systems after 1997 and that Great Britain would exercise full authority until June 1997, Beijing tends increasingly to meddle in Hong Kong policy. For example, alarmed by the widespread support among the local populace for democracy in China and fearful of Hong Kong's political reform, Beijing effectively vetoed a British plan for a quicker pace of democratic reform. Thus, in June 1990, the Basic Law Drafting Committee drafted, obviously at the behest of the PRC leadership,[8] a Basic Law that would limit to 18 the number of elected seats in Hong Kong's 60-member legislature, leaving the rest to be manipulated by Beijing. The elected total would rise to only 30 by the year 2003. The response from Hong Kong citizens was highly critical.[9]

Another example was the persistent attempt by the PRC to influence a new airport project. Beginning in December 1990, Lu Ping, the newly appointed director in charge of Hong Kong affairs at the State Council, and other officials repeatedly criticized the project and its financing. On 9 February 1991, Hong Kong media prominently reported Deng Xiaoping's remarks to other CCP leaders, as published in a pro-PRC Chinese magazine, allegedly calling for vigilance against British "bad plots" to squander Hong Kong's coffers on the $20 billion-plus airport and harbor projects and "leave behind a heavy burden" for China after 1997.[10]

CAPITAL FLIGHT AND BRAIN DRAIN

Many in Hong Kong have been alarmed by increasing Chinese attempts to interfere with local affairs, attempts that they construe as breaches of the 1984 Sino-British joint declaration. Martin Lee, a Legislative Council member and a leader of the democratic forces, voiced this widespread concern when he pointed out that if China meddles in Hong Kong's affairs now, with Britain present, it is questionable that after 1997 China will keep its promise of allowing Hong Kong " 'a high degree of autonomy.' "[11]

Such sentiment, coupled with the loss of confidence in the future of Hong Kong in the aftermath of Tiananmen and the perceived British betrayal, has resulted in a severe brain drain and flight of capital. People, especially the more skilled, are leav-

8. The Basic Law Drafting Committee is appointed by and responsible to the Chinese National People's Congress rather than to any Hong Kong or U.K. body. Of 59 members in the committee, 36 are from China and 23 are from Hong Kong, mostly representing big business and groups sympathetic to Beijing.

9. Barbara Basler, "Hong Kong Leaders Criticize Beijing-Dominated Draft of Charter," *New York Times*, 22 June 1990, p. 3.

10. *China Times* (Taipei), 10 Feb. 1991, p. 9.

11. Nicholas D. Kristof, " 'Meddling' by Chinese Is Worrying Hong Kong," *New York Times*, 28 Dec. 1990.

ing in large numbers: about 45,000 annually in the past three years, or roughly double the rate of 1984. The rate is expected to reach 55,000-60,000 in 1991. This high rate of emigration disrupts offices and creates skill shortages.

Many companies have relocated their legal domicile to more trustworthy jurisdictions. The reincorporation of the Hong Kong and Shanghai Banking Corporation, the colony's quasi-central bank, in early 1991 could only further exacerbate the crisis of confidence in the international business community in Hong Kong and induce more companies to reincorporate elsewhere in order to maximize possible legal protection. Many companies have diversified their businesses geographically beyond what would seem to be justified by purely business-oriented calculations.

CHANGING RELATIONS BETWEEN THE PRC AND TAIWAN, 1949-78

Although the establishment of the PRC was proclaimed in October 1949, China's civil war did not end. Defeated by the CCP, the KMT nonetheless relocated the government of the Republic of China (ROC) in Taiwan, claiming to be the sole legal government of China and challenging the legitimacy of the "bandit" regime in Beijing. President Chiang Kai-shek vowed to retake the mainland by force. Thus to capture Taiwan and destroy the KMT regime became one of the most important leadership priorities of Mao Zedong and other CCP leaders.

Before the Chinese Communists could launch an invasion across the Taiwan Strait in the first half of 1950, Kim Il Sung's North Korean troops marched south on 25 June 1950 seeking to unify the two Koreas by force, thereby preempting what the CCP might have done to Taiwan. Two days later, President Harry Truman sent U.S. troops to Korea to fight the North Korean invaders. Equally important, he dispatched the Seventh Fleet to "neutralize" the Taiwan Strait—this was a complete about-face in U.S. policy toward China.[12] The U.S. action meant a renewed American intervention in the civil war, causing an indefinite postponement of a Communist "liberation" of Taiwan.

As soon as the Korean War ended, the Communists turned their attention toward the unfinished task, and during the years 1954-58, Beijing mounted several military campaigns against Nationalist island outposts off the East China coast. In 1955, the United States signed a treaty of mutual defense with the Republic of China, committing itself to the defense of Taiwan against Communist invasion.[13]

When Beijing threatened to liberate Taiwan in the summer of 1958 by launching a large-scale bombardment of Quemoy and Matsu, two Nationalist outposts off the shore of Fujian province, Washington's reactions were correspondingly firm. The U.S.

12. Foster Rhea Dulles, *American Policy toward Communist China: The Historical Record: 1949-1969* (New York: Thomas J. Crowell, 1972), pp. 94-95.
13. Ibid., pp. 152-56.

Seventh Fleet provided a convoy for the Nationalist ships supplying the offshore islands, for example. In the face of the strong U.S. reaction, Beijing soon backed down and called for negotiation with the United States.

For more than three decades, since the fall of 1958, Beijing has not made another attempt to use force against the offshore islands, let alone invade Taiwan. Instead, the Communists and the Nationalists have continued to wage propaganda war across the Taiwan Strait. Likewise, both sides have fought many diplomatic battles in various international arenas, competing for diplomatic recognition and membership in international organizations.

BEIJING'S PEACE OFFENSIVES SINCE 1979

Since the signing of the Shanghai Communiqué between President Nixon and Premier Zhou Enlai in 1972, and especially since the establishment of U.S.-PRC diplomatic relations in 1979, Beijing has launched a series of peace offensives aimed at Taiwan's reunification with the mainland. On 1 January 1979, Beijing announced a cease-fire in the Taiwan Strait; it abandoned the slogan "liberation of Taiwan" and proclaimed a policy of peaceful reunification. Moreover, it also called for the establishment of transportation and postal services, the reunion of relatives, the exchange of visits, and direct trade between the mainland and Taiwan.

During the 1980s, the Beijing authorities made a series of peace offers to induce the Nationalists to settle the issue of Taiwan's reunion with

the mainland at the negotiation table. In an interview with the Taiwan-based *China Times* on 24 September 1990, PRC President and CCP Politburo member Yang Shangkun reiterated all the main points that other Communist officials had made earlier and called for the CCP and the KMT to negotiate "on the basis of equality." Key passages of Yang's remarks follow:

To realize reunification we put forward the position of "one country, two systems," a position raised by Deng Xiaoping. . . .

"One country, two systems" means Taiwan will not be the same as the other provinces in the mainland, but a special administrative region under the jurisdiction of one China. It will enjoy a higher degree of autonomy than the autonomous regions in the mainland and will be able to carry out a different social system from that of the mainland. . . . In addition, Taiwan can retain its armed forces. The mainland will not send any person to Taiwan to take part in governmental administration. However, we welcome Taiwan sending some personnel to the mainland to participate in the central government. . . .

How to realize the goal of "one country, two systems" should be negotiated by the KMT and the CPC on an equal basis.[14]

The response from Taipei to Yang's gesture and, for that matter, to earlier proposals has been a resounding no, and for good reason. First of all, the Nationalist government still claims to be the sole legitimate government of China, of which Taiwan is

14. Quoted from the official version of the interview, "Yang Shangkun on China's Unification," *Beijing Review*, 26 Nov.-2 Dec. 1990, pp. 11-12, 14.

only a province. Based on this claim, it justifies its authoritarian rule over the native Taiwanese, who comprise 85 percent of Taiwan's population. To accept Beijing's proposal for negotiation—not to mention its terms of reunification, which would reduce the Taipei regime to the status of a local authority—would, by the KMT's own standards, affirm the legitimacy of Beijing as China's rightful ruler and at the same time destroy its own main claim to power in Taiwan.

Second, few among Taiwan's 20 million people desire reunification under the prevailing circumstances. By Asia's standards, most people in Taiwan are doing well economically, certainly much better than people in the PRC. The large number of Taiwanese who have visited the mainland know what China is like after four decades of Communist rule. In addition to economic backwardness, the purges, the large-scale sociopolitical turmoil of the Cultural Revolution, and the fresh memory of the brutal suppression of pro-democracy students do not win over hearts and minds in Taiwan. Unification is seen as a mission impossible under KMT auspices and a catastrophe if brought about by the Communists. These considerations underlie the KMT policy of Three Nos—"no contacts, no negotiation, and no compromise" with the Communists.

TAIWAN'S "MAINLAND FEVER" AND "FLEXIBLE DIPLOMACY"

Yet, in spite of Taipei's officially proclaimed policy, reality dictates otherwise. Beginning in the mid-1980s, illicit trade between Taiwan and the mainland grew and many residents visited the mainland in defiance of the official ban. The Three Nos policy quickly became untenable when a cargo plane of China Airline, the ROC flag carrier, flew to Canton on 3 May 1986 as the pilot defected. Taipei had no choice but to authorize the China Airline representatives in Hong Kong to sit down and negotiate with the officials of the China Civil Aviation Corporation, the flag carrier of the PRC, over the return of the plane and its crew. In fact, the reaction of most commentators in Taiwan, including the opposition politicians, to Taipei's flexible response were highly favorable and showed little if any of the adverse consequences feared by the government.

A far-reaching change in Taiwan-mainland relations came in November 1987 when the Nationalist authorities officially lifted the travel ban and permitted retired soldiers to visit their mainland relatives. Since then, approximately 2 million people—most of them Taiwanese and a small portion of retired soldiers—have visited the mainland, a development that has enormous consequences and implications for future Taiwan-mainland relations.

In March 1988 the ROC officially sanctioned indirect trade and began publishing its statistics. Two-way trade exceeded $1.5 billion in 1988, $2 billion in 1989, and over $4 billion in 1990. Meanwhile, an increasing number of Taiwanese business firms are investing in China, especially in Fujian province. It is estimated that at the end of 1989 Taiwan's cumulative investment in China was about $1 billion—5 percent of a $20 billion total foreign investment—representing about 9 percent of Taiwan's direct investment abroad. In September 1990, Taiwan also sent a large delegation of athletes to Beijing for the Asian Games.

Taipei's newly found flexibility is also reflected in its external relations. In May 1988, the ROC delegation returned to the Asian Development Bank annual meeting in Manila after several years of absence in protest of the bank's having changed the ROC name to "Taipei, China," at the behest of the PRC. In 1989, Taipei dispatched an ROC delegation led by Dr. Shirley Kuo, minister of finance, to the Asian Development Bank meeting held in Beijing. Moreover, Minister Kuo rose with the delegates of other countries when President Yang arrived to deliver welcoming remarks and the PRC national anthem was played. In 1988-89, Taiwan established full diplomatic relations with Grenada, Liberia, and Belize, all of which already had diplomatic ties with the PRC. The new policy is a significant departure from the Nationalists' previous claim that the ROC is the sole legal government of China; the policy permits countries to recognize both regimes simultaneously.

The implication of Taipei's new tack was not lost on PRC leaders, and they quickly terminated relations with these countries in order to forestall the emergence of "two Chinas" or "one China, one Taiwan." Moreover, to offset Taipei's diplomatic initiatives and to dilute the adverse impact of the international sanctions in the wake of Tiananmen, the PRC launched a diplomatic counteroffensive. Beijing's establishment of formal ties with Saudi Arabia, Indonesia, and Singapore in the second half of 1990 was the tangible result and put Taipei in a highly unenviable position. The PRC seems to be targeting South Africa, and South Korea could switch its diplomatic recognition from Taipei to Beijing if the PRC decides to opt for formal ties with Seoul.

INTERACTIONS BETWEEN
TAIPEI AND BEIJING

The death of Taiwan's President Chiang Ching-kuo and the takeover by Lee Teng-hui since January 1988 presented new worries for Beijing. Although a member of the ruling Nationalist Party, Lee is an ethnic Taiwanese and may thus appear to the CCP leaders to have weaker ties to the mainland than his predecessor. During the presidential election in Taiwan in March 1990, Beijing sought to intervene against Lee's reelection and on 7 March issued a pointed statement by an "authoritative person" supporting his rivals,[15] but to no avail. In an informal meeting with CCP gerontocrats and Politburo members in September 1990, Deng Xiaoping reportedly criticized Lee for "advocating Taiwan independence and failing to take active measures to promote China's unification."[16]

The PRC leaders have also been disturbed by Taiwan's progress toward a democratic, pluralistic system. They are particularly apprehensive about the Democratic Progressive Party (DPP), as its membership is

15. The statement was carried by NCNA the same day.
16. *South China Morning Post* (Hong Kong), 19 Sept. 1990, p. 1.

mostly Taiwanese-born, its platform calls for self-determination for Taiwan, and many party members speak openly of independence. The mainland press has waged a relentless campaign against the DPP and other advocates of self-determination and Taiwanese independence.[17]

From time to time, Beijing has resorted to saber rattling, threatening to use force to coerce Taiwan to accept reunification with the mainland. In October 1984, for instance, Deng told Japanese visitors that the PRC would not renounce the use of force in "taking back" Taiwan and that the Chinese military had the capability to blockade the island. In May 1985, CCP General Secretary Hu Yaobang stated, " 'If we are economically powerful in seven, eight, or ten years, we shall be in a position to modernize our national defense. If the broad masses of the Taiwan people wish to return and a small number of people do not wish to return, it will be necessary to use some force.' " Hu added, " 'If we have the strength to enforce a blockade and if Taiwan vehemently opposes reunification, we shall have to consider enforcing a blockade.' "[18]

Chinese Communist leaders are reported to have on various occasions specified conditions under which the PRC would attack Taiwan: If Taipei leaned toward Moscow instead of Washington; if Taipei decided to develop nuclear weapons; if Taiwan claimed to be an independent state; if Taipei lost internal control as a result of the succession process; or if Taipei continued to reject reunification talks "for a long period of time."[19]

In the interview with *China Times* cited previously, President Yang stated:

Today, Taiwan's position is not stable and there is a danger of its being taken over by others. Thus, we cannot promise to [forgo] the use of military force in order to prevent Taiwan splitting off from China. This doesn't mean we intend to attack Taiwan. The Taiwan people are our compatriots. How can we attack our compatriots? Our possible use of military force is mainly aimed at foreign countries, countries which want to take Taiwan away from China.[20]

Which foreign countries would try to take Taiwan away from China? There is no reason to believe that Moscow would be interested in forging political or security ties with Taiwan. Likewise, Japan is in no such position nor does it have the intention to take Taiwan from China. The United States, however, has maintained extensive and close economic, cultural, and security ties with Taiwan due to past relations and the 1979 Taiwan Relations Act, in spite of

17. See, for example, Tian Di, "Why the Noise Again Clamoring for Taiwan Independence," *Renmin ribao* [People's daily], overseas ed., 20 Oct. 1990, p. 2; Tang Ming, "Taiwan Independence Is Dead End: A Commentary on the So-called 'Taiwan's Sovereignty Resolution,' " ibid., 6 Nov. 1990, p. 5; Tao Shian, "March toward Peaceful Unification, Stop the Spread of 'Taiwan Independence,' " ibid., 8 Dec. 1990, p. 2.

18. "Hu Yaobang Interviewed by Pai Hsing's Lu Keng," *Pai Shing* (Hong Kong),

1 June 1985, in Foreign Broadcast Information Service, *FBIS Daily Report—China*, 3 June 1985, p. W7.

19. Guocang Huan, "Taiwan: A View from Beijing," *Foreign Affairs*, 63(5):1608 (Summer 1985).

20. "Yang Shangkun on China's Unification," pp. 15-16.

not recognizing the ROC since January 1979. The Taiwan Relations Act mandates continued U.S. arms sales to Taiwan, and Washington has frequently expressed its interest in a peaceful process through which Beijing and Taipei might settle their dispute.

Beijing has blamed the United States for the lack of progress in Taiwan's unification with the mainland and sometimes has blatantly accused the United States of instigating and supporting Taiwan independence. Obviously, the Chinese Communists do not want to concede that a large number of Taiwanese oppose reunification with the mainland and want independence. The frequency with which the Communists have denounced Taiwanese independence and threatened the use of force suggests they take the matter rather seriously. Beijing has targeted both the DPP and the KMT government, putting heavy pressure on the Nationalist authorities to clamp down on the independence activists.

Besieged by calls for reunification from the Communists, right-wing KMT politicians, and unification advocates in the media and by demands of the democratic forces and the DPP for democratization, President Lee has had to walk a tightrope. It was in this context that he proposed to do away with the official policy of the Three Nos and talk with the Communist regime. In his inauguration speech on 20 May 1990, Lee declared,

If the Chinese Communist authorities can implement political democracy and a free economic system, renounce the use of military force in the Taiwan Strait, and not interfere with our development of for-

eign relations on the basis of a one-China policy, we would be willing—on a basis of equality—to establish channels of communication.[21]

Predictably, Beijing rejected the overture.

Lee has since taken additional measures to demonstrate flexibility. In the autumn of 1990, a bipartisan National Unification Council was set up under the office of the president to devise strategy concerning peaceful unification and to mobilize popular support. Two additional organizations, the Mainland Affairs Council and the Strait Exchange Foundation, have also been set up to handle Taiwan-mainland relations. The former is a cabinet-level council of senior officials under the Executive Yüan, charged with policymaking and coordination of implementation of mainland policy by various government agencies. The latter is a quasi-official agency to deal with daily issues in mainland relations and to serve as a communication channel across the Taiwan Strait.

For some time to come, Taipei will still ban direct trade across the Taiwan Strait and direct investment on the mainland, notwithstanding the complaints by the PRC and Taiwanese businesspersons. KMT officials believe that the relaxation of controls must be gradual so as not to undermine the island's stability and security. They also see direct trade and direct investments as Taiwan's leverage or bargaining chips to secure concessions. ROC spokespersons have time and again called on Beijing to meet the three conditions laid down

21. *Free China Journal*, 22 May 1990, p. 3.

in President Lee's inauguration speech, which the PRC has steadfastly rejected.

As Yang stated in his *China Times* interview, the CCP leaders "pin [their] hopes on two factors in Taiwan"—the Taiwanese authorities and the Taiwanese people—for reunification.[22] As a matter of fact, the CCP authorities have striven to cultivate both Taiwanese and mainlander intellectuals, journalists, businesspersons, and politicians of different persuasions in an overall united-front operation. The Communists have learned to use an open and pluralistic society to their advantage and to influence public opinion to effect change in government policy. There are numerous signs that Beijing will increasingly resort to such tactics to induce and compel the KMT authorities to expand the Taiwan-mainland ties, including direct trade and investment along with exchanges of air and shipping services.

Taiwan's relations with the mainland will become troublesome as 1997 approaches. Beijing can be expected to intensify the campaign for unification before then, putting heavy pressure on Taipei to come to the negotiating table. Conceivably, the old

22. "Yang Shangkun on China's Unification," p. 16.

guard, the political dinosaurs in Beijing, if they have not died by 1997, will try very hard to achieve some result before they go. Should they attempt the use of force, the United States would be put on the spot because the Taiwan Relations Act and numerous U.S. statements oppose such a measure. Beijing and Washington would be on a collision course.

Beyond that, relations between Taiwan and the mainland may become smoother. With the civil-war generation out of the picture, the leadership in both Taipei and Beijing will be more pragmatic and more rational and could learn to coexist peacefully. Unification is not a foregone conclusion. Whether the outcome will be two nations with two systems, a loose confederation, or some kind of a commonwealth under the name of China is an open-ended question.

Given the long history of hostility and distrust, and the vast difference between the two societies in their ways of life and value systems, not to mention the differences in political and economic systems, Humpty Dumpty cannot be put back together again. Therefore, talk about peaceful unification seems unrealistic. The more practical issue is whether the two sides can work out some kind of modus vivendi so that both can benefit from growing interactions and expanding ties.

ANNALS, *AAPSS,* **519,** January 1992

International Organizations in Chinese Foreign Policy

By SAMUEL S. KIM

ABSTRACT: Despite China's much-heralded entry into the United Nations in late 1971, a comprehensive network of linkages between China and the rest of the world was not established until the 1980s, when Beijing joined practically all important international organizations. Growing participation in international organizations, made possible by the open-door policy, has created new opportunities, payoffs, and penalties. Chinese foreign policy behavior, manifest in the various domains of global politics, follows a real, if unstated, maxi/mini principle, maximizing China's rights and minimizing China's responsibilities. It also seeks to maximize state interests and minimize normative costs by making the world of international organizations safe for the drive for modernization and status. Policy pronouncements and adjustments over time on various global issues and problems show international organizations in general and economic and functional organizations in particular to have shortened the Chinese global learning curve. The prospects of post-Tiananmen Chinese global policy remain uncertain as the old limitations have been greatly increased and the new possibilities greatly reduced.

Samuel S. Kim (Ph.D., 1966, Columbia University) teaches in the Woodrow Wilson School of Public and International Affairs, Princeton University. He has published widely on East Asian international relations and world-order issues. His most recent publications include The United Nations and a Just World Order *(edited with Richard Falk and Saul Mendlovitz, 1991);* The Constitutional Foundations of World Peace *(edited with Richard Falk and Robert Johansen, 1992); and* China's Quest for National Identity *(edited with Lowell Dittmer, forthcoming). He is currently completing a book on Chinese perspectives on international relations.*

NOTE: Research for this article was supported by the Peter B. Lewis Fund of the Center of International Studies, Princeton University.

DESPITE China's much-heralded entry into the United Nations in late 1971, its participation in international organizations—both international intergovernmental organizations (IGOs) and nongovernmental organizations (NGOs)—remained rather self-consciously parsimonious and largely symbolic during the Maoist period. A comprehensive network of global linkages with China was not established until the 1980s when Beijing joined practically all IGOs in the U.N. system. Even more surprising was the astonishing tenfold growth in NGO membership in the years 1977-89. An equally significant rise in multilateral treaty commitment is another indicator of this expanding nexus with the outside world.

Thus China, for the first time in modern history, has finally joined the global political system, and international organizations have clearly established their presence in Chinese foreign policy. Post-Mao China's great leap outward and the resulting globalization of its foreign policy, coupled with the ongoing global communication/transparency revolution, have linked domestic and external factors as two interactive sides of the same complex system. As a result, engagement in the multiple games of multiple international organizations presents a more difficult task of generalizing about Chinese foreign policy behavior. Still, participation in international organizations has broadened the empirical base for the study of Chinese foreign policy. Proceeding from the premise that China's growing participation in global politics, made possible by the

globalization of the open-door policy, has created myriad new opportunities, payoffs, and penalties, this article examines Chinese foreign policy behavior as manifest in the domains of global normative politics, global high politics, and global low politics.

THE DOMAIN OF GLOBAL NORMATIVE POLITICS

There is little doubt that Beijing sees many global political IGOs in general and the U.N. General Assembly in particular as congenial platforms from which to project its own world outlook. The annual general debate in the General Assembly's plenary session affords Beijing free global prime time—and global prime arena—to pronounce its own definition of the international situation in the form of its annual state-of-the-world report. In the unique domain of this quasi-global parliamentary meeting, many normative proposals are adopted in the form of recommendatory resolutions with few implementing actions. This may be the primary reason why the General Assembly is so important to the Chinese style of dramatizing its moral righteousness. The General Assembly is the surest and cheapest way to China's international forum shopping and to the politics of collective legitimation and delegitimation.

We cannot fully grasp the logic of compulsive and mindless moralizing in Chinese multilateral diplomacy—and the behavioral style of always promoting state interests disguised in the name of defending abstract international principles—without first recognizing the normative imperative of legitimation challenge and response in Chinese politics. Of course, legitimation is an integral, if not always the most salient, part of any political system. In the Chinese case, however, the quest for legitimation has enduring resonance. Historically, China has remained a multinational empire supersensitive to the rise and fall of the mystical but legitimating Mandate of Heaven. Even in our time, after its founding in 1949, the long exclusion of the People's Republic from the international community and the still-unsettled nature of the multiple-Chinas problem have made international legitimation an essential objective of foreign policy. Deng's authoritative pronouncement of three key objectives for the 1980s—anti-hegemony, reunification, and modernization (in this order in 1980); and modernization, reunification, and anti-hegemonism (in the reprioritized order of 1982)—can be said to be three competing principles of legitimation. They also show the interdependence of domestic and external factors in the Chinese quest for legitimation. Viewed in this light, IGOs become the continuation of the legitimation struggle by another name.

During much of the 1970s, Chinese behavior was generally marked by the discrepancy between symbolic activism and participatory aloofness. The self-styled moral regime had shown the greater interest in the making of new principles for the establishment of a new international order, shying away from many of the functional and technical committees and subsidiary bodies of the United Nations. Maoist China managed to

retain a measure of credibility for its support of the Third World's call for the establishment of a New International Economic Order. China stood out as the only Third World country that gave but never received any bilateral and multilateral aid. The three institutional pillars of the capitalist world system—the World Bank, the International Monetary Fund, and the General Agreement on Tariffs and Trade (GATT)—were assaulted as the last stronghold of resistance to the New International Economic Order. Global interdependence was likened to the relationship "between a horseman and his mount" and as such an ideological cover for imperialist penetration. China thus followed the Maoist version of *dependencia* theory on a trinity of (1) maximizing self-reliant autocentric internal development, (2) minimizing external dependency, and (3) transforming the capitalist world system.

Substantial slippage occurred in post-Mao China's symbolic diplomacy in global IGOs. The modernization drive redefined the central challenge of Chinese foreign policy: how to make the outside world safe for the march to modernity. In 1978, post-Mao China suddenly changed its national identity, from a model of self-reliant socialist development to a poor global power actively seeking most-favored-nation treatment from multilateral economic and technical institutions. China's abrupt termination of its aid programs to Albania and Vietnam also occurred in 1978, recalling the sanctions that China's traditional tributary—vassal—states had to suffer when they showed improper behavior or insufficient deference to the Middle Kingdom. The invasion of Vietnam in February 1979 evidenced the extent to which the post-Mao leadership was willing to bend the pledge never to act like a hegemonic power. These geopolitical and geo-economic reversals in 1978 and 1979, coupled with the harsh repression of the first wave of post-Mao democracy movements, began the decay of China's moral regime in the domain of global normative politics.

Despite the ritualized attack on power politics and ritualized rhetorical support of Third World causes, *People's Daily*, echoing the dominant Dengist line, unabashedly declared in mid-1980 that "China and the United States hold identical views on the overall matter of resolutely meeting strategic challenges in the 1980s."[1] Even in the U.N. politics of collective legitimation and delegitimation, China and the United States followed parallel strategies on many global geopolitical issues. For such transformed role playing, the United States paved the path for China's grand entry in 1980 into the cockpit of the capitalist world economic system nested in the World Bank and the International Monetary Fund.

As if to recover lost normative ground during the Sino-American entente period, Beijing's line began to shift in the latter half of 1981. Under the banner of an "independent foreign policy," Beijing began once again to project its symbolic identification with the Third World, voting with the Third World majority on most global

issues, commenting from the sidelines, or responding rhetorically to superpower overextension in Third World trouble spots. China publicly touts its role in the Security Council as the only developing country among the Big Five fighting for the causes of the Third World. Its automatic support of a Third World candidate in the five-year electoral cycle in the Security Council for the post of U.N. secretary-general suggests low respect, if not outright contempt, for the world organization.

The recurring projection of China's national identity as a socialist country belonging to the Third World notwithstanding, one thing has remained consistent in Chinese international organizational behavior. China has indeed succeeded in turning itself into the most independent actor in global group politics, a veritable group of one, by refusing to join the two leading Third World organizations—the Group of 77 in global developmental politics and the Non-Aligned Movement in global geopolitics. The ambiguities and contradictions of Beijing's Third World policy may be accounted for by the deepening crisis of national identity and status, a crisis that stems not only from China's dual and inconsistent status in the international pecking order but also from an inordinate demand placed on foreign policy to gain absolute international legitimation to make up for growing legitimation deficits at home.

Still, China shares with the Third World a sense of common past, a strong collective memory of imperialist exploitation. China's identification with the Third World reflects

1. *Renmin ribao* [People's daily], 8 June 1980, p. 4.

and dramatizes its nationalistic sentiment of being unjustly denied its rightful place in the international system for so long by those more powerful, bespeaking a deep sense of historical grievances and ideological and economic vulnerability. China deftly exploits this collective guilt to the full in the pursuit of most-favored-nation treatment and exceptions in the global community. Meanwhile, declining Third World leadership has become a Chinese way of proving its pledge never to be or act like a hegemon in international relations. The Chinese style of assuming championship without leadership is to demonstrate fidelity to staying firm in principle but flexible in practice. Or, perhaps more accurately, it is another way of squaring the circle of deviant—anti-Third World—behavior. Indeed, it may well be a device to disguise the lack of any sense of a common future or respect for the Third World. Racist anti-African student demonstrations in Nanjing and elsewhere in China a few years ago—and their escape from the government's crackdown—also speak directly to ambivalent attitudes about the Third World in general and Africa in particular. China for its own self-serving reasons can neither fully embrace nor completely reject its identification with the Third World, and, in the domain of global normative politics, it cannot afford to ignore the Third World's power of numbers.

These counterpurposive pressures and demands make Beijing's Third World policy prone to wild swings from overly assertive to overly defensive behavior. The normative and cognitive strains incurred in the course of fulfilling its repeated commitment as the champion of the global underdogs before the global audience without compromising its state interests explain these erratic twists and turns. China's rhetorical endorsement of the Third World and of the United Nations as the world organization is always couched in vague and abstract terms subject to multiple interpretations and often within its larger concern of enhancing its own political status and leverage in world politics. Herein lies the logic of a multifaceted and multiprincipled multilateral diplomacy allowing China to be all things to all nations on all global issues.

More than any event in modern Chinese history, the June 1989 massacre, in a single stroke, dealt a severe blow to the credibility of the make-believe moral regime in global normative politics. Almost overnight, the People's Republic acquired a new national identity as a pariah anti-people regime. Tiananmen has made it possible, even if temporarily, for the United Nations to accomplish a human rights mission impossible—condemning a permanent member of the Security Council for human rights abuses at home. In August 1989, the U.N. Subcommission on Prevention of Discrimination and Protection of Minorities, a subsidiary expert body of the Commission on Human Rights, passed by a secret vote of 15-9 the first resolution in U.N. history criticizing one of the Big Five of the Security Council for human rights abuses at home. In February 1990, the International Labor Organization added international delegitimation by endorsing the findings of an expert committee extremely critical of China's mistreatment of workers who had supported the pro-democracy movement. A narrow escape at the 46th session of the Commission on Human Rights in early 1990 occurred when a procedural resolution to "take no action" about human rights in China was adopted in a close vote of 17-15-11. The worst was avoided, only just, due to abstention by Argentina, Brazil, Colombia, Mexico, Peru, Venezuela, and the Philippines, among others.

Yet the greatest damage of all is not so much from the content or duration of the international sanctions themselves as from the collapse of international reputation and credibility that the sanctions reflected and effected. Suddenly, the China factor in global geopolitics was reduced to its nuisance—veto—value in the Security Council. Its place in global normative politics became marginalized, and, above all, its national identity as a people's republic was besmirched beyond redemption. Like Picasso's great painting *Guernica*, which so powerfully captured the dehumanization of Spanish fascism and the terror bombing of the city of Guernica, the many pictures and images of what happened in and around Tiananmen Square captured and transmitted by 1200 foreign journalists in May-June 1989 revealed the true color and identity of the Chinese Communist regime for the world to see and judge.

Post-Tiananmen China returned to the General Assembly with calls for a new international political and economic order (NIPEO). This was another desperate attempt to shore up legitimacy at home via international legitimation. As Foreign Minister Qian Qichen assured the domestic audience, Deng Xiaoping was the first to advocate the establishment of an NIPEO based on the Five Principles of Peaceful Coexistence.[2] The five main points of the proclaimed new order, however, are remarkably like the old, pre-Nuremberg statecentric international legal order: how each sovereign state, including China, terrorizes or makes war on its people and minority nationalities was absolutely none of the United Nations' business.

It should be noted here that China by 1982 seemed to have recognized that human rights had become an integral part of global normative politics, and it decided to enter the fray. In this spirit, China ratified or acceded to seven U.N.-sponsored multilateral human rights treaties on women, racial discrimination, refugees, apartheid, genocide, and torture. Clearly, the classical Westphalian notion that how each state mistreated its own citizens was not part of international concern became progressively less compelling in Chinese thinking. There was, until Tiananmen, growing recognition and acceptance of the proposition that a country's human rights performance was closely keyed to its international image and reputation. Thus China's human rights promise and performance were regarded as an integral part of its status drive in global politics. More telling, some Chinese international relations scholars ad-

2. Qian Qichen, "The Changing World Situation and China's Foreign Relations," *Qiushi* [Seeking truth], 16 Dec. 1990, pp. 8-11.

vanced the Wilsonian, not Leninist, explanation that democracy at home is the cause of peace. Global activities to promote human rights became major contributions to the cause of world peace. The major lesson of World War II to be drawn from the fascist capacity in Germany, Italy, and Japan to launch a war of aggression was said to be the absence of a democratic system in these countries. But post-Tiananmen China simply took a great leap backward on human rights. Beijing's learning curve collapsed or slid back to the 1979 position, while many prominent students and intellectuals made a great leap outward, thinking and acting globally.[3]

In sum, crying wolf on the peaceful-evolution strategy of the West, appealing to the Third World for the NIPEO, launching a global diplomatic blitz to get off the hit list of the World Bank, and still propagandizing for international cooperation in the name of global economic interdependence have become the competing themes in post-Tiananmen China's Jekyll-and-Hyde diplomacy.

THE DOMAIN OF GLOBAL HIGH POLITICS

More than in any previous period, the adoption of an independent line in 1981-82 and a world peace and development line in 1984 brought about a drastic reinterpretation of Marxist theory of international relations. Whatever the theoretical refor-

3. For further discussion and documentation, see Samuel S. Kim, "Thinking Globally in Post-Mao China," *Journal of Peace Research*, 27(2):191-209 (1990).

mulation, however, China's security behavior in the domain of global high politics—the Security Council, the Special Sessions of the General Assembly on Disarmament (SSOD), and the Conference on Disarmament in Geneva—is fraught with ambiguities and contradictions inherent in its balancing act between normative and geostrategic concerns. The real, if unstated, code of conduct is a maxi/mini principle, maximizing China's own security interests while attempting to minimize normative costs. The maxi/mini principle also works in the service of maximizing rights and minimizing responsibilities in global high politics. Beijing is constantly cultivating expectations about the multiple possibilities and dangers of the China factor in world affairs. Herein lies the key to understanding how an impoverished China can act as if it had become a great global power and is indeed being treated as such by the rest of the world, including the superpowers.

Despite the habitual and now ritualized assault on power politics and the public espousal of participatory decision making in IGOs, China since 1970 has become one of the most unabashed practitioners of behind-the-scenes power politics. Indeed, China's realpolitik in the grand Machiavellian tradition has captured the strategic imagination of the high priests of global geopolitics everywhere, especially in the United States. The same logic found its way to the post-Tiananmen strategy of overcoming U.S. sanctions. In late 1990, an internal policy analysis prepared for the leadership revived the allure of the China card with a new geopolitical twist. The United States was said to have little leverage due to its fear of driving China into the Soviet orbit and especially due to its anxiety to keep "electronic monitoring stations" in Xinjiang (Sinkiang) that are very important for gathering information on Soviet missile tests.[4] Apparently, the leadership accepted this line of reasoning, as Foreign Minister Qian repeatedly proclaims "China's strategic position and great potential" as the global reality that Western countries can ignore only at their own peril.

Although there occurred a shift from hard realism to soft realism in Chinese security behavior, the maxi/ mini principle remains, expressed in the espousal of differentiated and proportionate responsibilities in global arms control and disarmament (ACD) processes. Since the two superpowers account for 95-97 percent of all nuclear warheads in the world, we are told, it is they who must bear the primary responsibility by drastically reducing their nuclear arsenals before other nuclear states can join the disarmament process. In this way, China projects its role as a constructive and positive player in the U.N. disarmament game without constraining its own nuclear development. At the SSOD II in mid-1982, China modified its ambiguous stand: the superpowers should reduce their nuclear weapons by 50 percent before China and the other nuclear powers would join in further nuclear disarmament negotiations. This position was softened in 1984, thanks to the

4. Nicholas D. Kristof, "Strained U.S. Ties Reported in China," *New York Times*, 5 Oct. 1989.

inauguration of the world peace and development line: the superpowers needed only to take the lead in halting the testing, development, and manufacture of nuclear weapons and come to an agreement on a 50 percent reduction before China would join in a five-power nuclear disarmament talk.

China was a major free-ride beneficiary of the 1988 Soviet-American Intermediate-Range Nuclear Forces Treaty. Yet the treaty seems to have come as a rude awakening that Beijing may have committed the fallacy of premature specificity. China rather quickly relapsed into a "who, me?" refrain. While welcoming the treaty as the first genuine disarmament treaty of the postwar era, China omitted its 50 percent reduction proposal from the position paper presented at SSOD III in mid-1988, calling instead for a "drastic reduction" in the strategic nuclear stockpiles of the superpowers. A 50 percent reduction would not meet China's new measure of a "drastic reduction." At the same time, an old Chinese ACD line had been resurrected: while the superpowers have the special responsibility for drastic nuclear disarmament, all countries, big or small, strong or weak, have the right to take part in any future disarmament negotiations.

The contradictions of the world peace and development line are underlined in China's sudden and rapid rise as a major-league arms exporter in the 1980s. It ranked first in the Third World, and fifth in the world behind the Soviet Union, the United States, France, and Britain. Since mid-1983, the post-Mao Chinese military-industrial complex has mounted ambitious public relations and marketing campaigns through its participation in or sponsorship of international arms exhibitions. China, as well as the rest of the Big Five in the Security Council, sold arms to both belligerents during the Iran-Iraq war. Nearly 70 percent of China's arms exports went to Iran and Iraq in the years 1981-87. Despite its refusal to recognize Israel until the Palestinian question is solved, Beijing has maintained covert military ties with that country since 1980. Indeed, Israel helped China to improve the accuracy of the intermediate-range Silkworm missiles that have been sold to Saudi Arabia, putting Tel Aviv within firing range from Riyadh. Most recently, the Central Military Commission is reported to have held a series of meetings to explore new ways and means of boosting China's arms sales to the Middle East in the aftermath of the Persian Gulf war. China is now well poised to launch another great leap into the postwar Middle East munitions market with its new M-9 and M-11 medium-range ballistic missiles. Yet the old habit of remaking the facts of realpolitik so as to validate its "principled stand" persists. On 21 February 1991, the Chinese Ministry of Foreign Affairs, in a letter to the Kyodo News Service bureau in Beijing, categorically denied that China ever sold any arms to either Iran or Iraq during the eight-year Iran-Iraq war!

Thus Chinese ACD behavior is marked by selective activism on global ACD issues—for example, chemical weapons, space weapons,

and superpower nuclear disarmament—selective aloofness on Asian-Pacific regional ACD issues, and an unabashed "who, me?" refrain on global arms trade. In essence, then, Chinese ACD behavior is dictated by the maxi/mini strategy of making virtue out of necessity—the maximization of its security interests free-riding off superpower ACD negotiations and the minimization of its own commitments to a few safe, or nonpriority, areas. Apparently, the seabed nuclear arms race has become another safe or nonpriority area, as the Chinese government, on 28 February 1991, acceded to the 1971 seabed treaty, increasing to eight its commitments to the U.N.-sponsored multilateral ACD treaties. Its participation in the global politics of disarmament has become more engaging and deft, but the old nationalistic resolve that in a dangerous and nuclearized world a China without the bomb does not count persists. Moreover, there is now a new twist to the Maoist resolve to stand up in world politics with economic and military muscle power growing out of arms sales to the Third World.

The same neorealist maxi/mini principle is manifest in Chinese thinking on U.N. peacekeeping. Until late 1981, China generally showed a negative attitude toward such operations. Then policy changed as part of renewed identification with the Third World and putative strategic dealignment from the United States. On 14 December 1981, China for the first time voted for the extension of the U.N. peacekeeping force in Cyprus. By late 1982, Beijing had safely projected itself as a champion of U.N.

peacekeeping: "The more tumultuous the international situation, and the more seriously threatened are world peace and international security, the more important and pressing becomes the task of strengthening the United Nations."[5]

In 1988-89, China's support of U.N. peacekeeping and the Sino-Soviet renormalization process progressed in tandem. With Soviet prodding and support, China formally made a request in September 1988 to become a member of the U.N. Special Committee on Peacekeeping Operations, and it was unanimously accepted two months later. In China's first official statement issued as a new member in April 1989, Ambassador Yu Mengjia urged the international community to give "powerful political support" to U.N. peacekeeping, because facts have proved convincingly that it had become an "effective mechanism" in realizing the purposes of the U.N. Charter and an integral part of its efforts in finding a political settlement for regional conflicts.[6]

The Persian Gulf crisis put China's support of U.N. peacekeeping on the spot. Characteristically, Beijing's initial response was no response, waiting to see how others would react and perhaps hoping this invasion, like Saddam Hussein's 1980 invasion of Iran, would pass away as another international nonevent. This wishful wait-and-see attitude was tempered by a sense of multiple dangers: for example, losing Iraq as a valuable customer in its global arms trade, a vanishing antihegemonic line in the face of naked aggression of one Third World country against another, and losing inordinate investments in sponsoring the Asian Games scheduled to be held in September. Despite the initial vacillation and ambiguous posturing, Beijing soon awakened to the "dialectical" possibility of seizing the crisis for diverting the world's attention away from China and once again throwing its weight in global high politics. By abstaining rather than voting for or against Security Council Resolution 678 on 29 November 1990, China allowed itself ample room for multiple interpretations of its "principled stand," a public demonstration of China's multiprincipled diplomacy of projecting itself as all things to all nations.

Despite the repeated pronouncements in the course of the Security Council proceedings that "China does not have nor wishes to seek any self-serving interests in the Middle East region, and its only concern is to maintain peace and stability of that region,"[7] China managed to extract maximum payoffs from the United States with minimum support. In the end, through its never-never fence-straddling strategy—never say no and never say yes—Beijing managed to force Washington into becoming an overly anxious supplicant seeking

5. "UN Should Play a More Effective Role," *Beijing Review*, 1 Nov. 1982, pp. 11-12.

6. Xinhua [New China News Agency], in Foreign Broadcast Information Service, *FBIS Daily Report—China*, 13 Apr. 1989, p. 4. For a glowing scholarly account, see Liu Enzhao, "UN Peacekeeping Forces," *Guoji wenti yanjiu* [Journal of international studies], 1989, no. 2, pp. 53-61.

7. UN Doc. S/PV. 2963, 29 Nov. 1990.

help. A Washington quid for a Beijing quo exemplified the maxi/mini code of conduct. The Bush administration, ignoring a then-current crackdown on political dissidents, agreed to the resumption of high-level diplomatic intercourse—a long-sought White House visit by Foreign Minister Qian was granted—and to support the World Bank's first "non-basic human needs" loan, for $114.3 million, since Tiananmen. All the same, Beijing can still claim its championing the Palestinian cause while at the same time looking forward eagerly to sending thousands of construction workers and exporting major weapons systems to the postwar Middle East.

During the Maoist period, abstention, as against nonparticipation, was a *rara avis* in Chinese voting behavior because it was said to be a sign of unprincipled foreign policy behavior. In this case, however, China voted in favor of 11 Security Council resolutions on various measures including economic sanctions against Iraq but made an unprincipled escape by abstaining on Resolution 678 on the use of "all necessary means" as its own way of "adhering to principles and upholding international justice."[8] What China cannot support is the use of force in the name of the United Nations on the grounds that the "United Nations, as an international organization for the maintenance of peace and security, is responsible both to international security and to history."[9] Being "responsible to history," Foreign Minister Qian later explained in his interview

for the home audience, means that "the Chinese people still clearly remember that the Korean War was launched in the name of the United Nations."[10] A Hong Kong source offers a more revealing surrealist commentary on the official foreign policy mind-set. According to this source, Deng is reported to have said to his four bridge partners, Yang Shangkun, Wan Li, Song Renqiong, and Chen Pixian:

When I saw on the television news that Qian Qichen unhurriedly raised his hand in "abstention" I nodded to him and saluted him. By holding up his hand he again showed the whole world that China has a decisive say in solving major disputes in the world. Our foreign policy is firm and principled. We will not follow any other country or act according to another people's baton; we will not threaten other countries with force, nor are we afraid of other countries' threat of force; we will not give up our principled stand by accepting exchanges or compromises. If we violate this principled stand, it will mean an out-and-out betrayal of Marxism-Leninism and a betrayal of the behests of millions of martyrs, and our posterity will not forgive us.[11]

Indeed, Security Council Resolution 678 can be said to be a Chinese textbook case of hegemonic manipulation of the United Nations, a 1950 U.N. police action in Korea revived and revised, as it were, deviating from all U.N. peacekeeping operations from 1956 to the present. Yet China did not propose an alternative multilateral nonhegemonic peacekeep-

8. Ibid.
9. Ibid., p. 62.

10. See *Renmin ribao*, 17 Dec. 1990, p. 7.
11. Meng Lin, "Deng Xiaoping Salutes Qian Qichen," *Ching pao* (Hong Kong), 10 Feb. 1991, p. 36, in *FBIS Daily Report—China*, 12 Feb. 1991, p. 17.

ing force to deal with the gulf crisis. Despite the self-characterization of its role in the Security Council's management of the gulf crisis as at once principled and influential, China's actual role can be better described as unprincipled fishing in troubled waters, making the best of all worlds and seeking an escape from international sanctions by allowing the Security Council to legitimate an American war in the gulf. China failed to capture the high moral ground. Despite the moral support of U.N. peacekeeping in 1982-89, the first litmus test shows that China remains part of the global problem in the post-Cold War high politics in the Security Council. More specifically, China is a problem for the revival of American hegemony in the United Nations and for the implementation of the Charter-based collective security system in the post-Cold War era.

THE DOMAIN OF GLOBAL LOW POLITICS

In the post-Mao era, China's modernization drive has begun to transform both the style and the substance of Chinese participation in international organizations. Expanding participation in low-politics, or functional, IGOs is driven by this spirit of nation building, not by any sudden conceptual conversion to the functional approach to world order. In intent, if not in consequence, China is pursuing state-enhancing, not state-diminishing, functionalism. In the wake of America's high-tech military victory in the gulf war, Beijing has decided to reprioritize its vaunted four modernizations by putting science and technology as the top priority pursuit. The post-Tiananmen return to ideological orthodoxy at home and the calls in the General Assembly for an NIPEO seem to have no bearing on the dogged pursuit of "international cooperation and exchanges in science and technology" in the domain of global low politics. China continues to talk and act as if it could not live by socialism alone. A global campaign seeks more direct foreign investments and more concessional loans from bilateral and multilateral governmental sources. It wants more technical aid from developed countries and specialized functional IGOs. It calls for more free trade and less protectionism to fuel China's export-oriented—and import-substituting—developmental strategy, and for quicker entry into the GATT to receive the General System of Preferences treatment. All this is euphemized as "international cooperation" and "global interdependence," which now becomes an integral part of fulfilling the Eighth Five-Year Plan (1991-95) and the Ten-Year Economic Blueprint (1991-2000).[12]

The major turning point, as noted earlier, occurred in 1978-79 when China made a sudden and dramatic reversal from giving aid to seeking aid. In an unprecedented move, Beijing abandoned its tradition of self-reliance to request aid from the United Nations Development Programme, the largest multilateral technical aid organization. That this request from a poor Third World

12. See Yu Lixin, "An Analysis of China's Balance of International Payments during the Eighth Five-Year Plan," *Jingji ribao* [Economic daily], 16 Feb. 1991, p. 3.

country was received in the U.N. community as a complete surprise and with mixed reactions reflected China's ambiguous status. Having thus crossed the Rubicon on multilateral aid, Beijing continued its aid-seeking diplomacy unabated. Post-Mao China also joined the race to outbid Third World countries in the exportation of cheap labor, and since 1979 it has been promoting the business of "international labor cooperation" to capitalize on its human resources. In a short span of three years, China had renounced its unique status as the only developing country to decline multilateral aid and had instead acquired the largest number of multilateral technical aid projects.

Thanks to the rise of post-Mao neofunctionalism, technology, once regarded as an easy path for structural penetration and plundering of the national economy by foreign imperialists and multinationals, is now claimed to have no class character. It is treated as a kind of global collective goods—the more free rides China takes, the better. Even among the most liberal Chinese political influentials "soft normative globalism" seems absent. Instead, virtually all of their futuristic and globalist writings and policy pronouncements can be called "hard technocratic globalism." The heated and short-lived debate on "global citizenship" (qiuji) that the nonofficial World Economic Herald initiated in 1988 can easily fool outside world-order activists. There is now a new wave of the scientific and technological revolution, we are told, creating complex global networks of mutual influence and infiltration. In

this new era, China's development has only two options. Either it does not emancipate its political economy thinking and falls behind in the technological race, forfeiting its "global citizenship" in the process, or it becomes more fully integrated into and makes more creative use of the world market whereby it will leap into the front ranks of world development.[13] In effect, functional IGOs and NGOs are treated as filling stations on the way to the promised land, providing technical expertise and information as well as cost-effective fuel for China's accelerated modernization drive.

The rise of post-Mao neofunctionalism is most dramatically evident in China's changing attitude and policy toward the World Bank group. By the end of 1988, China had transformed itself into the only great power that stood first in the receiving line of foreign aid and investment and was one of the largest recipients of the most concessional multilateral interest-free loans of the World Bank's soft-loan window, the International Development Association. In 1989, China overtook India, becoming the world's biggest recipient of official foreign aid, bilateral and multilateral, at $2.2 billion per year, which is about 5 percent of the net global total.[14] The World Bank, that quintessentially capitalist organization, continues to receive good press in the Chinese media as having provided US$9.6 billion for 87 projects in the

13. See Lu Yi et al., eds., Qiuji: Yige shijiexing de xuanze [Global citizenship: A global choice] (Shanghai: Baijia chubanshe, 1989).

14. Economist (London), 13-19 Apr. 1991, p. 98.

decade ending January 1991. The feasibility studies that the World Bank conducts prior to approving any project have been welcomed as "a kind of free technical assistance, not available from other commercial banks" and hence "essential to China for making good use of its foreign loans."[15] For the first time in the history of the People's Republic of China, a draft of a five-year plan, the Seventh Five-Year Plan, was produced early enough to allow extensive debates and analyses by a wide variety of officials, scholars, and technical experts both inside and outside the normal planning channels and mechanisms. The State Council's Technical Economics Research Center, which was set up in 1981 as former Premier Zhao Ziyang's think tank, began to cooperate with the World Bank in 1983 in collaborative research on the topic of China in the year 2000.

The June 1989 military crackdown instantly placed Beijing on the sanctions hit list of the World Bank and the Asian Development Bank; billions of dollars' worth of concessional loans was placed on hold. Yet, in the face of this international reaction, Beijing has self-consciously avoided criticism of these multilateral financial institutions, even in polemical assaults on the "peaceful evolution" strategy. Instead, it has taken a desultory damage-limitation approach of wriggling off the hook. Fang Lizhi, the most celebrated dissident, became both carrot and stick for pressuring the United States to help lift the sanctions. One of Beijing's original conditions for allowing Fang to leave was the resumption of some World Bank loans. When this condition was met, Beijing is said to have demanded that Washington resume export of military goods and high-technology products.[16] In the end, as noted earlier, Hussein's aggression came as a godsend in Beijing's prodigious search for an escape route. By making the resumption of World Bank lending a central issue in Sino-American relations and by giving just enough support to the United States in the Security Council, Beijing has indeed acknowledged Washington as the global hegemon it can antagonize only at its own economic peril.

Before Tiananmen, China's entry into GATT was only a matter of time. In the past two years, the conjunction of several new developments has muddied the waters. In December 1990, the four-year Uruguay Round of global trade talks to rewrite the rules for the GATT-based global trade regime collapsed in a shouting match between the United States and the 12-member European Community, the world's two biggest trading powers, over farm subsidies. The new phenomenon of growing protectionism, bilateralism, and regionalism is matched by declining confidence in the multilateralism anchored in the GATT. As a result, the China issue was pushed to the back burner. Tiananmen has also greatly energized and emboldened Taiwan's

15. "World Bank Aids Modernization," *Beijing Review*, 24 Mar. 1986, p. 36.

16. Nicholas D. Kristof, "Storm Signals Flying on U.S.-China Relations," *New York Times*, 4 Mar. 1990; Robert Pear, "China Ties New Demand to Dissident's Fate," *New York Times*, 4 Apr. 1990.

"flexible diplomacy." On 1 January 1990, Taiwan declared its entry into the global politics of competitive legitimation by applying for membership in GATT. More serious and dangerous, China's soaring trade surplus with the United States—$6.2 billion in 1989, $10.4 billion in 1990, and projected to hit $15 billion in 1991—has highlighted the hidden hands of Chinese mercantilism: import restrictions; export subsidies and dumping; use of prison inmates to produce goods for export; software piracy; and other intellectual-property issues. The Super 301 Sword of Damocles in the Omnibus Trade and Competitiveness Act of 1988 hangs over China.[17] In response, socialist China has now posed itself as the champion of free trade, claiming that it will never engage in protectionism and that its imports declined because of Western economic sanctions!

For a while it seemed that the concept of global interdependence had received a lethal theoretical blow after Tiananmen. But it soon became apparent that the return of Marxist fundamentalism, as far as Chinese international organizational behavior is concerned, was more smoke than fire, as the policy of reform and opening to the capitalist world continued undiminished. Tellingly, the concept of global interdependence practically vanished from the Chi-

17. Nicholas D. Kristof, "New Tension over Trade with China," New York Times, 4 Mar. 1991; "Beijing Is Said to Allow Prison-Made Exports," New York Times, 19 Apr. 1991; Asia Watch, Prison Labor in China (New York: Asia Watch, 1991); Paul Magnusson, Amy Borrus, and Dinah Lee, "China's Ugly Export Secret: Prison Labor," Business Week, 22 Apr. 1991, pp. 42-46.

nese press for the home audience and also from Li Peng's 1990 report of the government, but it was still alive in the 1990 Chinese state-of-the-world report. The world economy was said to be an "inalienable whole" and the "global division of labor in industrial production is becoming a more and more important part of international cooperation."[18]

CONCLUSION

Chinese foreign policy thinking and behavior, manifest in the attitudes and policy toward IGOs in general and the United Nations in particular, has changed over the years. The post-Mao great leap outward both reflected and effected a shift from system-transforming and system-reforming to system-maintaining—and system-exploiting—approaches in the service of China's modernization drive. Despite the now-on and now-off calls for a new international order, Beijing has been asking more and more what IGOs can do for China, and less and less what it can do to reform or transform the world of international organizations. Remarkably, at least until the Tiananmen carnage, Beijing successfully applied the maxi/mini principle in the conduct of its multilateral diplomacy. Indeed, doing less seemed like achieving more in China's new role as a system-maintaining global status quo power. The key to this success is a notional one. As if to emulate Sun Zi's strategy of winning a war without firing a single shot, China has skillfully cultivated the notion that

18. For the full text of Qian's speech, see Renmin ribao, overseas ed., 29 Sept. 1990, p. 4.

the mere presence of the world's most populous country is a sufficient contribution in and of itself to bless each international organization as a legitimate international institution with universal membership. The rise of China's global standing in the hegemonic world order and its unique status as a poor global power entitled to special—that is, double-standard—treatment can be explained by the putative change in China's national identity from a revolutionary system-transforming actor to a neorealist system-maintaining actor.

Through generous aid and friendly policy advice, always with special sensitivity to the pretenses and claims of the self-styled moral regime, IGOs managed to enter the castle of Chinese state sovereignty, thereby influencing the processes by which Chinese national interests are redefined and Chinese modernization requirements and priorities are reformulated. International organizations have certainly helped post-Mao China to bridge information, knowledge, capital, and technology gaps with a minimum of political control. In the process, international organizations may have also helped post-Mao China to invent a new global reality: that in the still-statecentric world, international organizations and international law are, or at least can be made to be, empowering instruments rather than constraining norms in the service of China's own state-enhancing modernization drive.

This engagement with global economic IGOs has produced the spillover effect of prompting changes in policies, policy processes, and institutions within China.[19] Participation in the global politics of arms control and disarmament has spawned an embryonic ACD community in the Chinese foreign policy establishment. Some IGOs reshape Chinese foreign policy behavior by creating transparency in the behavior and expectations of member states, thus making any rule-defying, uncooperative behavior more detectable and costly. The price that China has to pay to maintain membership in good standing and to maximize its benefits is compliance, at least rhetorical, with the norms and policies of IGOs. This may explain Chinese refusal to exercise its veto power in the Security Council and its generally positive voting behavior in the General Assembly. Such compliance can also reflect and effect some readjustment or restructuring of certain principles of Chinese foreign policy, such as world peace and development or global interdependence. Of course, this is what global learning and adaptive foreign policy are all about. The astonishing growth of Chinese IGO and NGO membership was followed by positive press coverage, supportive policy pronouncements, and a number of policy adjustments and shifts on such issues as arms control and disarmament, U.N. peacekeeping, North-South relations, human rights (until Tiananmen), free trade, and science and technology. Thus some Chinese global learning has indeed occurred. From a post-Tiananmen

19. See Harold K. Jacobson and Michel Oksenberg, *China's Participation in the IMF, the World Bank, and GATT: Toward a Global Economic Order* (Ann Arbor: University of Michigan Press, 1990).

perspective, however, it seems obvious that this learning rested upon the fragile coalition of reformers headed by Hu Yaobang and Zhao Ziyang in the years 1982-88.

What are the prospects for Chinese foreign policy? Only a few years ago, most observers, the present writer not excepted, offered a rather optimistic forecast for the continuity of reform and open policy or at least argued that the outer reaches of wild shifts and swings were greatly narrowed. Indeed, Deng's China had already established an all-time record of continuity and stability in the turbulent history of the foreign relations of the People's Republic. But now as never before it appears more relevant, urgent, and problematic for outside analysts to speculate about the shape of China's international role in the 1990s and beyond. The Tiananmen massacre instantly conflated the deepening, unresolved, and suspended legitimation and identity difficulties into a megacrisis. Conceptually and ideologically, post-Mao China had gotten itself into a bind. The post-Mao socialism with Dengist characteristics could no longer cope with deepening and widening systemic problems without giving up its identity as a socialist state. And yet, to abandon the legitimating prop of socialism is and becomes an act of ideological and political suicide. Worse, the renewed quest for national identity as a socialist state without positive international reference groups can only lead China back into the future of a Stalinist "socialism in one country" state.

Of course, the China-qua-China factor as the most populous country in the world continues to cast long shadows on most international organizations. China can still do better in recovering international than domestic legitimation. Yet the post-Tiananmen government barely wriggled off the hook, only to find itself confronted with new global realities. Despite the resumption of lending by the World Bank, the Asian Development Bank, and Japan, the halcyon days of automatic entitlement to China-specific special treatment and exemptions are over. Even more threatening is the fact that the capitalist world system has already begun shifting its major concerns to Eastern Europe as if to demonstrate how the peaceful-evolution strategy is working. The total demand for capital by Eastern Europe, Latin America, and the Middle East is now projected to exceed the Western world's supply by more than $200 billion.[20] Such a shortage and the resulting rise in interest rates come when the regime is banking on more concessional loans from the West to fuel its Eighth Five-Year Plan as well as to cope with its own approaching debt crisis.

By sheer necessity, Beijing still cherishes and lives by the illusion that it can—indeed, must—eat a socialist cake and have a capitalist one, too. The notion that a socialist China can piggyback on the world capitalist system to race into communism first so as to prove the inevitability and superiority of socialism over capitalism characterizes the post-Mao system. But this system resembles a hy-

20. Steven Greenhouse, "World's Finances Facing Strains As Troubled Areas Try to Rebuild," New York Times, 26 Mar. 1991.

brid mutant, mixing and accentuating the worst features of traditional Chinese authoritarianism and modern Soviet Stalinism. It does not work for socialism or capitalism, let alone for the Chinese people. Post-Tiananmen China has indeed become its own worst enemy. Wherever the Dalai Lama goes, Beijing's protests only call attention to continuing oppression in Tibet that most governments and international organizations would rather forget. The government's formula for socialist stability and prosperity seems like moving the multiple goalposts: expanding the role of the market, fighting the Western peaceful-evolution strategy of subverting the Communist Party's leadership, upholding "the people's democratic dictatorship," increasing the military budget, and concocting 12 major principles to build communism. In short, the party-state dictatorship at home and the reform and open policy for the outside capitalist world have become two ways of pursuing a Jekyll-and-Hyde diplomacy. Shakespeare, in *Julius Caesar*, offers a better policy advice to the prisoners of Zhongnanhai:

The fault, dear Brutus, is not in our stars,
But in ourselves, that we are underlings.

Domestic Factors of Chinese Foreign Policy: From Vertical to Horizontal Authoritarianism

By ZHAO QUANSHENG

ABSTRACT: Foreign policy decision making in China is no longer the domain of a paramount leader acting through a vertical command channel with a fundamentally unified policy. Foreign policy decisions are now made by several discrete power bases coordinated at the center, with multiple command channels reflecting different interests and policies. Bureaucratic interests, agendas of policy issues, local-central authority relations, intellectual and think-tank influences, and the domestic political-economic environment differentially affect policy input and output. The change from vertical to horizontal authoritarianism parallels that which occurred in South Korea and Taiwan, but whether it evolves similarly toward democratic pluralism remains to be seen.

Zhao Quansheng is currently a peace fellow at the United States Institute of Peace, Washington, D.C., on leave from Old Dominion University in Norfolk, Virginia, where he is chairman of the Asian Studies Committee and a faculty member of the Political Science Department. He is also adjunct research associate of international relations at the East-West Center and adjunct professor of political science at the University of Hawaii. Dr. Zhao is coeditor, with Robert Sutter, of and contributor to Politics of Divided Nations: China, Korea, Germany and Vietnam—Unification, Conflict Resolution and Political Development.

NOTE: The author would like to thank Doak Barnett, Deborah Davis, Thomas Fingar, Alexander George, Harry Harding, Carol Hamrin, Mancur Olson, and Shaoguang Wang for comments or discussions, Paula Smith for research assistance, and the Ohira Memorial Foundation for a Pacific Basin academic grant. The views expressed here are those of the author alone. They do not necessarily reflect the views of the United States Institute of Peace.

I N a television program on a national public broadcasting station, an American traveler who bicycled through China from east to west made this comment: "Considering China's 'one child policy,' it is hard to imagine that in the future China will go to war without domestic resistance because no Chinese parent would be willing to send his or her only child to the battlefields."[1] This comment offers a remarkable example of the linkages between Chinese domestic policy and foreign policy. These linkages are based on broad social, political, economic, and cultural conditions and on the assumption that the domestic environment will indeed affect a country's foreign policy. As Chinese Foreign Minister Qian Qichen put it, "Diplomacy is the extension of internal affairs."[2]

This article, however, will not address such broad domestic sources of Chinese foreign policy. Rather, it will concentrate on the relationship between political development and the changing process of foreign policy-making. It will examine domestic politics and their impact on foreign policy, including such elements as general political and economic conditions and popular demands, political leaders and institutions, policy-making mechanisms, policy-issue agendas, bureaucratic interests, and the relationship between the central government and local authorities.

With regard to the current events surrounding China's external relations, it will try, through the perspective of domestic politics, to explain such questions as why Chinese foreign policy has not drastically changed since the Tiananmen incident of 1989.

There are several schools of thought regarding the issues of international relations and foreign policy. Realism, for example, believes that the primary goal of a country's foreign policy is its own survival in the international system; therefore the major issues concerned are security, military capability, the diplomacy of political alliances between states, and the pursuit and balance of power.[3] Interdependency theory analyzes the multiple channels and multiple actors in the interaction of world politics, the role of nonmilitary instruments of statecraft, and the role of economic variables in the international system.[4] Domestic politics and questions such as how the development of domestic affairs and ideology could change the basic perception of national interest and diplomatic strategy are not the major concerns of these approaches.

The importance of international constraints on Chinese foreign policy has often been emphasized in the study of Chinese foreign policy, specifically the extent to which the inter-

1. *Travel*, WETA, Washington, DC, 28 Jan. 1991.

2. "China's Important Role in World Affairs," *Beijing Review*, 15-21 Oct. 1990, pp. 11-12. Qian states that a stable political situation and growing economy "[create] favorable conditions for diplomatic work."

3. See, for example, Hans Morgenthau and Kenneth Thompson, *Politics among Nations*, 6th ed. (New York: Knopf, 1948, 1985); Kenneth Waltz, *Theory of International Politics* (Reading, MA: Addison Wesley, 1979).

4. See, for example, Robert Keohane and Joseph Nye, *Power and Interdependence* (Boston: Little, Brown, 1977).

national environment, superpower bipolarity in particular, frames Chinese foreign policy options.[5] Indeed, international conditions have clearly played an important role in the dramatic changes that have taken place in China's enemy-alliance orientation since 1949.

On the other hand, domestic politics are not unimportant to foreign policy issues. On the contrary, as Alexander George points out, a country's foreign policy decisions "may be more responsive to the internal dynamics of such a policy-making process than to the requirements of the foreign-policy problem itself."[6] The examination of domestic factors in foreign policy by connecting political and economic development and the policymaking process is different from the previously mentioned schools of thought; therefore, it will provide an alternative framework for the study of foreign policy issues and linkages between domestic and foreign policy.

PROCESS OF CHANGE

It is increasingly clear that after more than a decade of political and economic reforms, the Chinese political system and decision-making process have remained fundamentally

authoritarian in nature. This is particularly true in the formation of Chinese foreign policy. The policymaking process in China has remained highly centralized and personalized and lacks institutionalization.

Nevertheless, noticeable changes took place during the decade-long political and economic reforms, changes that are significant enough to affect the process of foreign policymaking. This phenomenon of halfway change that stops short of transforming the basic authoritarian nature of Chinese politics has been analyzed by a number of China specialists. Harry Harding, for example, called the post-Mao period a "consultative authoritarian" regime. He argues that China has experienced "a significant departure from the totalitarianism of the recent past, but not a truly pluralistic, or even quasi-democratic, political system."[7] In an analysis of political development in Asia, Robert Scalapino advocates a pattern of "authoritarian pluralism": "by keeping a rein on political rights yet enabling initiatives to operate in such areas as enterprise and religion, governments achieved a mix of stability and dynamism suitable to indigenous conditions." Scalapino believes that the Asian Leninist states, primarily China, "are now gravitating in this direction."[8] This general trend of political development has had an impact on the making of Chinese foreign pol-

5. See Michael Ng-Quinn, "The Analytical Study of Chinese Foreign Policy," *International Studies Quarterly*, 27(2) (June 1983); Jonathan Pollack, "China and the Global Strategic Balance," in *China's Foreign Relations in the 1980s*, ed. Harry Harding (New Haven, CT: Yale University Press, 1984).

6. Alexander George, *Presidential Decisionmaking in Foreign Policy* (Boulder, CO: Westview Press, 1980), p. 114.

7. Harry Harding, *China's Second Revolution: Reform after Mao* (Washington, DC: Brookings Institution, 1987), p. 200.

8. Robert Scalapino, *The Politics of Development: Perspectives on Twentieth-Century Asia* (Cambridge, MA: Harvard University Press, 1989), p. 127.

icy; namely, Beijing has attempted to depart from the Maoist era, when there was a single paramount leader who dominated foreign policymaking. This process has been described by Doak Barnett as change "from individual to collective decision making."[9]

What we have seen is a gradual process of change in which the formation of Chinese foreign policy could be characterized as shifting from vertical authoritarianism to horizontal authoritarianism. The terms used here refer primarily to the policymaking process rather than to the nature of the regime itself, although the two may have a close connection.

Vertical authoritarianism refers to a policymaking process where the paramount leader dominates through a vertical command system. Vertical authoritarianism is often seen in Communist countries, such as the Soviet Union under Stalin, China under Mao Zedong, Romania under Ceausescu, and North Korea under Kim Il Sung. Under vertical authoritarianism, as during the period of Mao Zedong, the paramount leader makes virtually every strategically important decision regarding foreign policy issues, such as policy toward the United States or the Soviet Union. The premier, in this case, Zhou Enlai, in consultation with related members of the Politburo and the central small group of foreign affairs specialists, is primarily "in charge of the conduct of foreign af-

fairs."[10] Implementation of concrete foreign policy is conducted by governmental bureaucracies, particularly the Ministry of Foreign Affairs (MFA).

The basic characteristics of vertical authoritarianism are one-man domination, one vertical command channel, and one fundamentally unified foreign policy. The participation of political institutions and governmental bureaucracy in the policymaking process is passive and highly personalistic. People outside of the country may hear only one voice on foreign policy issues.

Horizontal authoritarianism refers to a policymaking process that is essentially authoritarian and highly centralized but with several power centers at the top level representing and coordinating various interests and opinions. There are also multiple command channels at both institutional and ad hoc bases. Under horizontal authoritarianism, one sees more players and participants in the foreign policymaking process, and from time to time one may hear conflicting voices representing different interests and policies. In this sense, it may also be called collective authoritarianism.

In a comparison of the two, horizontal authoritarianism seems less personalized and more institutionalized and therefore may develop into a more pluralistic policymaking system. I will discuss this possibility in detail in the latter part of this article. To avoid confusion with regard to terminology, it is necessary to notice that the words "vertical" and "hori-

9. Doak Barnett, *The Making of Foreign Policy in China: Structure and Process* (Boulder, CO: Westview Press, 1985), p. 16.

10. Ibid., p. 7.

zontal" as used here refer only to the scope, character, and nature of participation in the foreign policymaking process—for example, collective decision making versus one-man domination—and not to the structure of the command systems of foreign policy. Indeed, foreign policy formulation and implementation in virtually every country, authoritarian or democratic, takes place within a vertical command system.

The primary driving forces behind the process of transformation in China include economic development and modernization efforts; the emerging power and influence of technocratic bureaucrats at the top level; the passing away of the old revolutionary generation; lessons learned from recent history, particularly the upheavals of the Cultural Revolution; China's opening up to the outside world; the enormous increase in the diversity and complexity of foreign policy decisions; and, finally, the political awakening of the Chinese people. Despite the severe setback since 1989, economic reforms and other developments of the Deng era, as Michel Oksenberg points out, "have continued after the Beijing massacre."[11] The continuing existence of these driving forces will keep this transformation process going and will prevent China from returning to vertical authoritarianism.

The examination of the process of changing from vertical authoritarianism to horizontal authoritarianism in the area of foreign policymaking or linkages between domestic and foreign policy requires a close look at the following key domestic elements:

— power centers at the top levels;
— bureaucratic interests within functional institutions;
— agendas of policy issues;
— the involvement of local interests and the relationship between the central government and local authorities;
— the participation of intellectuals and think tanks; and
— general political and economic conditions and popular demands.

These elements have worked collectively in the transformation process from vertical to horizontal authoritarianism. The focus of this article is more on political institutions and elite politics than on mass politics because of the nature of the Chinese regime and the nature of the foreign policy issues concerned. As Mancur Olson suggests, in Soviet-type societies and autocratic environments, "it is usually better to look at the regime and at the civil and military officials rather than only at the preferences of the people to understand what happens."[12] This, however, does not mean that the demands of the people are not important. Both China's domestic politics and its foreign policy have been effectively influenced in recent years by the people's political demands in the form of the changing of political culture and new forms of political participation, namely, demonstrations and passive resistance. These

---

11. Michel Oksenberg, "The China Problem," *Foreign Affairs*, 70(3):4 (Spring 1991).

12. Mancur Olson, "The Logic of Collective Action in Soviet-Type Societies," *Journal of Soviet Nationalities*, 1(2):26 (Summer 1990).

changes and developments will be discussed later.

LEADERSHIP DIFFERENCES

It is well known that there have been various factions at the top level in Chinese politics. Kenneth Lieberthal described three schools of thought prevalent in the Chinese foreign policymaking establishment. The first is the nativist. Supporters of this line of reasoning encourage a closed-door foreign policy and a reign of virtue domestically. Advocates of the second school, the eclectic organizers, want to strengthen China by using foreign technology, while at the same time they want to shield the country from the cultural influences that accompany the technological imports. Adherents to the third school of thought, the "all-around modernizers," strive to alter the fundamental nature of Chinese culture in favor of rapid economic development in order to speed up the country's modernization process.[13]

That there are differences between top leaders is not new. For example, it is believed that there were a number of differences between Mao Zedong and Zhou Enlai, both in perceptions of the outside world and on foreign policy issues. Under the vertical authoritarianism of the Maoist era, however, it was possible for the paramount leader to silence different opinions. According to "some Chinese who were close to Zhou at that time," Mao's influence in the making of broad strategic decisions on foreign policy "greatly overshadowed that of Zhou."[14]

Another good example of one-man domination is the case of Peng Dehuai, the former marshal and defense minister. Peng voiced different opinions on domestic and foreign policy issues at the Lushan Conference in 1959 and was immediately removed from the top military position. Later he was placed under house arrest and was tortured to death during the Cultural Revolution. Under the system of vertical authoritarianism, different opinions on both domestic and foreign policy issues were usually silenced.

Due to the process of changing from vertical to horizontal authoritarianism, the top leader—in this case Deng Xiaoping—has less authority and power than did Mao. It is now relatively difficult to silence or eliminate political leaders who have different opinions but similar political power.[15] Therefore, Deng may have to tolerate different opinions at the top level.

The best current example is the case of Chen Yun, another senior leader, who for a long time prior to the Cultural Revolution ranked higher than Deng within the Party hierarchy. Deng and Chen have shared many similar ideas on a broad range of domestic and foreign policy issues. There are, however, differences between the two. Domestically,

13. Kenneth Lieberthal, "Domestic Politics and Foreign Policy," in *China's Foreign Relations in the 1980s*, ed. Harding, pp. 44-45.

14. Barnett, *Making of Foreign Policy in China*, pp. 7-8.
15. Leaders with less power, such as Hu Yaobang and Zhao Ziyang, however, may still be removed from the leading position.

Chen is known to favor a more centrally planned economy than Deng. Internationally, Deng has had long experience in dealing with the Soviet Union and is deeply concerned about Soviet expansionist intentions. Therefore, he favors a foreign policy that would draw China closer to the West. By contrast, Chen is virtually the only top Chinese leader who has not made a single public statement criticizing the Soviet Union since the Sino-Soviet split became open in the early 1960s. Long before the formal normalization of relations between China and the Soviet Union in 1989, Chen advocated a more conciliatory policy toward Moscow.

From the mid-1980s on, Beijing has advocated an "independent foreign policy," one that would be somewhat independent from both of the superpowers. This policy has in general reflected China's national interests at the time, but it can also be regarded as a compromise between the two schools of thought represented by different power centers for major foreign policy issues. These power centers, however, are not institutionalized; rather, they are based on personal prestige and connections and therefore are quite personalistic. But the very fact that there is more than one power center is already a major change from the previous regime of domination by one person.

As if to emphasize the existence of another power center in Beijing, since the middle of 1990 there has been open support for the so-called Chen Yun thought, which calls for studying and mastering "Comrade Chen Yun's economic thinking about

the correct relationship between planning and market."[16] Moreover, Chen's son Chen Yuan, who is currently a deputy governor of the Chinese People's Bank—a position equal to vice-minister—and widely regarded as spokesperson of the Chen Yun power center, has been increasingly active in advocating his or his father's ideas on economic and political issues in Beijing's political circle.[17] Therefore, in addition to seeing a power center headed by Chen Yun, one can actually hear clear differences of opinion on policy issues between Deng and Chen.

Openly voiced differences at the top level require more time for consultation, coordination, and compromise, so that a new and imaginative policy that will fit the changing situation can be worked out. Therefore, the best temporary solution on many occasions is to maintain the status quo, to stick to existing policy. This is especially true in the field of foreign policy because foreign policy issues are often seen as less controversial and less relevant to power struggles at the top compared to domestic issues such as political and economic reforms. It is not surprising that the Seventh Plenum of the Chinese Communist Party's Central Committee, which was held in December 1990, a year and a half after the Tiananmen incident, produced nothing of substance in either domestic or foreign

16. Robert Delfs, "Thought Control, Conservatives behind Chen Yun in Reform Struggle," *Far Eastern Economic Review*, 8 Nov. 1990, pp. 19-20.

17. *World Journal*, 19 June 1991, p. 10; ibid., 27 July 1991, p. 10.

policy. A China watcher points out that "this lack of substance underlines the present paralysis gripping the policymaking process."[18] The inability to generate new initiatives in either domestic or foreign policies due to the temporary balance between power centers at the top level partially explains why Chinese foreign policy remains more or less unchanged, despite a period of major turmoil in domestic politics. This phenomenon can be explained further by an examination of other domestic factors.

BUREAUCRATIC PARTICIPATION

We now shift to the bureaucratic interests of functioning institutions, such as the Party-governmental apparatuses of foreign affairs. In China, every political institution is led by the Communist Party. Nevertheless, the Party and the government have separate agencies for dealing with foreign affairs, each with different functions. Under the Party's Central Committee, there is the International Liaison Department, which is in charge of the Party's international activities, while the State Council represents the Chinese government. The State Council controls several ministries that have jurisdiction over foreign policy issues, most notably the MFA. Many other institutions may also have functioning organizations dealing with foreign affairs. For example, there is a Foreign Affairs Committee under the National People's Congress (NPC).

Political and administrative reforms in the 1980s brought a generation of technocrats into the ranks of the government bureaucracy. These technocratic bureaucrats are relatively young, well educated, and therefore more confident and assertive in their own fields of specialization. David Bachman argues that the younger generation of leaders such as Li Peng, the current premier, has a smaller power base and less authority compared to the older generation, which includes Mao and Deng. Therefore, it is probable that politics will be based more on persuasion and compromise and that bold, new initiatives harming entrenched bureaucratic interests will be less likely.[19] In other words, this new group of bureaucrats has participated more actively both in the policymaking process and in the protection of bureaucratic interests. Foreign affairs bureaucrats are no exception in this regard.

This participation of bureaucrats in the policymaking process is primarily reflected in day-to-day affairs. Within their own jurisdiction, foreign affairs bureaucrats may play an active role. This trend has also been strengthened by the increased expertise of a professional foreign service team. Within the Chinese embassy to the United States, for example, Chinese diplomats have gradually improved their working efficiency by fo-

18. Tai Ming Cheung, "Policy in Paralysis: Deng's Cameo Fails to Tilt the Delicate Balancing Act," *Far Eastern Economic Review*, 10 Jan. 1991, pp. 10-11.

19. David Bachman, "Domestic Sources of Chinese Foreign Policy," in *China and the World: New Directions in Chinese Foreign Relations*, ed. Samuel S. Kim (Boulder, CO: Westview Press, 1989), p. 37.

cusing their attention on key institutions of American foreign policy, including not only the White House and the executive branch but also the legislature. In the mid-1980s, the Chinese embassy began to establish the Division of Congressional Affairs with about seven or eight staff members headed by a senior diplomat. The division was formed to conduct extensive research and diplomatic activities.[20] This kind of development has naturally enhanced the influence of foreign affairs bureaucrats in the policymaking process.

After the Tiananmen incident, there was a downturn in Sino-American bilateral relations. The MFA, however, has been seen as having worked hard within its jurisdiction to improve relations with the United States.[21] One example was Beijing's agreement to a visit by Richard Schifter, the U.S. assistant secretary of state for human rights, in December 1990. The assistant secretary held 16 hours of talks with his Chinese counterparts and submitted a list of 150 political prisoners about whom the Americans were particularly concerned.[22]

The MFA not only hosted this visit but also arranged meetings with a broad range of high-level government officials from ministries or agencies of public security, justice, minority nationality affairs, birth control and

family planning, religious affairs, and the Supreme Court. The discussions were quite broad and frank.[23] The visit itself was regarded as a compromise by Chinese authorities since Beijing has always insisted that human rights issues are internal affairs and that no foreign power should intervene.

Another example of increased bureaucratic participation in the policymaking process is the changing nature of the NPC, under which there is a committee on foreign affairs. In China, staff members of the Party, the government, and the congress are all regarded as cadres—that is, as government employees—so they are all part of the central bureaucracy. The NPC Foreign Affairs Committee is largely staffed by retired high-ranking diplomats; therefore, it can be regarded as a part of the bureaucratic establishment. The NPC has long been regarded as a rubber-stamping body, but for the last several years it has increased its influence. For example, during the 1989 student-led, pro-democracy movement, approximately forty members of the standing committee of the NPC were active in working out a petition for the lifting of martial law.

Studying the NPC's potential influence in China's policymaking process, Kevin O'Brien argues that the NPC is "neither a classic conservative legislature, nor a dynamic base for mobilization that propels social groups into the political process." O'Brien believes that the NPC "is an

20. Interview with a high-ranking diplomat in the Chinese embassy to the United States, 8 Feb. 1991.
21. Interview with a U.S. White House official, 5 Feb. 1991.
22. Susumo Awanohara and Tai Ming Cheung, "Abusive Treatment: China Hedges Response to US Human Rights Pressure," *Far Eastern Economic Review*, 3 Jan. 1991, pp. 8-9.

23. Interview with a U.S. State Department official who participated in this visit, 25 Feb. 1991.

arena couched in overall approval of existing policies, and semi-retired central elites, regional leaders, and mass representatives express minority opinions and exert a moderating influence, largely by adverse public opinions and by insisting on procedural regularity and a systematic approach to problems."[24] In the field of foreign policy as well as domestic politics, the NPC may eventually become a place for bargaining and compromise.

EXPANDED POLICY AGENDAS

Horizontal participation in the policymaking process is bound to increase as the number of issues on the policy agenda increases, especially in cases where these issues do not involve major strategic or political decisions. As China opened to the outside world, foreign policy decisions became much more diversified and complicated than ever before, especially in the areas of foreign economic and cultural exchange. Since these issues tend to involve more participants in the policymaking process, it is likely that there are more players representing a greater variety of interests. In addition, these players tend to have a more autonomous status than that possessed by those who were links in the vertical-authoritarianism system. In the field of foreign economic relations, for example, a number of government institutions, such as the Ministry of Foreign Economic Relations and Trade and the

National Planning Commission, have played prominent roles. Other ministries related to economic development have also increased their direct dealings with foreign countries. Institutions in the field of international cultural and educational exchange, such as the Academy of Sciences, the Academy of Social Sciences, the National Commission of Education, and the National Commission of Sciences and Technology, have all broadened their power in external activities since China started its open policy in the late 1970s.

One other remarkable development in this regard is in the field of arms sales in the international market. The People's Liberation Army (PLA) has become a major arms supplier to the world. China has quickly become the fourth-largest seller in the arms trade, behind the United States, the Soviet Union, and France. This rapid development has both a long-term and a short-term goal. In the long term, it will provide a basis on which to build political influence in regional and global affairs. In the short run, however, those arms sales must generate foreign exchange for the PLA's own modernization.[25] The seeking of profit by means of arms sales abroad is a direct result of domestic political and economic changes. The Chinese military has experienced significant budget cuts throughout the 1980s. For example, in 1979 China spent Rmb22 billion, or 17.5 percent of its total budget, on defense expenditures. By 1987, this ratio had

24. Kevin O'Brien, "Is China's National People's Congress a Conservative Legislature?" *Asian Survey*, 30(8):793-94 (Aug. 1990).

25. John Calabrese, "From Flyswatters to Silkworms: The Evolution of China's Role in West Asia," *Asian Survey*, 30(9):873 (Sept. 1990).

been reduced to Rmb20.4 billion, or 8.2 percent of the total budget.[26] Therefore, the PLA has been encouraged to make its own profit through internal and external economic activities, particularly by conducting arms sales abroad in order to earn foreign currency for its modernization. The most noticeable customer for the PLA's profitable business was the Middle East. For example, during the six-year Iraq-Iran war, more than 70 percent of China's arms exports were purchased by these two combatants alone.[27]

The military's autonomy in external relations, however, has its limitations. Although the PLA has traditionally had enormous influence over political issues, it is in no position to challenge the authority of the Party. If there are conflicting interests between the MFA and the PLA, the issue will be referred to a special group supervised by the highest leadership of the Party, which will coordinate the various interests and make the decisions. Interestingly enough, beginning in the late 1980s the MFA for the first time was allowed to send its representative to participate in the group's discussion of arms sales. However, once a decision is made, it will normally be accepted by all subordinate groups.

By the end of the 1980s, after a series of high-level negotiations between China and the United States, Beijing agreed that it would not sell Silkworm missiles to the Middle

East. The MFA made this pledge openly. It is believed that in general the PLA has cooperated with this policy rather well, although it sometimes has attempted to test the policy's limits by inquiring about possible buyers without actually signing contracts.[28] In February 1991, the MFA formally denied allegations that China was continuing to sell arms to Iraq during the ongoing Persian Gulf war,[29] and in June Beijing agreed to participate in a U.S.-sponsored conference to get the world's top arms suppliers to establish guidelines limiting the sale of arms and nuclear-related technology to the Middle East.[30] From 27 to 31 July 1991, the PLA's foreign affairs working conference was held in Beijing, directly following the State Council's foreign affairs working conference.[31] This reflects Beijing's effort to coordinate foreign policy and international activities among key institutions, particularly the military and the State Council.

LOCAL INPUTS

The relationship between the central government and local elites and the emerging role of entrenched local interests in foreign relations—in foreign economic relations in particular—is another element worthy of examination. Under vertical authoritarianism, central authority tightly

26. Eberhard Sandschneider, "The Chinese Army after Tiananmen," *Pacific Review*, 3(2):118 (1990).

27. Ibid., p. 119.

28. Interview with a U.S. White House official, 5 Feb. 1991; interview with a U.S. State Department official, 25 Feb. 1991.

29. *Renmin ribao*, 2 Feb. 1991.

30. Tai Ming Cheung, "Missile Refrain," *Far Eastern Economic Review*, 27 June 1991, pp. 12-13.

31. *Renmin ribao*, 1 Aug. 1991.

controlled local activities in virtually all aspects—political, economic, and even social. Central authorities have a wide range of mechanisms with which to contain the activities of local elites: control over the appointment and dismissal of major provincial officials, such as the first Party secretaries, governors, and military commanders; control over certain mobile military forces, notably the field armies; control of the propaganda apparatus; and, finally, control over key economic resources, such as metals and transportation.[32]

These tight constraints on local interests and activities were gradually loosened during the period of reform prior to the summer of 1989. There are open areas, in particular coastal cities or provinces such as Guangdong, Hainan, Fujian, Shandong, Shanghai, and Tianjing, together with the four special economic zones of Shenzhen, Zhuhai, Xiamen, and Shantou. Local governments in these areas have obtained a higher degree of authority in terms of local economic activities and external economic relations. The central government, for example, permits these local governments to retain a proportion of the foreign exchange they earn in order to encourage exports and local economic development. With greater access to foreign currency, provinces such as Guangdong and Fujian can enjoy unprecedented autonomy in conducting external economic activities. Some China specialists believe

that in these cases the relationship between the center and the provinces has become more interdependent.[33] Vertical authoritarianism tends to favor the center, whereas under horizontal authoritarianism the balance of power may favor the province. This shift in favor of the provinces gradually took place in the 1980s.

The struggle to retain and strengthen local power has not stopped in the 1990s. There have been frequent reports of resistance on the part of provincial officials to the efforts of the central government to tighten control over local economic and external activities. In some cases, several provincial governors have worked together to oppose recentralization of certain economic policies. Provincial power has also been strengthened by the fact that more provincial governors or first Party secretaries have been promoted to leading positions at the center. For example, before becoming premier of the State Council and, later, the Party general secretary, Zhao Ziyang served for a long time as provincial boss in Guangdong, Inner Mongolia, and Sichuan. The current general secretary, Jiang Zemin, was previously first secretary of Shanghai. Li Ruihuan, member of the Party's standing committee, was promoted from the positions of mayor and first Party secretary of Tianjing. These promotions have inevitably increased the influence of local interests and strengthened the ties between the center and the local level.

After the Tiananmen incident, the United States suspended bilateral of-

32. Kenneth Lieberthal and Michel Oksenberg, *Policymaking in China: Leaders, Structures, and Process* (Princeton, NJ: Princeton University Press, 1988), pp. 339-53.

33. Ibid., p. 352.

ficial exchanges. Few high-level Chinese officials were invited to visit the United States. In July 1990, a Chinese mayoral delegation paid an official visit to "enhance mutual understanding and improve bilateral relations."[34] This delegation was headed by Zhu Rongji, mayor of Shanghai,[35] the highest official to visit the United States at that time. Zhu, although a local official, conducted extensive diplomatic activities, meeting with National Security Adviser Brent Scowcroft, State Department Deputy Secretary Lawrence Eagleburger, and Speaker of the U.S. House of Representatives Thomas Foley.[36] These activities further confirmed the more visible participation of provincial officials in foreign relations.

Nevertheless, one cannot overemphasize local authorities' autonomy. Considering China's highly centralized political system, the participation of local elites is primarily limited to local affairs and can be further limited by the central government at any time. Indeed, as of 1 January 1991, Beijing has decided to remove export subsidies, a measure designed to crimp the growing independence of regional governments.[37]

34. "Quarterly Chronicle and Documentation," *China Quarterly*, Dec. 1990, no. 124, p. 780.

35. Zhu was promoted to vice premier in the spring of 1991.

36. Interview with a U.S. State Department official, 25 Feb. 1991.

37. Elizabeth Cheng, "Power to the Center: China Removes Export Subsidies to Curb Regional Privileges," *Far Eastern Economic Review*, 24 Jan. 1991, pp. 34-35.

THINK TANKS

Think tanks and intellectuals are also assuming an increasingly important role in foreign policymaking. During Mao's era of vertical authoritarianism, the voices of intellectuals were largely silenced. Since the early 1980s, however, foreign affairs think tanks have expanded remarkably in terms of both number and scope of participation. Under the State Council, there are the Center for International Studies and the Institute of Contemporary International Relations. In addition, every foreign-policy-related ministry, such as the MFA and the Ministry of Foreign Economic Relations and Trade, has its own research institute. At the Academy of Social Sciences there are also several internationally oriented research institutions concentrating not only on world political and economic relations but also on regional studies, such as concentrations on the Soviet Union and Eastern Europe, the United States, Japan, Latin America, South Asia, the Middle East and Africa, and Western Europe. There are also research institutions of international studies at major universities located in Beijing, such as Beijing University and the People's University.

Most of these research institutions engage primarily in two kinds of activities: preparing background information on international affairs by conducting basic research, and providing proposals and analysis on foreign issues. They may also have institutional or private internal channels to various levels of authorities to present their own analyses on foreign policy issues and even opinions different from official lines. In this way, think tanks and intellectuals have more or less played an advisory and consulting role in the foreign policy-making process. From 1978 to 1985, for example, there were long-lasting debates about Soviet socialism among these think tanks and intellectuals as well as among government bureaucrats.[38] These debates fostered the internal preparations necessary for Beijing to normalize its relations with Moscow by the end of the 1980s.

Nevertheless, the political influence of think tanks and intellectuals over foreign policy issues has remained weak. They may have a fairly high degree of freedom to conduct discussions on a variety of issues internally, but it is difficult, if not impossible, for them to voice their different points of view openly. In China, there is no open forum for international affairs experts to discuss foreign policy issues. If a scholar is allowed to discuss these issues in public, he is expected to give a positive explanation of the official line, thereby justifying the policy. For example, in the mid-1980s Deng Xiaoping repeatedly stated that large-scale world war would not break out for a relatively long period of time because the forces for peace in the world had grown and that, therefore, it was justifiable to accord defense a low priority in the budget and to put the military through a wrenching overhaul. In a published interview with foreign

reporters in Beijing, Huan Xiang, a leading expert in foreign affairs and director of the State Council's Center for International Studies, made the following comment:

"Deng Xiaoping's peace thoughts are based on China's economic development and the political and economic reforms which form the core of Deng's thought. . . . The basic things that China relies on in order to safeguard peace are political and economic reforms and development. I think that this is Deng's thought."[39]

This is typical of the open statements made by Chinese think tanks on foreign policy issues in order to explain the top leader's thoughts and to justify a certain policy. In this sense, intellectuals have not yet become an independent entity in China's political life. They have gained more freedom to discuss policy issues internally, but, externally or publicly, they have to support official lines. This is an important characteristic of horizontal authoritarianism.

GENERAL POLITICAL AND ECONOMIC CONDITIONS

The final elements—but not the least important—changing the nature of the foreign policymaking process are popular demand, or mood, and general political and economic conditions. Because of the society's authoritarian nature, the expression

38. For detailed accounts, see Gilbert Rozman, The Chinese Debate about Soviet Socialism (Princeton, NJ: Princeton University Press, 1987).

39. Huan Xiang, interview with foreign reporters in Beijing, 21 June 1985, in Wen wei po, 22 June 1985, in Foreign Broadcast Information Service, FBIS Daily Report—China, 24 June 1985, quoted from Carol Hamrin, China and the Challenge of the Future: Changing Political Patterns (Boulder, CO: Westview Press, 1990), p. 141.

of political demand in China is different from that in democratic societies, where there are institutionalized articulated means of expressing these demands, such as popular elections, referenda, opinion surveys, interest groups, and lobbying activities. In China, two basic unofficial forms of political participation have developed in recent years: open demonstrations such as the ones that took place during the spring and summer of 1989, and passive resistance. Both are effective in communicating popular demand to the authorities. This development can be regarded as a direct result of the ten-year political turmoil of the Cultural Revolution (1966-76), and it represents a gradual change in China's political culture.

Passive resistance has been widely adopted since the military crackdown of 1989. An article in the *Far Eastern Economic Review*, for example, included this comment a year after the Tiananmen incident:

There is a conspiracy . . . perhaps strongest in Peking [Beijing] but extending throughout China. . . . It is a conspiracy of silence, the sum of thousands of individual decisions not to inform on friends, neighbors or colleagues. This spontaneous mass refusal has stymied attempts to mount a full-scale investigation and purge of participants in last year's disturbances.[40]

Many political discussions organized by the authorities for the purpose of "purifying thinking" turned into occasions for people to criticize the Party for its inept leadership and clumsy handling of the demonstra-

tions.[41] A more dramatic example of passive resistance took place in an official, controlled election for the city's People's Congress in Beijing in December 1990. In the Haidian district, where most of the city's universities are concentrated, 300 people voted for disgraced Party chief Zhao Ziyang, even though the only choices on the ballot were carefully screened Communist Party loyalists.[42]

In order to maintain Communist rule and domestic stability, the Beijing leadership has to consider this kind of political demand. This consideration of domestic mood has inevitably had an impact on China's foreign policy. For example, the release of several hundred political prisoners and the permission extended to top dissident Fang Lizhi to go abroad in 1990 were no doubt responses to international pressure, as many people outside of China believed. But one cannot overlook the fact that it was also a response to the domestic demand that Beijing badly needed a gentler image toward its own people.

Domestic political and economic conditions are always important in understanding Chinese foreign policy. There have been cycles in China's political atmosphere throughout the history of the People's Republic. Lucian Pye has analyzed these unique cycles, stating that China's distinctive state-society relationship has contributed to the "peculiar breadth of its politics." Pye believes that the

40. *Far Eastern Economic Review*, 31 May 1990, p. 17.

41. Hong Shi, "China's Political Development after Tiananmen: Tranquility by Default," *Asian Survey*, 30(12):1210 (Dec. 1990).

42. *Far Eastern Economic Review*, 24 Jan. 1991, p. 9.

factional struggles within the ruling elite have produced not a Western pendulum that swings between liberal and conservative "but an up and down motion of centralizing and decentralizing, or tightening and loosening, the state's penetration of society."[43] The making of foreign policy in China is closely related to this "up and down motion." It is also reflected in the speed and process of transformation from vertical to horizontal authoritarianism.

The most recent example of this "up and down motion" is the difference in Chinese political life before and after the Tiananmen incident of 1989. During the period of political disturbance since the late 1980s, the first priority in the making of foreign policy has been to maintain the domestic stability necessary for the survival of the regime. This concern will inevitably be reflected in China's policy toward major powers.

For example, if the Beijing leadership feels that the United States is a subversive political force rather than a constructive partner, then Sino-American relations are likely to remain at a lower level. An article in the *Beijing Review* revealed this concern. It suggested that in the post-Cold War era a shift in the balance of power in favor of the West surfaced as a result of dramatic changes in the Soviet bloc and the ever-widening North-South gap. It argues that "such a new situation may tempt some Western countries [read: the United States] to recklessly impose their will on others interfering in the internal affairs of other countries [read: China] and practising power politics and hegemony in international relations."[44] An internal Chinese Communist Party document circulated among high-ranking Chinese officials has made this point more clearly. The document summed up the views of He Xin, one of the few Chinese academics who openly supported the violent suppression of 1989, depicting "the United States as an enemy nation bent on destroying China's communist system and replacing it with capitalism."[45] Even though this viewpoint perhaps only reflected Beijing's hard-liners' ideas, it indeed illuminated the linkages between domestic political situations and Chinese leaders' perceptions of the outside world.

Economic conditions are another domestic factor that could affect foreign policy. For example, China's foreign debt increased from zero in 1979 to $16 billion in 1985, to $40 billion in 1988, and then to more than $50 billion in 1990.[46] Such a development may give conservatives sufficient leverage to alter China's international borrowing policy substantially and thus dramatically slow the pace of China's integration into the world capitalist market.

43. Lucian W. Pye, "China: Erratic State, Frustrated Society," *Foreign Affairs*, Fall 1990, p. 73.

44. Jin Dexiang, "Peace and Development, A Strenuous Task in '90s," *Beijing Review*, 18 Feb.-3 Mar. 1991, pp. 13-17.

45. Dan Southerland, "A Glimpse of Beijing's Suspicions of U.S.," *Asian Wall Street Journal Weekly*, 22 July 1991, p. 15.

46. Samuel Kim, "Chinese Foreign Policy after Tiananmen," *Current History*. Sept. 1990, p. 248.

THE EFFECT OF CHANGE

This article has been concerned with the changes of foreign policy-making in China represented by the transformation from vertical authoritarianism to horizontal authoritarianism. Under vertical authoritarianism, which is characterized by one-person domination, foreign policy tends to be more rigid and more concerned with ideology. It is not surprising that early works on the Maoist era all emphasized the revolutionary nature of Chinese foreign policy, bearing such titles as *Revolution and Chinese Foreign Policy*[47] and *Revolutionary Diplomacy*.[48]

By contrast, under horizontal authoritarianism, more players and more diverse issues are involved in the process of foreign policymaking. There is more collective decision making. It is true that the policy outcome is not always connected to the policymaking process; therefore the horizontal type of policymaking does not necessarily produce only positive policy outcomes. But with more interests and players involved, Chinese foreign policy does appear to be relatively less rigid and more pragmatic. In recent years, foreign analysts have noted this change in Chinese foreign policy and have expressed such notions as "growing flexibility and pragmatism [have] characterized China's foreign relations in recent years"[49] or

"the very flexibility of Chinese pragmatism can at times raise problems, particularly in foreign relations, as the agility of Chinese leaders can leave the more cautious and ponderous American (and Soviet) decision making process a step or two behind."[50]

The development of horizontal participation in foreign relations has its limitations, however. In China, for example, every governmental institution or agency is controlled by the Communist Party. In order to be promoted to positions of higher authority, officials must rise through the ranks of the bureaucratic hierarchy. As a result, an individual seeking greater autonomy may be placing his or her political career in jeopardy. The risk is greater if the specific policy involves strategic or political issues. Indeed, sensitive and strategically important issues such as China's relations with major powers can be handled only by a small group of top leaders. For example, the issue of Taiwan not only involves foreign powers such as the United States but is also a sensitive issue in China's domestic politics.[51] Any major decision regarding Taiwan, therefore, is believed to be made by Deng and Yang Shangkun—Deng's close associate and China's president—themselves.

47. Peter Van Ness, *Revolution and Chinese Foreign Policy* (Berkeley: University of California Press, 1970).

48. A. D. Armstrong, *Revolutionary Diplomacy* (Berkeley: University of California Press, 1977).

49. Harding, *China's Second Revolution*, p. 243.

50. Lucian Pye, *The Mandarin and the Cadre: Chinese Political Cultures* (Ann Arbor: University of Michigan, Center for Chinese Studies, 1988), p. 106.

51. For detailed accounts of the Taiwan issue, see Zhao Quansheng, "One Country Two Systems and One Country Two Parties: PRC-Taiwan Unification and Its Political Implications," *Pacific Review*, 2(4):312-19 (1989); idem, "The United States New Initiatives and Beijing's Dilemma," *United Daily News*, 25 July 1991.

Horizontal authoritarianism can be regarded as a progressive political development, a gradual departure from the regime of one-person domination. We have seen similar processes occur in other parts of East Asia. In both Taiwan and South Korea, horizontal authoritarianism was a step between the previous vertical authoritarianism and the ongoing process of political democratization characterized by parliamentary politics.

Even though prior to 1989 China was moving in much the same direction as South Korea and Taiwan, it differs from them in important respects: basic economic settings with special reference to policy toward private enterprise; the degree of external political influence, particularly from the West; and the quality of top leadership in terms of level of education and awareness of democracy and political development. Therefore, one cannot say that China will automatically follow the footsteps of other East Asian societies. There will be a long period of uncertainty in China's domestic politics, which will bring a certain degree of uncertainty to its foreign policy.

ANNALS, *AAPSS*, **519**, January 1992

China's Foreign Economic Relations

By GUOCANG HUAN

ABSTRACT: China's foreign economic relations dipped sharply after Tiananmen. International agencies and governments suspended loan negotiations while foreign investors lessened new commitments. Tourism plunged. The net effect cut foreign exchange earnings. But retrenchment measures to cool the overheated economy reduced imports, as did the lessened availability of credit, while exports increased. The balance of trade markedly improved. By mid-1990 foreign economic sanctions had been eased or lifted altogether. Various measures favored special economic zones and coastal enclaves for foreign investment, especially from Taiwan and Japan. Conservative attacks on policy, the recentralization of foreign exchange control, and stagnation in economic reform cause concern abroad, however. The differential development of interior versus coastal areas affects marketing and competitiveness. A likely succession struggle and the possible emergence of popular unrest continue to cloud foreign views.

Dr. Guocang Huan is a nonresident senior fellow of the Atlantic Council of the United States and associate research fellow of the East Asian Institute, Columbia University.

CHINA'S foreign economic relations have changed significantly since the summer of 1989. During the second half of 1989 and the first quarter of 1990, despite the depreciation of the renminbi, the Chinese currency, by 21.2 percent on 16 December 1989, China generated a substantial foreign trade deficit, caused mainly by its volatile domestic politics and changed economic strategy. But the spring of 1990 was a turning point; Beijing restructured the foreign trade system, imposed tough restrictions on imports, and increased fiscal subsidies for exports. During the following three quarters, China's imports dropped significantly while exports began to pick up. On 16 November 1990, Beijing further depreciated the renminbi by 9.75 percent, providing a strong incentive to exports. For the entire year, China enjoyed a trade surplus of $8.7 billion.[1]

Similarly, with the exception of Taiwanese and Hong Kong investment, overseas direct investment in China dropped sharply during the second half of 1989 and the first half of 1990. It then began to increase. Taiwanese companies have shown a strong interest in labor-intensive manufacturing operations and chemical factories in Fujian province, and Hong Kong investment in Guangdong province has remained strong. In April 1990, when Beijing announced its plan to establish the Pudong Development Zone (PDZ) in Shanghai, the international business community responded positively. Yet, to date, the central government and

the Shanghai municipal government have not made significant moves to ensure foreign investors that the zone will enjoy more privileges than other special economic zones (SEZs). Meanwhile, the central government has carried out a number of key personnel changes in some SEZs and has cut their fiscal and other privileges in other parts of the country. It has continued to grant more autonomy to Hainan province for expanding business ties abroad, however.

From mid-1989 to mid-1990, most nations of the Organization for Economic Cooperation and Development (OECD) imposed economic sanctions on China, banning the transfer of high technology and governmental loans. Subsequently, most OECD nations, led by Japan, lifted these sanctions. Moreover, Tokyo decided to resume the third round of its $5.2 billion loan to Beijing. A number of West European countries followed suit, as did the World Bank. The only exception was the United States, which continued its sanctions. Yet, in certain areas, U.S. economic policy toward China also softened. These developments have had a strong impact on the international banking community's lending policy toward China.

A few questions arise. First, in what direction and to what extent have China's domestic politics and economics affected its foreign economic relations? Second, what other major factors have had an impact? Third, what are the future trends and prospects? To answer, we will review changes and continuity in China's foreign economic policy since the Tiananmen tragedy, examine new

1. *People's Daily*, 12 Apr. 1991.

problems, and then project future trends.

FOREIGN TRADE, TECHNOLOGY, AND IMPORTS

During the third quarter of 1989, the central government lost control over economic affairs, including foreign trade. Imports of consumer goods rose suddenly and significantly while exports fell substantially. In particular, China's imports of capital goods from and exports to Hong Kong, its number-one trade partner, declined sharply, due partly to China's highly unstable economic and political developments and partly to Hong Kong's slowed economic growth. Worried about possible changes in Beijing's policies on foreign trade and foreign exchange, local authorities, enterprises, and individuals rushed to spend their hard currency. Meanwhile, enterprises along the Chinese coast were discouraged from conducting business with their foreign counterparts, who were shocked by China's political turmoil. As a result, the trade deficit jumped.

The situation began to change in the fall of 1989 when Beijing gradually regained control over the society and began to impose new economic policies. In October, it decided to recentralize decision making concerning foreign trade by imposing a new tough import license system. Moreover, the government raised import tax rates on some consumer goods. It no longer allowed local authorities to approve applications for establishing foreign trade companies, and it closed over 1000 local foreign trade companies. At the same time, the central government raised interest rates, reduced the money supply, and cut fiscal spending, pushing the economy into recession. As a result, the increase in demand for imported goods began to slow down. Meanwhile, lower inflation and the recessionary environment induced corporations from Taiwan and South Korea to increase imports from China and to set up export-oriented and labor-intensive manufacturing operations on the Chinese coast. These developments have gradually stabilized foreign trade, although the 1989 trade deficit reached $6.6 billion.[2]

In late spring 1990, however, the central government suspended its so-called readjustment strategy by increasing the money supply and investment in infrastructure and basic industries. Nonetheless, in the first half of 1990 it continued to tighten its foreign trade policy. In addition to newly imposed import restrictions, Beijing further raised import taxes on both consumer and capital goods. It also increased fiscal subsidies for exports and strengthened control and monopoly over the exports of key commodities such as oil, coal, cotton, and mine products. Having reduced its pressure on the private sector and provided a strong incentive for trade with Taiwan, the government further depreciated the renminbi by 9.75 percent on 16 November. These policies encouraged enterprises that conduct exports and improved China's balance of trade. Finally, in December, Beijing announced that it would terminate fiscal subsidies for exports on

2. Ibid., 15 Apr. 1990.

1 January 1991. This new move made foreign trade enterprises financially independent and reduced the central government's fiscal burden. It was also designed to increase the chance for China to win the competition against Taiwan for membership in the General Agreement on Tariffs and Trade. Nevertheless, this policy is likely to reduce local government revenue generated from foreign trade. In 1990, China's total exports rose 18.1 percent to $62.1 billion and imports declined 9.8 percent to $53.4 billion, resulting in a net surplus of $8.7 billion.[3]

In 1989, due largely to the OECD nations' tightened restrictions on technology transfer to China and to the government's readjustment strategy, imports of technology and industrial equipment declined sharply. Some OECD nations suspended cooperation with China in defense-related industries. Before June 1989, about 80 percent of China's important and large technology-import projects were paid for by loans provided by OECD governments. From June 1989 to June 1990, most OECD nations stopped lending money to China. Consequently, the number and value of technology-import projects in 1989 fell 25 percent and 18 percent, respectively. China's technology imports from the United States were particularly hurt, their number and value falling 48 percent and 42 percent from 1988, respectively.[4] The interruption in lending was also an

important cause for the increase in China's trade surplus with the United States.

The situation began to change in mid-1990 when most OECD nations decided to lift their sanctions against China. Washington authorized the U.S. Export-Import Bank to resume trade-related credit and guarantes to China and approved Australia's using Chinese missiles to deliver U.S.-made satellites. These developments improved China's ability to receive technology from the OECD nations and will continue to do so.

FOREIGN
DIRECT INVESTMENT

Due largely to China's high degree of political instability in the spring and summer of 1989, many overseas corporations put their investment plans for China on hold. Yet most overseas corporations that already had operations there did not withdraw. Rather they decided to wait and see. After the fourth quarter of 1989, the political situation gradually stabilized, but the readjustment strategy and recentralization programs pushed the economy into a recession. As a result, OECD corporations were discouraged from increasing investment.

In the late spring of 1990, Beijing adjusted its domestic economic policies as well as its policies on foreign investment. In April, the government announced its plan for the PDZ in Shanghai, signaling its commitment to attracting direct foreign investment. But it specifically indicated that the PDZ should not repeat the models and experiences of four SEZs

3. Ibid., 12 Apr. 1991.
4. Li Lanqin, "The Current Situation and Tasks of Our Country's Foreign Economic and Trade Work," *International Trade Journal* (Beijing), 1990, no. 9, p. 6.

in the south that developed export-oriented and labor-intensive manufacturing industries based on a market mechanism. Rather, it should try to build a high-technology, trade, and finance-oriented SEZ under the existing planning system. Because the newly founded PDZ does not have much comparative advantage in attracting foreign direct investment with high-technology industrial and financial projects, the Shanghai municipal government has begun to talk about the necessity to develop manufacturing industries in order to earn hard currency.

During the following few months, the European Economic Community (EEC) and Japan decided to lift economic sanctions against China, so the economy and industrial production began to recover. Inflation declined while the supply of capital goods and raw materials became stable. More important, the central government further adjusted its policies on foreign direct investment by offering the rest of China similar privileges—low tax and tariff rates, special rights for importing and exporting, domestic market shares, and access to foreign exchange—previously enjoyed only by coastal open areas to attract foreign investment. These policies improved the investment environment in areas outside the SEZs and open cities, and they narrowed the gap in investment conditions between different parts of the country. In October 1991, when the SEZs celebrated their tenth anniversary, Beijing reendorsed its support, indicating that the previous political debate within the leadership over the SEZs was temporarily suspended.

According to official figures, in 1990, foreign capital invested in China rose to $10.1 billion from 1989's $7.9 billion.[5] The total value of new loans increased 3.4 percent to $5.4 billion.[6] During the year, Beijing approved 7276 foreign direct investment projects, which constituted an actual investment of $3.4 billion, a 0.6 percent increase from 1989.[7] Among these projects, 4093 were joint ventures, 1317 were cooperative-management projects, and 1861 were solely foreign-owned enterprises. More important, about 90 percent were industrial, and many were export-oriented. Foreign-funded enterprises sold $5.9 billion of goods to the international market, contributing 9.5 percent of China's total exports.[8]

Nineteen open cities and Hainan province continued to play an important role in attracting foreign direct investment, signing 3578 investment contracts with overseas corporations, an 18.2 percent increase from 1989. Overseas corporations' investment commitments rose 14.5 percent to $3.7 billion, of which about $1.7 billion was actually used. In 1990, the industrial output of foreign enterprises in these areas reached 25 billion yuan, or about $5 billion.[9]

Since fall 1989, Taiwanese companies have actively invested in the Chinese coast. Hundreds of business delegations have visited the mainland, often meeting with senior government officials. In 1990, the Na-

5. *People's Daily*, 23 Feb. 1991.
6. Ibid.
7. Ibid.
8. Ibid.
9. *Beijing Review*, 34(14):26 (1991).

tional People's Congress passed a law on investment from overseas Chinese that gave rights and privileges to investors from Taiwan and Hong Kong similar to those for foreign investors. According to official sources, the total Taiwanese direct investment in China surpassed $3 billion in 1990.

INTERNATIONAL FINANCIAL ORGANIZATIONS AND THE INTERNATIONAL FINANCIAL MARKET

China's political instability and its slowed economic reform have had a strong impact on relations with international financial organizations and its position in the international financial market. Due to the OECD nations' strong objection, the World Bank suspended its loans to China following the June crackdown in 1989. In addition, it delayed or suspended some going projects because of the unstable political and economic environment. The Bank did not close its representative office in Beijing, however, nor did it cut off its working relations with the government. Between September 1990 and the summer of 1991, the World Bank has approved three loans to China for "humanitarian considerations." Following the Group of Seven's conference in Houston in July 1990, the World Bank took a more positive attitude toward its relationship with China, looking forward to resuming its activity there.

Nevertheless, besides the political consideration of some OECD nations, especially the United States, China's economic performance and reform have also caused new problems with

the World Bank's operations in China. Due to Beijing's delay of many reform programs, for instance, the Bank has had to cut some of its programs to promote institutional reforms. The gap in economic strategy and philosophy between the Bank and the Chinese leadership has also created difficulties for the former to provide policy recommendations to the latter on how to further China's economic reform and open-door policy. Moreover, the World Bank has reduced training programs for Chinese officials in charge of economic affairs.

China's working relations with the International Monetary Fund (IMF) have also changed. Because of its positive balance of international payments, China has not actively borrowed money from the IMF. Before June 1989, the IMF joined the World Bank's efforts to conduct policy research for the government and train Chinese officials. Since June 1989, these programs have been reduced.

The Asian Development Bank is an exception here. With the support of Japan and other Asian countries, the Asian Development Bank has provided two loans to China since the autumn of 1989. Its working relationship with China, which started in 1988, has continued to expand. To date, Taipei and Washington have not objected to this development. Nonetheless, China's position in the international financial market significantly weakened after mid-1989 because of internal political instability and economic difficulties. The June crackdown shocked the international banking community, which previously had treated China as a special case based upon its high expectation for continued reform and impressive economic growth. Moreover, the OECD nations' economic sanctions prevented international banks from conducting new business with China. From June 1989 to mid-1990, almost all international banks stopped their lending to Beijing. A number of international rating agencies lowered China's standing. In the international capital market, investment banks stopped helping Beijing issue bonds.

This situation has gradually changed since spring 1990, when a few Japanese banks, with Tokyo's encouragement, began to make loans to China again. Beijing has decided to allow foreign banks to increase their presence in Shanghai and other coastal cities. China's expansion of financial markets in a number of cities has also attracted more attention from the international banking community. To date, there are 33 foreign bank branches established in four SEZs and Hainan province.[10] In addition, a few foreign banks have also opened branches in Shanghai's PDZ. Since mid-1990, tension between China and the OECD nations has eased as economic performance has improved somewhat and the balance of trade has begun to show a surplus. As a result, more foreign banks have again become willing to lend money to China. Nevertheless, they have raised interest charges. In most cases, they now demand a guarantee from central agencies to back local borrowing. At the end of 1990, China's foreign debt totaled $41 billion,

10. Ibid.

of which 11 percent was short-term. According to the government, from 1990 to 1995, the debt-service ratio is between 12.48 and 14.6 percent, just under the warning line of 15-20 percent.[11] To serve its foreign debt, China will have to maintain its surplus of trade and international payments.

TOURISM AND
THE EXPORT OF
LABOR SERVICES

China's tourist industry has been seriously affected by the country's political turmoil, especially during the second half of 1989. That year, the total number of tourists arriving dropped 22.7 percent to 24.5 million, resulting in a 19.4 percent decline in hard-currency revenue, to $1.8 billion.[12] In 1990, despite China's hosting the Eleventh Asian Games, tourism did not return to the 1988 level, the number of visitors totaling 27.5 million, with a hard-currency earning of $2.19 billion. These figures are lower than 1988's 31.7 million tourists and $2.25 billion, respectively.[13]

During the past two years, China's political instability appeared to have only limited impact on its export of labor services, because they go mainly to the Persian Gulf and the Soviet Union, where Chinese domestic politics are not a major concern. In 1989, the revenue from the export of labor totaled $1.69 billion.[14] In 1990, due to the Persian Gulf war, China's

11. Ibid., p. 25.
12. *International Trade Journal,* 1990, no. 9, pp. 12, 38-39.
13. *Beijing Review,* 33(9):vi (1990).
14. Ibid., 34(3):19 (1991).

export of labor services to the Middle East dropped sharply. While the Soviet Union's share increased slightly, the total income rose only 0.8 percent, to $1.70 billion.[15]

KEY FACTORS

Four major factors have affected China's foreign economic relations since June 1989. First, political turmoil and unstable politics have had a strong impact on policy. They have also damaged economic ties with other parts of the world, especially the OECD nations and Hong Kong. This was particularly true during the second half of 1989, when Beijing was preoccupied by crisis management, most OECD nations imposed economic sanctions against China, and Hong Kong's economic growth dropped sharply. The heightened political struggle both within the leadership and between the state and society has not only interrupted the implementation of the open-door policy but also has significantly increased the country's political risk, discouraging overseas corporations from committing themselves to the Chinese market. Moreover, conservative political trends since June 1989 have strongly affected the morale of local officials and professionals who work in foreign trade and investment.

Before mid-1990, the conservative leaders tried to alter the open-door policy, especially in the SEZs. At both a general level and a policy level, there were serious debates within the

15. Sui Duo, "Trends in International Service Market and China's Countermoves," *International Trade Journal*, 1990, no. 5, p. 64; *Intertrade* (Beijing), 1990, no. 5, pp. 29-30.

bureaucratic establishment about what political and economic relations China should build with the West. While China's internal political instability and the sanctions imposed by the OECD nations against China were certainly taken into account, the fundamental changes in Eastern Europe and the Soviet Union frightened the leadership. Some believed that the collapse of Communist systems was due to a Western plot and that China should cut back its ties with the West in order to prevent China's system from being overthrown. More important, these leaders, especially those in charge of economic affairs at the center, tried to form a new foreign economic strategy to fit their conservative political policy and readjustment economic strategy. Nevertheless, due partially to Deng Xiaoping's personal intervention and partially to local authorities' strong resistance, the conservatives' efforts failed.

Technically, however, the degree to which China's political development affects its foreign economic relations varies according to the nature of different industrial and business operations. The impact is also influenced by the overseas business environment. For those foreign companies that do not depend on China's domestic market but rather take advantage of its cheap labor and resources and conduct labor-intensive manufacturing operations in China for overseas markets, the political risk is limited. Labor costs, tax rates, the cost of raw materials, and rent are major considerations. Moreover, their investment-return cycle is relatively short in comparison with high-technology and heavy industrial projects. These were the primary reasons why most Hong Kong and Japanese companies did not withdraw their operations and many Taiwanese companies rushed to move their operations to China after the Tiananmen crackdown.

In addition, to repair the damage to its policies toward Hong Kong and Taiwan and its relations with the OECD nations caused by the Tiananmen crackdown, Beijing set up the PDZ in Shanghai and continued the development of Hainan's ties with the international market. It has granted more favorable fiscal treatment—low tax rates, cheap land prices and rents, greater domestic market shares, and so forth—and business deals to many Taiwanese companies and Hong Kong and foreign corporations that did not pull out after June 1989. Meanwhile, China's investment in Hong Kong has continued to increase, and, since the second quarter of 1990, its trade—both imports and exports—with Hong Kong has recovered.

The second major factor—in addition to the conservative attack on the open-door policy, which, contrary to some Western analysis, was not fully transformed into policy—is that Beijing has changed its foreign economic policy in some areas. It has tried to recentralize decision making and regain control over foreign trade and investment. More important, the central government's macroeconomic policies have had a strong influence on the implementation of the open-door policy. For instance, from mid-1989 to mid-1990, it fully imposed its readjustment program, pushing the economy into a recession. Conse-

quently, supplies of capital goods, raw materials, and energy to foreign enterprises improved significantly. Anti-inflationary policies also reduced foreign production costs.

On the other hand, however, the strong pressure from the central government on local authorities and enterprises weakened the latter's ability to respond to changes in the international marketplace. In particular, between mid-1989 and mid-1990, Beijing significantly reduced the credits and foreign exchange provided to local authorities and enterprises that conduct export-related business activities. It also tightened its control over imports of capital goods and raw materials that may be used for export-oriented manufacturing operations.

Moreover, beginning in 1986, overseas investment in China gradually shifted from service sectors—especially tourism and real estate—to labor-intensive manufacturing industries. By 1989, many of these industrial projects had begun to operate, enabling the Chinese coast to increase foreign exchange earnings. Because these projects are mainly export-oriented and their management and marketing are conducted by either foreign managers alone or Chinese and foreign managers jointly, the events of 4 June had only limited influence on these newly established facilities.

Third, since mid-1988, the central government has delayed or suspended many of its economic-reform programs, such as price reform, the reform of the share-hold system, and financial reform. With limited success, it has tried to recentralize economic decision making and budgetary power by weakening provincial authorities and imposing new restrictions on local economic activities, including foreign investment and trade. These policies have had a strong impact on foreign economic relations. The increased central-government control over foreign trade has reduced the competition between local authorities and enterprises for overseas markets and for the supplying of raw materials used for export-related manufacturing. This development, in turn, has strengthened China's position in the international manufacturing-goods market. It has significantly reduced the import of consumer goods in particular. Recentralization has also narrowed policy gaps between the SEZs and other parts of China, thereby increasing the latter's ability to attract foreign investment.

The central government has not been able to reverse most reform programs and open-door policies that were introduced and implemented before June 1989, however. It does not have the ability to force local authorities, especially those on the coast, whose economic and financial power increased significantly during the 10-year reform period, to cut back their ties with the international market. In many areas, local authorities and enterprises have effectively resisted those central-government policies that would hurt their interests.

Fourth, the international environment with which China must deal has undergone dramatic changes during the past two and a half years. As noted earlier, from mid-1989 to mid-1990, the OECD nations imposed sanctions against China. Thus, with the exceptions of a few projects concerning humanitarian needs, China could no longer receive loans and economic aid from the West, Japan, and the international financial organizations. Sanctions also seriously damaged trade ties with these countries as export of high-technology to China was banned. In the United States, serious struggle arose over the extension of China's most-favored-nation status. These developments have had a strong impact on the international business community's decision making. Most international banks have stopped lending to China, especially to local authorities and enterprises without the central government's guarantee, while others have raised their interest rates. Except for Taiwanese companies, most foreign corporations have reduced their investment commitments to the Chinese market.

In early 1990, however, most OECD nations entered recession. Their demand for manufactured goods from the newly industrializing countries and developing countries declined. A global capital shortage came partly from this recession and partly from differentiated interest rates. In addition, most American and European commercial banks that played a key role in China began to pull back from Asia while high interest rates in Japan constrained the Japanese banks' ability to increase their lending to China.

In mid-1990, President Bush vetoed a bill that the Congress had passed to discontinue China's most-favored-nation status. At the Group of Seven's Houston conference, Japan announced that it would stop economic sanctions against China. Following the conference, Tokyo resumed its $5.2 billion loan to China, and the EEC also decided to end its economic sanctions. But, in August, Iraq invaded and occupied Kuwait. The gulf war sharply cut local demand for Chinese goods and labor services, mainly construction teams. As a government spokesperson put it in November, "China has lost . . . more than $2 billion [in hard currency income] since the war broke out."[16]

Then on 18 November 1990, a few days before the United Nations Security Council vote implicitly authorizing force against Iraq, Secretary of State Baker personally telephoned Minister of Foreign Affairs Qian Qichen in Beijing, inviting him to visit Washington, D.C. A week later, Qian met President Bush in Washington, ending the ban on high-level exchanges between the two countries. Meanwhile, some American corporations actively lobbied for expanded business ties while others argued for taking protectionist measures to reduce the U.S. trade deficit vis-à-vis China. At the same time, however, Chinese student lobbying groups and international human rights organizations urged the administration to continue its economic sanctions against Beijing. These political developments have had and will continue to have strong implications for the future development of Sino-American economic relations.

There are also a few economic issues between China and the OECD

16. Liu Baorong, "Sino-Soviet Trade: Its Present Situation and Prospects," *Intertrade*, 1990, no. 8, pp. 28-30.

nations. In the United States, for example, the Congress set up a special team in November 1990 to investigate the trade deficit with China, estimated to have exceeded $10 billion in 1990. Since mid-1990, the U.S. Commerce Department has reduced China's export quota of textile products to the United States. In Japan, the business community has complained about China's sharp reduction of imports from Japan, most of which comprise industrial equipment and technology. Beijing, however, has criticized Japan's imposition of economic sanctions. Similarly, China has reduced its imports from the EEC.

THE DOMESTIC SCENE

Changes and developments in China's foreign relations are also influenced by China's domestic political and economic development. China is no longer a pure central-planning economy. Rather, it is a mixed economy with a relatively weak central government and strong local authorities. This economy is based on a semi-market mechanism and a high degree of enterprise autonomy. Moreover, China now has a private sector that is particularly active in the coastal area.

Such an economic system will continue to have a mixed impact on China's foreign economic relations. Local authorities, especially those on the coast, will continue to enjoy great autonomy in managing business ties with other parts of the world, although the central government will surely further tighten its control over the foreign exchange regime, customs, and taxation on foreign direct investment. These policies will narrow the regional gaps and rationalize the competition between various regions in China and Chinese corporations for access to foreign investment and markets.

Such a development will also force the central government to redefine its overall strategy toward the international market and its policies in those open areas of the country. The basic strategy should no longer be to put overwhelming emphasis on the development of the coast. Rather, the relationship between those open areas and other parts of China will have to be balanced, enabling the government to unify the domestic market and to force the open areas to be more competitive without depending on their special privileges. Beijing will also be gradually forced to resume the delayed or suspended economic-reform programs, although, given its relatively weak ability and authority, the process will be a slow one. For instance, it will have to further narrow the price gap between the Chinese domestic market and the market abroad and make its foreign exchange regime more flexible. In order to increase Chinese enterprises' international competitiveness and their ability to respond to the dynamics in the international manufacturing-goods market, it will have to increase their autonomy, especially allowing them to approach the international market directly, and reform the banking system and foreign exchange regime. Moreover, foreign economic policies will have to be coordinated with the country's overall development strategy, macro-economic management, and economic reform in light of changes in the international marketplace.

The government has set a target of a growth rate of between 5 and 6 percent for real gross national product for the next five years.[17] The relatively slow economic growth, the existing handicapped taxation system, and the irrational price structure will continue to constrain Beijing's ability to increase investment in infrastructure and will discourage multinational corporations from increasing their commitments to the Chinese market. The slow economic growth also will continue to restrict China's ability to import industrial equipment and technology.

On the other hand, however, the slower economic growth may create a more stable economic environment. Inflation may decline further, supplies of both capital goods and consumer goods may improve, and the irrational domestic competition could decline. At the same time, unemployment and underemployment will likely surge, lowering labor costs. This will increase Chinese enterprises' ability and incentive to expand exports. It will also reduce overseas corporations' production costs in China and attract more tourists.

Domestic politics will continue to have a strong impact on China's foreign economic relations. High tension within the leadership will weaken its ability to form rational foreign economic policies and implement them effectively. Uncertainty around the forthcoming succession to—but not limited to—Deng Xiao-

17. *People's Daily*, 23 Nov. 1990.

ping and ideologically conservative trends will discourage professional policymakers, local authorities, and managers from committing themselves to the open-door policy.

Moreover, it is unlikely that the central government will gain much strength over local authorities. Conflicts of interest between them will continue to heighten. While local authorities may continue to implement their own policies in dealing with members of the overseas business community, the central government will continue to use policies of taxation, foreign exchange, customs regulations, supply of capital goods and raw materials, and banking credit as means to compete with local power.

Political risk will remain high. The suppression of the pro-democracy movement and the subsequent conservative trends have heightened tension between state and society. The ideological crisis has aroused strong antagonism against the current conservative leadership. Corruption has continued to spread widely. If the government fails to provide more jobs and consumer goods and to keep the inflation rate low, the country may face a high degree of social chaos. Yet, no matter how the current government tries to consolidate its power, fundamental changes will eventually take place during and soon after the real succession struggle.

The high degree of political uncertainty will discourage multinational corporations from increasing their long-term investment commitment to the Chinese market. The government's inability to further economic and political reform will maintain the wide institutional gap between the Chinese economy and market economies abroad, thereby weakening China's competitiveness in the international market. If tension between the central government and local authorities continues to rise and if the government fails to form and implement a more rational and effective foreign economic strategy, China's ability to obtain capital investment, technology, and market share abroad may decline.

China's political development has a special impact on Hong Kong's economic growth and its economic ties with China. Hong Kong investment in and trade with China will continue to recover. China's investment in Hong Kong and its other economic and political presence, in turn, will expand as well. Meanwhile, Hong Kong's local capital outflow and brain drain will continue to accelerate, although Japanese investment there will increase further in the next few years. The key issue, however, is the possible conjunction of China's succession crisis with Hong Kong's 1997 transition. If succession remains uncertain two or three years prior to 1997, Hong Kong's local politics and economy may become highly volatile. As a result, China's foreign economic relations would be seriously damaged.

THE FOREIGN CONTEXT

Finally, the dynamics of the international environment will further influence China's foreign economic relations. The Persian Gulf confrontation has driven oil prices down substantially. China's oil revenue has thus declined. Postwar reconstruction in the gulf, however, may provide China opportunities to send its construction teams back. More important, with the end of recession in many OECD nations, at least in North America and Japan, the demand for labor-intensive manufacturing goods from China may increase while more financial resources will be available.

China will have difficulty entering EEC markets after 1992. Yet, due to its comprehensive industrial system and its cooperation with Hong Kong and Taiwanese corporations, who know the European manufacturing-goods market well, it will continue to enjoy certain comparative advantages over other developing economies in the West European market. Unless China's human rights record worsens significantly, most OECD nations will not impose sanctions again. China's substantial trade surplus against the United States, however, will most likely cause new tensions between Washington and Beijing.

China's trade relations with the Soviet Union and Eastern Europe will continue to expand. Low-priced Chinese consumer goods and foodstuff will continue to be competitive in these countries. In return, China will continue to buy industrial equipment and technology from the Soviet Union and Eastern Europe. But the prospects for this trade will be determined by both sides' domestic economic development. The ongoing political turmoil and economic crisis in the Soviet Union and Eastern Europe may further weaken their ability to provide industrial goods that the Chinese are interested in importing.

Sino-Soviet border trade will likely expand in the east. It may not expand in the west—central Asia—if nationality tensions on the Soviet side, which have a strong impact on China's Muslim population living in Xinjing, continue to heighten. China may close the border.

In Asia, Japan and the four tigers—Hong Kong, Singapore, South Korea, and Taiwan—will continue to transfer their labor-intensive industries to China and to Southeast Asia as well. In this regard, China will have to compete against countries of the Association of Southeast Asian Nations for investment, technology, and overseas market shares. Whether or not China can successfully win this competition will depend largely on China's competitiveness as well as on its domestic development.

If China's domestic political and human rights situation does not deteriorate significantly, the World Bank and other international financial organizations will expand their activities there. Yet, unless Beijing makes great progress in reforming its economic system in the near future, these activities may not reach the level obtained before June 1989. The international banking community will increase its lending to China, but it will no longer treat it as a special case. Foreign banks will also be reluctant to make long-term loans to local authorities and enterprises without the central government's guarantee.

China is still at a historical turning point as are the post-Cold War international political and economic systems. If China's domestic political and economic developments over the next few years preceding the succession to Deng Xiaoping continue their current course, its ability to expand foreign economic relations will be limited. Yet as long as China's political ties with the OECD nations remain stable, it will continue to enjoy access to the latter's financial resources, technology, and market shares. Nevertheless, other Asian countries will surely heighten their economic competition against China in the international marketplace. The degree of China's competitiveness in the international market will be determined by its economic performance, its political stability, the effectiveness of its economic policies, and the progress made in reforming its political and economic system.

ANNALS, *AAPSS,* **519,** January 1992

Chinese Military Strategy Revised:
Local and Limited War

By PAUL H. B. GODWIN

ABSTRACT: In 1985, the Chinese People's Liberation Army (PLA), as all three armed services are collectively known, was required to redirect its military strategy from a focus on general war with the USSR to the more probable source of military conflict: small-scale and potentially intense wars around China's periphery. New enemies did not emerge; instead, the kinds of conflicts that could arise required a revised defense policy and military strategy. These changes, although important in themselves, left the PLA even more conscious of its technological obsolescence. Developing concepts of military operations in which speed and lethality were to be the principal characteristics of combat, rather than defensive operations based upon attrition warfare and a society mobilized for war, served only to highlight the PLA's technological weaknesses. As in all the years since the beginning of Chinese defense modernization in the late 1970s, these technological weaknesses led the armed forces to demand swifter modernization of their arms and equipment.

Paul H. B. Godwin is associate dean of faculty and academic programs at the National War College. He received his Ph.D. and M.A. from the University of Minnesota, and his B.A. from Dartmouth College. He has published extensively on Chinese defense and security policy. In the fall of 1987, he served as a visiting professor at the Chinese People's Liberation Army National Defense University in Beijing, China.

NOTE: The views expressed in this article are those of the author and are not to be construed as those of the Department of Defense, the National Defense University, the National War College, or any other agency of the U.S. government.

THE threat perceptions of the Chinese leadership changed dramatically over the years 1978-85. The Third Plenum of the Eleventh Central Committee, meeting in December 1978, concluded that although the Soviet Union was not an immediate military threat to China's security, the USSR's aggressive foreign policy and Soviet forces deployed along the Sino-Soviet border and in the Mongolian People's Republic were distinctly menacing. Defending against a massive Soviet assault deep into the political and industrial heart of northern China was the principal objective of the military strategy and concepts of operations developed by the Chinese armed forces over the years 1978-85.[1]

As this military strategy was being developed and refined, Chinese threat perceptions changed in response to alterations in the global balance of power. By the early 1980s, Chinese strategists were concluding not only that the Reagan administration's security policies were creating a shift in the military balance of power but also that there was a new American resolve to oppose what Beijing had long viewed as a predatory Soviet foreign policy. In essence, Chinese analysts saw a superpower military balance wherein the United States had an edge, but which essentially placed Moscow and Washing-

ton in a stalemate. Neither could attack the other and be confident of victory. This superpower stalemate would continue into the 1990s and perhaps into the twenty-first century, thereby making a world war very unlikely.[2] This same shift in the global balance of power and the superpower standoff would prevent the Soviet Union from attacking China.

The change in superpower capabilities was viewed as the central component in a transformation of the international system. The USSR and the United States were seen as being impoverished by their mutual competition. Their economic decline was diminishing their political influence, while the rapidly growing economic strength of Europe, Japan, and a number of Third World countries was granting greater independence from both Moscow and Washington. As early as 1983, Chinese analysts asserted that the dynamics of the international system were creating a multipolar world.[3]

This emerging multipolarity was not seen as favorable to China's security. Rather, whereas the balance of military power between the United States and the USSR made a global

1. See Paul H. B. Godwin, "Changing Concepts of Doctrine, Strategy and Operations in the Chinese People's Liberation Army 1978-1987," *China Quarterly*, Dec. 1987, no. 112, pp. 578-81; Ngok Lee, *China's Defense Modernisation and Military Leadership* (Sydney: Australian National University Press, 1989), pp. 146-74.

2. Banning Garrett and Bonnie Glaser, "From Nixon to Reagan: China's Changing Role in American Strategy," in *Eagle Resurgent? The Reagan Era in American Foreign Policy*, ed. Kenneth A. Oye, Robert J. Lieber, and Donald Rothchild (Boston: Little, Brown, 1986), p. 283.

3. Xing Shugang, Li Yunhua, and Liu Yingna, "Soviet-American Balance of Power and Its Impact on the World Situation in the 1980s," *Guoji wenti yanjiu*, Jan. 1983, no. 1, in Foreign Broadcast Information Service, *FBIS Daily Report—China* (hereafter *FBIS—Chi*), 21 Apr. 1983, pp. A1-12.

war unlikely, the probability of local wars flaring up was increased by the growing military strength of regional powers. The most threatening aspect of the future security environment perceived by Chinese analysts was the increased likelihood of small-scale wars around China's periphery.[4]

This new threat perception was reflected in a decision made by the Central Military Commission (Zhongyang Junshi Weiyuanhui) (CMC) of the Chinese Communist Party in June 1985. The CMC directed that China's war preparations would no longer be for an "early, major, and nuclear war" with the USSR but for what the CMC declared the most likely form of conflict in the foreseeable future—local limited war (*jubu zhanzheng*) around China's borders.[5]

The 1985 directive came shortly after Gorbachev became the general secretary of the Communist Party of the Soviet Union, but more than a year before his July 1986 speech in Vladivostok, with his first public gesture toward Sino-Soviet rapprochement. Thus the CMC's edict redirecting the focus of the armed forces' military strategy was not linked to any change in Soviet strategy or military capabilities along the Sino-Soviet border. Instead, it was in response to a modification in the global

4. Zong He, "Changes and Developmental Trends in the International Situation," *Shijie zhishi*, 1 June 1983, no. 11, in *FBIS—Chi*, 21 July 1983, pp. A1-5.

5. See Generals Zhang Zhen and Li Desheng's discussion of the CMC's May-June 1985 guidance at a meeting with the editorial board of *Jiefangjun bao* (*Liberation Army Daily*), reported in *Ta kung pao* (Hong Kong), 16 Feb. 1986, in *FBIS—Chi*, 18 Feb. 1986, pp. W11-12.

balance of power and Beijing's evaluation of the emerging dynamics of the international system. Six and a half years later, this CMC directive remains the authoritative guidance for Chinese defense policy and military strategy.

Ever since the Tiananmen tragedy, the People's Liberation Army (PLA) has been undergoing an intense political campaign designed to ensure its "absolute" obedience to the Chinese Communist Party. This campaign, combined with the internal security demands now placed on the armed forces, has undoubtedly reduced the amount of time spent on military training. But China's core military strategy has not been revoked, and what little reporting there is reveals that limited and local war remains the focus of the armed forces' preparation for armed conflict.

MILITARY STRATEGY
FOR LOCAL LIMITED WAR

With the CMC's new guidance, Chinese military strategists were tasked with preparing the People's Liberation Army, as all three armed services are collectively designated, primarily for small-scale and potentially intense limited war. Although the USSR remained capable of launching a major war with China, the chances of such a conflict were minimal. What Beijing believed it faced as it looked to the future was the possibility of small wars' erupting along its borders, including the remote possibility of a limited war with the Soviet Union. Such wars required preparations distinctly different from the principles of protraction and attrition that had dominated the armed forces' preparations for a total war with the USSR.

Chinese analysts view local wars and limited wars as a category of conflict circumscribed both in geographical scope and political objectives, but which can vary widely in intensity and duration. The purpose of military force when used in these wars is not to eliminate totally the adversary's capability and will to resist but to "assert one's own standpoint and will through limited military action. . . . This being the case, the further progression of modern limited warfare is mainly not decided through military action as such, but rather determined by the needs in the political and diplomatic struggle."[6] While recognizing that these kinds of wars can be quite lengthy in duration, as were the Korean War, the American war in Vietnam, and the Iran-Iraq war, the primary focus of Chinese military analyses has been on the operational requirements for localized wars of short duration.

Chinese military journals have designated five types of limited war to be of special importance: (1) small-scale conflicts restricted to contested border territory; (2) conflict over territorial seas and islands; (3) surprise air attacks; (4) defense against deliberately limited attacks into Chinese territory; and (5) "punitive counterattacks" launched by China into enemy territory to "oppose invasion,

protect sovereignty, or to uphold justice and dispel threats."[7] The characteristics common to all of these scenarios are the limited political objective behind the use of military coercion and the requirement that the forces used be able to respond quickly either to defeat the presumed political purpose of the attack or to gain the political objective sought by the limited use of force.

There is a definite ahistorical cast to Chinese analyses of limited local war appearing in military journals over the years following the CMC's decision. Most of the essays recognized the importance of the Korean War and China's 1979 incursion into Vietnam in their analyses of the different kinds of limited war and local conflicts that have occurred since the conclusion of World War II. They do not note, however, that all of the conflicts fought by the Chinese armed forces since 1949 fall into this category. From the Korean War in 1950 to the March 1988 seizure of atolls in the Nansha (Spratly) Islands, Chinese armed forces have been used in precisely the kinds of confrontations the CMC concluded would be the most likely form of military conflict for the foreseeable future.

Nonetheless, the new focus of the PLA's military training, both in the field and in China's centers of professional military education, did not

6. Jiao Wu and Xiao Hui, "Modern Limited War Calls for Reform of Traditional Military Principles," *Guofang daxue xuebao*, 1 Nov. 1987, no. 11, in Joint Publications Research Service (hereafter JPRS), *China Report No. 037*, 12 July 1988, p. 49.

7. Jia Wenxian et al., "Tentative Discussion of the Special Principles of a Future Chinese Limited War," *Guofang daxue xuebao*, 1 Nov. 1987, no. 11, in JPRS, *China Report No. 037*, 12 July 1988, p. 48, contains this particular categorization, but over the past three years a number of essays in a variety of journals have tended to focus on these types of potential conflicts.

exclude the Soviet Union. What changed was the nature of the possible conflict with the USSR, for the Soviet Union was included in the PLA's new concentration on local and limited wars that potentially endangered China's periphery. To be sure, there were others who could be adversaries, but the USSR remained the principal threat. No new enemies emerged to change the threat environment. Rather, the kinds of conflicts most likely to be fought required a new look at defense policy and military strategy.

Local wars and unanticipated military crises involving only limited political objectives require the swift and effective application of military force. Within this framework, the three-stage approach to campaigns, where the war is divided into defensive, stalemate, and counteroffensive stages or phases, is viewed as no longer plausible. In essence, Chinese analysts now state that modern military technology grants an aggressor the capability to seize the initiative in the opening battles of the war. The first battle will be of crucial importance in local wars. This means that mobilizing the entire country and people for war is no longer an appropriate policy.[8] The nature of contemporary and future warfare requires standing forces capable of a quick and lethal response to crises involving the threat or application of military force.

Local war and
  the military region

Preparation for local wars required the PLA to review its defense

posture around the periphery of China and to make an assessment of the most likely conflicts to be fought in each sector. Given the diversity of terrain, weather, and potential adversaries, different border areas were faced with different operational requirements. This led to the conclusion that each of China's seven military regions (MRs) should conduct independent training and field exercises for local war.[9] The concept of a "war zone" was introduced, with the observation that "war zone independent campaign operations will probably be the most frequently seen mode of action in the Army's campaign operations for some time to come."[10]

In 1988, four major MR exercises were conducted under the direction of their MR commanders. These were designed to test the extent to which the previous three years of preparation had developed new capabilities within the armed forces to respond to the changing threat environment. Three of the exercises focused on the USSR as the potential adversary: West-88, conducted by the Lanzhou MR in northwestern China; Yanhang-88,

8. Ibid.

9. Zhao Tianxiang, "Militia Reform and the Strategy of Theater Development," *Jiefangjun bao*, 10 June 1988, in JPRS, *China Report No. 069*, 4 Nov. 1988, pp. 29-30. The commander of a military region is in operational command of all the forces assigned to his region, regardless of which service they belong to. He may also have command of naval forces assigned to coastal defense of his MR. The MR should therefore be viewed as a unified command.

10. Xu Jingyao, "1988: A Year of Reform for the Chinese Army," *Liaowang*, overseas ed. (Hong Kong), 16 Jan. 1989, no. 3, in *FBIS—Chi*, 24 Jan. 1989, p. 36.

conducted by the Beijing MR in northern China; and Qianjin-88, conducted by the Shenyang MR in the northeast. Guangzi-88, conducted by the Guangzhou MR in the South China Sea, where the postulated enemy had to be Vietnam, rounded out the exercises.[11] The only potential adversaries not faced in these campaign-level maneuvers were India and Taiwan, and there has been no report of exercises equivalent to those directed at the USSR and Vietnam being designed for the Sino-Indian border or Taiwan.

The exercises primarily tested rapid-deployment and combined-arms operations responding to "border clashes, accidents, and local warfare."[12] Equally important, however, was the testing of theater operations fought by individual MR commanders as independent campaigns. In each of these maneuvers, the MR commander was clearly defined as being responsible for the campaign and, presumably, the concept of operations behind the campaign.[13] The three exercises directed against a Soviet attack focused on the ability to respond quickly to a blitzkrieg assault. There was no reference to a massive mobilization of the society at large. These exercises were not designed to test the PLA's ability to conduct a prolonged defensive war; rather, they were campaigns built around combined arms warfare to disrupt and eject Soviet forces as early in the confrontation as possible. The maneuvers reflected Beijing's

11. Ibid., p. 37.
12. Ibid., p. 36.
13. Beijing Domestic Service, 14 Oct. 1988, in *FBIS—Chi*, 19 Oct. 1988. p. 29.

concern that a Soviet attack could be conducted for immediate political objectives rather than to subdue and conquer China itself. For example, when China attacked Vietnam in 1979, the USSR could have considered a limited assault on the People's Republic to force Beijing to back down from the invasion and withdraw its forces from Vietnam.

Guangzi-15, conducted by the Guangzhou MR in the South China Sea, was designed to test the PLA's ability in both coastal defense and the protection of China's territory in the South China Sea. It was a combined-arms campaign like those in the north but was rendered more complex by the need to coordinate land, air, and naval forces, including the naval air arm, in a force-projection exercise. It should be noted that the PLA's brigade-sized Marine Corps—it comprises 6000 troops—is deployed in the Guangzhou MR on the island of Hainan, where it is trained specifically for force projection into the South China Sea.

The maneuvers all referred to the use of special forces as an integral part of the exercises. Such forces are quite new and have played a prominent role in Chinese analyses of local-war requirements. While the size of these units is not known, they are probably small, well-prepared combat packages. They are trained to fulfill four major functions in a campaign: as "door openers," striking at critical targets and widening a breach in the enemy's position; as "scalpels" to strike at targets that, when destroyed, will paralyze the adversary's combat potential; as "steel hammers" to seize crucial enemy positions; and as "boosters" to speed up the tempo of a campaign by opening up new battle areas within the invaded area.[14] American and co-alition special units were used in a similar manner during Operation Desert Storm against Iraqi forces.

Troops with these roles are often referred to as "fist" (*quantou*) units and have been the focus of consider-able discussion in Chinese military journals over the past six years. Air-mobile units are one focus of Chinese interest, and the airborne forces of the PLA have been selected for training as "fist" units and "rapid-response units" capable of being de-ployed anywhere in China within 12 hours.[15] Each military region has been reporting the development of fist units and rapid-deployment forces designed to fit its own local situation and potential adversary.

The PLA Marine Corps has re-ceived considerable publicity in these reports. Originally founded in 1953 but disbanded in 1957, the Marine Corps was reestablished on 5 May 1980 as the "fifth arm of the Navy." Headquartered at Zhanjiang, Guang-dong—the Fleet Headquarters of the South Sea Fleet—the Marines have received special attention as China's amphibious force capable of "sudden landings."[16] Their deployment with the South Sea Fleet and Chinese

analyses of the Marines' role in local war clearly identify them as the "fist" unit for operations in the South China Sea.

Each of China's military regions faces different geographical and cli-matic conditions under which it has to conduct operations, even if, as in the case of the three MRs facing the USSR, the potential adversary is the same. Thus the character and opera-tional demands of the campaigns will change from one MR to the next, the force structures employed in combat will differ, fist units and other special forces will vary in their size and com-position, and the intensity of the com-bat will vary. This being the case, there can be no common mold direct-ing each MR commander's prepara-tions. Each MR, seen as a potential theater of operations, will develop its campaign plans in view of its own unique conditions.

Nuclear weapons
and local war:
Linkages across the
spectrum of conflict

A 1987 *Liberation Army Daily* essay stated that China's strategy for national defense in the twenty-first century "should be based on fighting major wars and fighting nuclear wars."[17] China's focus on major war prior to 1985 was deemed of critical importance because these prepara-tions had prevented a major war and

14. Li Qianyuan, "A Cursory Analysis of the Characteristics of Limited War of the Fu-ture," *Jiefangjun bao*, 19 Dec. 1986, in JPRS, *China Report No. 048*, 23 Sept. 1987, p. 91.

15. Tan Jun and Hong Heping, "A 'Fist Battalion' of a Certain PLA Airborne Unit," *Jiefangjun bao*, 14 June 1988, in JPRS, *China Report No. 045*, 9 Aug. 1988, pp. 59-60.

16. Deng Huaxu and Li Daoming, "A Visit to the PLA Marine Corps," *Renmin ribao* [Peo-

ple's daily], overseas ed., 2 Aug. 1988, in *FBIS—Chi*, 3 Aug. 1988, pp. 30-31.

17. Zhang Jian, "It Is Still Necessary to Base Our Plans on Fighting a Major War," *Jiefangjun bao*, 24 Apr. 1987, in *FBIS—Chi*, 4 May 1987, p. A2.

it minimized the potential scale of such a war had it broken out. The author concludes that if China had focused only on preparations for limited and small-scale wars, then a major war could well have occurred. To be confident that future wars can be limited, preparation for large-scale and nuclear wars must continue.[18]

Chinese strategists analyzing linkages across the spectrum of conflict pay close attention to the role of nuclear weapons deployed by "medium" nuclear powers, such as Britain and France. It is asserted that at the root of any strategy pursued by a medium nuclear power is the belief that such weapons free them from manipulation by the superpowers.[19] In what may have been a reference to China's 1979 attack on Vietnam, this analysis holds that in border conflicts or small wars where lesser nations act as agents for great powers, the nuclear retaliatory capability of medium-sized powers can perhaps prevent interference by the great powers.[20]

Citing a Brookings Institution analysis, the Liberation Army Daily took note of the study's conclusion that in the 215 incidents involving American forces since World War II, the use of nuclear weapons was considered in at least 33 cases. Although nuclear weapons were not used, the author contends that China is surrounded by a "complicated environment, with more and more nations and regions possessing nuclear weapons in par-

ticular." Consequently, as China prepares for conventional local wars, it must also develop measures for dealing with limited nuclear wars.[21]

Perhaps reflecting these concerns, China's missile forces have conducted exercises in which they prepared for "nuclear counterattack operations" during maneuvers primarily designed to test conventional war capabilities; the 1988 exercises were of this type. Presumably, the responsibility of China's nuclear forces—the Second Artillery Corps—in these exercises was to be operationally prepared to launch a quick response to any use of nuclear weapons by the adversary, China's stated doctrine for the use of nuclear weapons. Such exercises would also fit Chinese military analysts' evaluation of their country's nuclear strategy. They view China's nuclear forces as preventing a major power from threatening the People's Republic with nuclear war in order to deter Beijing from a chosen course of action. In this manner, doctrine, strategy, and operations for nuclear weapons are integrated into theater-based campaign exercises where the central focus is conventional war fought for limited political objectives.

MILITARY TECHNOLOGY
AND SMALL-SCALE WARS:
THE PLA'S CONTINUING DILEMMA

The military requirements for small-scale wars place great emphasis on the need for mobility and lethality, and for command, control, communications, and intelligence capabilities to direct swiftly moving

18. Ibid.

19. Zhang Jianzhi, "Views on Medium-Sized Nuclear Powers' Nuclear Strategy," Jiefangjun bao, 20 Mar. 1987, in FBIS—Chi, 1 Apr. 1987, p. K29.

20. Ibid., p. K31.

21. Ibid.

combined-arms combat integrating air, land, and naval forces. The PLA's weaknesses in these areas are readily recognized by Chinese analysts, who state that "divorced from advanced military science and technology, we cannot possibly build an army capable of stopping and winning a modern war."[22]

Even if military force is not applied, a credible capacity to respond quickly to a crisis must be available if China is to maintain an effective deterrent posture at this level of warfare. Current levels of Chinese military technology severely limit both the mobility and lethality of the PLA, and, by implication, its credibility.

In spite of continual reporting in the Chinese press and journals of the extent to which the PLA is modernizing its combat aircraft, naval combat vessels, armored fighting vehicles, antitank/anti-air/antiship missiles and is developing computer-based command and control systems, Chinese equipment is not on a par with advanced Western systems. Furthermore, even with the one-million-man force reduction undertaken since 1985, the armed forces remain very large, perhaps some 3 million, with the ground forces accounting for 2.3 mil-

lion.[23] Equipment includes 7500-8000 main battle tanks; 2800 armored personnel carriers; some 6000 fixed-wing combat aircraft, including naval aircraft; 93 submarines, including one nuclear-powered ballistic-missile vessel (SSBN) and 4 nuclear-powered attack submarines (SSN); and 55 destroyers and frigates as the major naval surface combatants. This is a very large force to bring up to advanced Western standards, too big and too expensive a task to be completed in a short period of time. Once again, the Chinese readily admit this weakness and discuss it quite openly.

The approach taken by Beijing in recent years has been to modernize selectively. The military leadership has chosen to upgrade key units. It appears that fist units receive the most modern equipment and test it in field exercises.[24] This, the Chinese note, is the practice followed by advanced military forces in the West.[25] While undoubtedly the most sensible way to introduce new weapons and equipment into the armed forces, it will not result in a modernized PLA except over a very long period of time. But, as Chinese analysts observe, with the sole exception of the USSR, the most likely sources of local war around the periphery do not involve

22. Wang Chenghan, "On Coordinated Development of National Defense and the Economy," *Hong qi* [Red flag], 1 Sept. 1987, in JPRS, *China Report No. 011*, 7 Dec. 1987, p. 18. This essay in what was until 1989 the Communist Party's theoretical journal is but one of many over the past decade stressing that the need to modernize the PLA's military equipment in coordination with its modernization of strategy and operations requires greater defense outlays than Beijing is willing to provide.

23. These figures and the others used in this section are taken from *The Military Balance 1990-1991* (London: International Institute for Strategic Studies, 1990), pp. 148-52.

24. He Chong, "Let Some Units Modernize First," *Jiefangjun bao*, 6 Nov. 1987, in JPRS, *China Report No. 006*, 19 Feb. 1988, pp. 85-86.

25. Dongfang Tie, "What Can We Learn from Other Countries' Practice of Strengthening Key Troops?" *Jiefangjun bao*, 19 Mar. 1988, in *FBIS—Chi*, 6 Apr. 1988, p. 39.

countries whose forces have the capability to conduct high-technology warfare in the same capacity as do the major Western powers.[26]

Moreover, the capability of the armed forces to project military power much beyond China's borders is extremely circumscribed. With no in-air refueling capability for its aircraft and only limited at-sea replenishment for its naval vessels, the PLA is essentially restricted to defending China's borders. Even force projection into the South China Sea is severely limited by the inability of the air force to conduct sustained operations 600 miles from China.[27] Needless to say, the military leadership continues to press for larger budgets for the acquisition of advanced military technology and force-projection capabilities. The operational requirements of local wars provide yet another arrow in their quiver of defense-budget demands.[28]

MILITARY STRATEGY IN THE 1990s

With the normalization of Sino-Soviet relations in 1989, steady progress being made in force reductions, and confidence- and security-building measures with the USSR in 1990, China's northern border is more secure than it has been in the past 20 years.[29] Although not openly stated by Chinese analysts, the economic problems and internal political stresses faced by the USSR and the reductions in Soviet defense spending also reinforce their sense that the Soviet military threat is quickly dissipating.

Nonetheless, analyses of Soviet military strategy in January and March of 1990 adopted very cautious and conservative positions. They stressed that Soviet forces were in transition to a more defensive military doctrine and that they remained offensive in character and capability.[30] Nor were such wary evaluations limited to military publications. *Shijie zhishi* (*World knowledge*), a journal focused on international politics and security, was equally cautious about any near-term change in Soviet military strategy and capabilities. Force reductions were balanced by the technological upgrading of Soviet weapons and equipment, including space systems. The author concluded that "the forward-deployed offensive posture of the Soviet Union has not been fundamentally changed."[31]

26. Jia et al., "Tentative Discussion of the Special Principles," p. 48.

27. Tai Ming Cheung, "The Growth of Chinese Naval Power" (Manuscript prepared for the Major Powers in Asia Project, Institute of Southeast Asian Studies, Singapore, Sept. 1990).

28. Zhang Taiheng, "Local War, and Development of Weapons and Equipment," *Jiefangjun bao*, 1 June 1990, in *FBIS—Chi*, 15 June 1990, pp. 26-27.

29. See the Agence France Presse, Hong Kong report, 27 Jan. 1990, in *FBIS—Chi*, 27 June 1990, p. 3; Foreign Minister Shevardnadze's interview with A. Bovin on Moscow Television Service, Foreign Broadcast Information Service, *FBIS Daily Report—Soviet Union*, 17 Sept. 1990, pp. 13-14.

30. Wang Haiyun and Zhou Yi, "New Trends in Soviet Army's Theoretical Study of Combat," *Jiefangjun bao*, 23 Mar. 1990, in *FBIS—Chi*, 18 Apr. 1990, p. 9.

31. Zhou Aiqun, "The Soviet Union Adjusts Its Military Strategy," *Shijie zhishi*, 16 Jan. 1990, in JPRS, *China Report No. 037*, 14 May 1990, p. 6.

Thus Chinese military strategists remain guarded in their interpretation of the potential threat on their northern border.

Chinese analysts also emphasize that because the international system remains in transition from the post-World War II bipolar structure, its future is quite unpredictable. In January 1991, Beijing's foreign minister observed, "In this transitional period, the international system is volatile and does not enjoy peace."[32] Chinese strategists reflect, especially in their military appraisals, a continuing sense of China's vulnerability within an increasingly unpredictable global security system. The Iraqi invasion of Kuwait and the brief but violent military campaign it spawned is precisely the kind of war that they argue China must be prepared to conduct.

What has emerged from the CMC directive of 1985 is a military strategy more capable of responding to a variety of potential conflicts around China's periphery. No doubt the USSR remains of concern to Beijing's military strategists, but the focus on local wars fought for limited political objectives is designed to provide a military capability to protect interests in addition to meeting specified threats. China's border disputes and territorial claims provide sufficient reason to acquire a more finely honed military instrument to conduct operations that fit with the limited political aims required by this category of conflict.

General war fought to preserve China is now viewed as so improbable that it is no longer the military's primary concern. Nonetheless, as Chinese strategists look to the long-term future, a major force-projection capability will be sought. The future military capabilities and security policies of Japan and India, in addition to those of the USSR and the United States, will also play a role in how China's defense policy emerges in the twenty-first century.

---

32. Foreign Minister Qian Qichen, interviewed in *Beijing Review*, 7-13 Jan. 1991, p. 9.

Book Department

INTERNATIONAL RELATIONS AND POLITICS

DANDEKER, CHRISTOPHER. *Surveillance, Power and Modernity*. Pp. ix, 243. New York: St. Martin's Press, 1990. $45.00.

In *Surveillance, Power and Modernity*, Christopher Dandeker celebrates war and state surveillance in ways that affirm, in a dry sort of way, the current exhilaration over Desert Storm. In his previous writings Dandeker has urged greater academic recognition of military sociology and acknowledgment of the pervasive and defining influence of war and the military's command and control system on the broader social bureaucracy. He has dismissed any moralizing on these verities as "agitprop," and in his latest book he goes about his analysis in a scholarly, no-nonsense fashion.

Dandeker's arguments derive in part from his earlier doctoral thesis on Max Weber's theory of bureaucracy. He leans heavily on the views of Weber and other "Machiavellian" social theorists, who view the modern state as "a rational structure of dominance and surveillance." The United States came by this new order when we evolved from nineteenth-century liberal capitalism, with its free market and "facilitative" state, to twentieth-century "organized" capitalism, characterized by an administered market and a "directive" state.

Dandeker views bureaucratic surveillance as a universal feature of the modern state, a superior form of administration that places the natural and social sciences within hierarchical systems of command and control. By "surveillance" Dandeker does not simply mean spying on people. He includes the entire range of information gathering and supervision of what he calls "subject populations." Dandeker presents a chilling, straight-faced parallel between the factory, the prison, and the asylum, each characterized by "analogous organizational structures, timetables and disciplinary systems." He describes bureaucratic surveillance in modern capitalism as part of a permanent and continuous transformation of the organization of knowledge, separating the scientist, technician, and scholar from the means of production of knowledge by inserting them into bureaucratic organizations like universities and research institutes. He briefly acknowledges the primacy of science and technology in extending the state's capacity for surveillance, but, curiously, he offers none of the abundant evidence of the state's control of science.

We are told that war has led to a tightening of the networks of surveillance in both the military and nonmilitary sectors of modern societies, creating what Dandeker calls the "security state." Dandeker assures us that this new order is inevitable and indispensable and, indeed, that periodic war is essential in modern societies because "the abolition of war would simply entail the spread of unregulated violence in the field of human conduct." This preference for war over terrorism seems naive in its trust that the technology of modern warfare represents no ultimate threat to the planet or the species, so long as the state maintains a monopoly on violence.

HERBERT FOERSTEL
University of Maryland
College Park

LIFTON, ROBERT JAY and ERIC MARKUSEN. *The Genocidal Mentality: Nazi Holocaust and Nuclear Threat.* Pp. 346. New York: Basic Books, 1990. $22.95.

Robert Lifton is well established, and Eric Markusen is becoming well established, for highly readable topical studies that do not sacrifice theoretical significance for timeliness or, for that matter, for trade-paperback potential. *The Genocidal Mentality* is another such interpretive essay, based on original interviews with crucial individual decision makers in the Nazi apparatus and in the U.S. security system, military, academic, and industrial. To the best of my knowledge,

this comparison of the linguistic—and, by extension, psychological—structure of the Holocaust with the U.S. theory of deterrence and with the various verbal defenses of the nuclear establishment is without parallel.

It is tempting, and wrong, to reject as passé this critique of our permanent potential for genocide and ecocide. Although we may at the moment bask in the false dawn of a new international order, both the structure and the ideological rationale of the old order will endure for some time. Hence the perpetual relevance of the study, including its application to the language of justification of the Persian Gulf war. While U.S. deterrence theorists must posit war fighting to maintain the credibility of the threat designed to prevent war, a logical problem for most of us, President Bush has informed us that the gulf war is just such a case of war fighting to maintain the peace.

This book should not be too narrowly construed. While it focuses on the language of nuclear weapons and extermination, its arguments extend to all political decision making in which people refuse to confront the scale of the consequences of their decisions. For example, UNICEF's estimate of the thousands of infant deaths in the wake of Third World austerity measures is easily dissociated from the debate about rationalizing economies and constructing stabilization packages, which just happen to have these little coffins in them.

The Genocidal Mentality lures the reader like a detective novel. It contains elegant, even lyrical passages and an occasional inspiration, albeit sometimes ungrammatical, such as the following: "At the heart of nuclear war planning is ignorance and fantasy." Notwithstanding the grimness of the title, this intellectually and emotionally engaging study should appear in all community and university libraries. It is especially recommended for instructors and practitioners

204 THE ANNALS OF THE AMERICAN ACADEMY

of foreign policy, defense strategy, and international relations.

THERESA C. SMITH
Mankato State University
Minnesota

NORTH, ROBERT C. *War, Peace, Survival: Global Politics and Conceptual Synthesis.* Pp. xii, 298. Boulder, CO: Westview Press, 1990. $48.50. Paperbound, $17.95.

In the foreword to his book, Robert North notes that the book was started in the 1960s, and it clearly represents his effort to provide a unified theory of international relations. The result of this approach is essentially a history book dealing with the development of international relations theory and, to a lesser extent, an attempt to make this theory useful in the practice of politics. In the process, *War, Peace, Survival* provides an excellent and complete picture of attempts to study and specify the mechanisms of international relations.

It is apparent, however, that North feels the theory of international relations has not provided definitive answers to many of the questions raised by common relations between nations. In an attempt to attack this problem, he proposes recasting current theories in a new framework containing four nested classes at the individual, state, international, and global levels.

The first three levels readily fit paradigms now used in international relations theory and, as such, they represent little innovation. The fourth, the global level, is meant to be the innovative contribution of the book; however, it is relegated to the last 25 pages of a 260-page text, and its treatment is less than compelling. First, a long series of obligatory references are made to all manner of global interdependencies. Then three

strategies are suggested: (1) altering environmental conditions in ways conducive to peace; (2) changing our own dealings to low-risk, peace-prone methods; and (3) relying on the first two strategies to strengthen institutions conducive to peace. To implement these strategies we must change people. All this is quite obvious, but it lacks any direction concerning one critical issue: how does one do it?

The book is also weakened by attempts to introduce rigor where none exists through diagrams and pseudo equations, neither of which are useful for other than analyzing historical events—and then only in a very general sense. It also presents a noncritical reiteration of many themes inherent in the recently fashionable assumption of declining superpower influence, themes that are much less attractive after the Persian Gulf war and the cooperation that occurred between the superpowers during that conflict.

In sum, this book is a bit of a mixed bag. Nonetheless, the excellent research and description in the first nine chapters are sufficient to ensure its place as an important international relations publication.

WILLIAM J. WEIDA
Colorado College
Colorado Springs

*AFRICA, ASIA, AND
LATIN AMERICA*

CHOUEIRI, YOUSSEF M. *Islamic Fundamentalism.* Pp. 178. Boston: Twayne, G. K. Hall, 1990. $29.95.

SONN, TAMARA. *Between Qur'an and Crown: The Challenge of Political Legitimacy in the Arab World.* Pp. xiii, 266. Boulder, CO: Westview Press, 1990. $42.50.

These two studies attempt to interpret, for nonspecialists like the present reviewer, contemporary political and economic events in the Muslim world in light of the more than 13 centuries of Islamic history. Neither author is an apologist for Islam. Both strive for an objectivity that emerges as an inclination in favor of the tradition, to counter the bias against it of the normal historiography that originates in the West. Choueiri is familiar in detail with the economic and political factors attending the religion while Sonn concerns herself with the history and philosophy of Islam and the religion itself. Both, however, seek to be total in outlook, as the nature of Islam requires. The American is the livelier stylist, the Lebanese the more dense and abstract in language although the master of a perfectly serviceable prose. Both deal summarily with the period 632-833 C.E., the death dates of the Prophet and the Caliph al-Ma'mun, then make different choices between the figures and movements between the ninth-century rise of the Hadithi, or Traditionalists, and modernity. Choueiri paints on the wider canvas in his concern for non-Arabic Islam; despite this, his attention to black Africa and Southeast Asia remains limited. Sonn focuses almost completely on Arab Muslims and their Turkic Ottoman masters, with a brief look at Iran and British India, the latter from which came Pakistan and Bangladesh.

Choueiri's first three chapters are on Islamic revivalism, reformism, and radicalism, the latter seen as the prelude to a direct response to the late-twentieth-century emergence of nation-states. After the relative decline of the Ottoman, the Indian, and the Persian empires—roughly 1700—religious revivalist movements sprang up to reinstate Islam in its pristine condition. 'Abd al-Wahhab in Arabia (d. 1792), Shah 'Abd al-'Aziz in northern India (d. 1842), 'Uthman Dan Fodio in northern Nigeria (d. 1817), and Ahmad b. 'Abdallah in the Sudan, the self-declared Expected Mahdi (d. 1885), were all committed to purifying Islam of pagan customs and foreign "accretions," notably the veneration of Islamic saints; to independent reasoning in legal judgments; to flight from those territories dominated by unbelievers; and to belief in a single leader or renewer who would declare the time for holy struggle (jihad) to be at hand.

Islamic reformism sought to bring the poor Muslim population that lagged behind in military, political, and technological skills up to a European standard. The Indians Jamal al-Din 'al-Afghani and Ahmad Kahn and the Egyptian educationist Muhammad 'Abduh were chief among these ultimately frustrated, nineteenth-century reformists. To them should be added the name of the Ottoman Sultan 'Abd al-Hamid (d. 1909) and Reza Khan (d. 1941), father of the late Shah of Iran. The Muslim Brethren Association, founded in 1928 by Hasan al-Banna as its Supreme Guide, went from purely religious origins to become a modern political party with a program of action. It spread to Syria, Lebanon, Palestine, Jordan, the Sudan, and Iraq, went underground in 1949 with al-Banna's assassination, and split into competing factions in Egypt. It was then that Sayyid Qutb, the future ideologue of Islamic radicalism, emerged as head of the association's propaganda department.

Choueiri chronicles the turbulent period of 1950-70, when all Islamic countries experienced the modern nation-state as the chief agency of renewal and transformation. These radical changes evoked a radical response, enshrined initially in the writings of Abu al-A 'la Mawdudi (d. 1979), who required that Islamic law (Shari'a) be established as the supreme law of the land in all Muslim countries. This may require "a universal, all-embracing revolution," he wrote, a "far-reaching struggle that continuously exhausts all forces and all possible means . . . called *jihad*." Qutb depended on al-Mawdudi and the Lucknow 'Ulama Institute Rector al-Nadawi in formulating the new ideology of Islamic radicalism. Convinced that the whole non-Islamic world was wallowing in religious ignorance, he saw in the flagrant disregard of God's legislative authority every resultant moral evil, leaving Islam a haven of individual and societal virtue. The comprehensive ideology of these religious radicals is spelled out over the last seventy pages, ending in the application made of it by Iran's Khomeini.

Sonn devotes the second half of her book to events in the Middle East since the successful Arab revolt against Turkish control and the broken British wartime promise to support Arab independence. What Choueiri does painstakingly as he reports on the infinite complexity of the situation Sonn does with the broad strokes of the informed historian who has the journalistic gift. Her calculated lack of nuance will at times distress the expert while Choueiri's multiplication of it will prove daunting to the simple.

We have in these books two distillations of an enormous body of scholarship and modern history that should prove serviceable to students and diplomats alike. Teachers of Islamic history—but not Muslim faith—should want both as library resources, and one or the other for class use if the trade can bear it.

GERARD S. SLOYAN

Temple University
Philadelphia
Pennsylvania

DEYO, FREDERIC C. *Beneath the Miracle: Labor Subordination in the New Asian Industrialism*. Pp. xiv, 259. Berkeley: University of California Press, 1989. $30.00.

DRYSDALE, PETER. *International Economic Pluralism: Economic Policy in East Asia and the Pacific*. Pp. 294. New York: Columbia University Press, 1989. $18.50.

The newly industrializing countries (NICs), particularly those of East Asia, have been the subject of considerable attention from scholars and policymakers in recent years. South Korea, Singapore, Taiwan, and Hong Kong have been four of the fastest-growing economies in the world, and their high growth rates have partly been attributed to their outward-looking trade and industrial development policies. Since 1962, their share of world trade has more than doubled, and it now represents one-fifth of the total. Both of the books under review examine the underlying factors behind this extraordinary economic performance and its regional implications.

Beneath the Miracle explores the dynamics of economic transformation of the newly industrializing countries of East Asia based largely on a supportive and submissive labor force and weak unions. Weakness and powerlessness of the labor movement and unions in East Asia are explained usually in terms of such factors as Confucianism, hierarchical cultural traditions, and high economic growth. This book goes beyond such conventional factors and suggests that weak unions may largely be the result of broader economic and political structural factors. Frederic Deyo's thesis that East Asian economic development was based on "patriarchal, paternalistic, and patrimonial systems of labor control" facilitated by the growth of light, labor-intensive, export manufacturing that is dominated by young, low-skilled, and, often, female workers is largely valid. This, along with elitist control of unions and their political exclusion, communal and bureaucratic paternalism, continued vitality of non-proletarian labor systems, and economic legitimization of authoritarianism, has seriously debilitated the union movement in these countries. Other structural factors adversely affecting unions, and common to East Asian countries, include the semiskilled nature of the labor, workers' lack of career mobility, a high rate of worker turnover, and the export industries' vulnerability to international market fluctuations.

International Economic Pluralism considers the question of commercial diplomacy raised by outward-looking trade and industrial development policies of countries in East Asia and the Pacific. Peter Drysdale argues for a Pacific policy of new commercial diplomacy within a multilateral framework relevant to East Asia and the Pacific region. Even if comprehensive multilateralism under the General Agreement on Tariffs and Trade (GATT) fails to maintain its vigor in the 1990s, he suggests that these countries proceed independently with multilateral negotiations and mutual reduction of trade barriers.

Drysdale agrees with other economists such as Richard Cooper that the three-way economic interdependence and complementarity of North America, Japan, and Western Pacific countries have grown significantly in recent years. Increasing divergence between Japanese and West European economic growth rates and the Asian NICs' vigorous pursuit of industrial growth and outward-looking policies have helped to accentuate and deepen this trend. The increasing limits that the diversity and pluralistic nature of East Asia and the Pacific impose on these countries' ability to take independent economic policy action, however, necessitate greater commonality and coordination in their economic policies. Drysdale favors a system of cooperation and coordination that is both open and nondiscriminatory toward the multilateral framework of GATT. According to him, a

heterogeneous group of countries that are nevertheless highly complementary in terms of economic activity can develop an intensive pattern of economic relations fostered by proximity, common political associations and a strong coalition of interests which both encourages and requires closer policy coordination and economic association; and this is occurring steadily among countries of the Pacific (p. 220).

He sees a great deal of consistency and convergence between the interests and policy objectives of the Pacific countries and the interests of the international economic system and international economic policy goals. Such regional trade policy based on consensus among Pacific countries is facilitated by Japan, willing to assume a crucial leadership role in the formulation of such consensus. Throughout the book, Drysdale argues that it is in the interests of the Pacific and East Asian countries to have a "non-discriminatory trade regime, supportive of their own industrialization and trade growth ambitions as well as the global GATT-based trade system."

Given the marked difference in comparative advantage, geographical proximity, and overall outward-looking policies, Drysdale finds greater scope for the growth of intra-Pacific trade. His enthusiasm for outward-looking policies in the development strategies of East Asian countries is undiminished. Such a policy has helped these countries to achieve greater economic integration into the world economy and thus accept major structural adjustments and promote inter-industry trade growth through international industrial and commercial activities and networks.

Another major topic of discussion in the book is the financing of economic development in these countries. The rapid growth of East Asian economies has been financed through the mobilization of both domestic savings and international, especially Japanese, capital. While the liberalization of the Japanese capital market is expected to strengthen Japan as a source of capital and center for financial intermediation, the liberalization of capital markets in the whole Pacific region is expected to further enhance these countries' capacity to exploit opportunities for regional trade and international specialization.

Both of these books are important contributions to the study of East Asian economic systems. By examining the weakness of East Asian labor mostly in terms of economic structures, *Beneath the Miracle* provides a perspective refreshingly different from those derived from much of the traditional scholarship on Asian labor. Frederic Deyo's analysis does not answer the fundamental question of why the Asian tigers' "economic miracle" is not replicated in other authoritarian Asian countries, and the book's style is somewhat tedious. But the book introduces a beginning student of East Asian economies to a basic comparison of East Asian labor and its role in the region's economic transformation. Peter Drysdale's *International Economic Pluralism* is a deeper and comprehensive study of East Asia and the Pacific economies. His incisive analysis and inescapable conclusions are necessary reading for any student of Pacific economics, especially in today's world, where the liberal multilateral economic regime based on GATT principles is constantly challenged by short-term parochial interests.

P. I. MATHEW

U.S. Coast Guard Academy
New London
Connecticut

RICHARDS, ALAN and JOHN WATERBURY. *A Political Economy of the Middle East: State, Class, and Economic Development.* Pp. xv, 495. Boulder, CO: Westview Press, 1990. $56.00. Paperbound, $21.95.

Seldom has a book been more timely. Appropriately dedicated to the late Middle Eastern scholar Malcolm Kerr, this volume for years to come will be one of the standard sources for those interested in the Middle East and North Africa. Richards and Waterbury have spent a considerable part of their careers in the Arab world, experience that contributes to the authority of their opinions.

The book is an outstanding example of authors' setting goals and accepting boundaries in an era when multidisciplinary approaches are rampant, and of not trying to do everything and ending up doing nothing. For that reason, some readers will find the approach too traditionally political and economic in light of developments in social history and psychohistory. On the other hand, some may argue that the book is too wide ranging and ambitious when it attempts to embrace an area stretching from Morocco to the Persian Gulf. Richards and Waterbury themselves admit that the region is especially one in which the psychological and religious variables that they do not discuss can be important, as well as an area where, most particularly, "personal foibles among leaders can lead to momentous changes in the course of events." They freely admit to the diversity of the Arab world.

Having acknowledged such problems, they still believe that the region can be studied "at large" and that a traditional approach can be useful—"the process of economic and social change in the Middle East and North Africa is not qualitatively different from that in most of the less-developed countries." Their success more than justifies "an approach to the Middle East as a whole" and the decision to leave a number of religious and cultural topics to others. The three topics that they do propose to treat are economic growth and structural transformation, state structure and policy, and social class. They succeed.

This is not a book to encourage optimism about the Middle East after the recent gulf war. It is a record of disillusionment and cynicism and of "leaders nearly obsessed with control [who] have emasculated the very political organizations they created to mobilize and integrate the masses." It is a gloomy story of severely stretched resources, fatigue, self-doubt, and an "organizational and ideological vacuum" in the Arab lands, which the worst sort of actors are attempting to fill. Much of the Arab political imagery and religio-nationalism is warmed-over 1930s European fascism. Among the unlovely participants in the region's tragedy is the president of Iraq: "Few Middle Eastern leaders have ever had as much experience with 'dirty tricks' as Saddam Hussein. . . . He has nurtured a cult of his own personality that is unparalleled in the Middle East."

This is a book packed with facts and full of insights. In the case of the oil-rich nations, Richards and Waterbury find, as other have, that they have been damaged by the way oil revenues have permitted the avoiding of hard decisions. With 10 years' experience as a government adviser in the gulf sheikhdom of Qatar, I can second that opinion.

Population growth is a major problem to which an entire chapter is devoted. The uncontrolled expansion in the region means that the population will double in the next 24 years. This increase is catastrophic, especially when coupled with constricting expatriate labor opportunities in the gulf and with the consequent reversal of labor flows. The political threat that so many unemployed youths now present is staggering. In the two-year period 1984-86, remittances from Egyptians overseas to their homeland

shrank from $4 billion to $2 billion; the safety valve has been shut.

Although written before the Iraqi invasion of Kuwait, A Political Economy offers many insights into the immaturity and lack of sophistication of Arab political life. Presidents are in fact monarchs, and the leader on the white stallion is a ubiquitous image: "He must propagate the belief that were he ever to disappear, the system would disintegrate into a chaotic war among all the petty contenders for spoils. 'Après-moi le déluge' is very much the motto of Middle Eastern monarchs."

The availability of a paperback edition should ensure extensive use of this book in college classrooms. There is an abundance of tables and graphs. To be provided with only two small maps in such an otherwise excellent volume is a shortcoming, however. There is no mention in the acknowledgments of who prepared the superb index; indexing in such a long and comprehensive book is sufficiently important that its authorship should be acknowledged.

PAUL RICH

University of Western Australia
Nedlands
Perth

SOBHANI, SOHRAB. *The Pragmatic Entente: Israeli-Iranian Relations, 1948-1988*. Pp. xxvii, 179. New York: Praeger, 1989. No price.

TANTER, RAYMOND. *Who's at the Helm? Lessons of Lebanon*. Pp. x, 262. Boulder, CO: Westview Press, 1990. $24.95.

In their scope and content these are two very different books. Sobhani offers a forty-year survey of Israeli-Iranian relations that rarely strays beyond their immediate confines. Tanter presents a concentrated analysis of American foreign policy options and choices when confronted with tensions between Israel, Syria, and Lebanon exacerbated and sometimes inspired by the Palestine Liberation Organization (PLO). He covers less than 18 months in 1981 and 1982.

They have their similarities, however. Both offer rather weak attempts at theoretical frameworks in which to place their subjects, and both authors claim more than their texts provide. In the end, both authors disappoint, being limited in their use of scholarly sources and, on occasion, in displaying awareness of how to evaluate sources. This is the more dismaying as both authors have academic credentials. Tanter is a professor of politics at the University of Michigan, and Sobhani is an adjunct professor of international relations at Georgetown.

Sobhani's is the stronger work. He gives an adequate outline of Israeli-Iranian relations, noting the mutual security concerns of the two countries in the face of Arab nationalism and how their ties served specific interests: Mossad paid Iran $240,000 in 1950 through an American go-between for de facto recognition in order to facilitate passage of Iraqi Jews through Iran; Mossad agents were active along with Savak in fostering Kurdish unrest in Iraq in the 1960s. Sobhani concludes with a discussion of Israeli ties to Khomeini's Iran. Relying on interviews with Israeli foreign ministry officials, he argues that Israeli arms shipments were motivated, despite Israel's denials, by a concern for arranging the departure of Iranian Jews to Israel, and because of the money to be gained.

Sobhani uses these interviews, along with the Iranian publication of documents taken from the American embassy in Tehran, to good effect. On the other hand, he frequently makes assertions of great interest with no substantiation. One example is his claim that Iran, Israel, and Saudi Arabia coordinated activities against Gamal Abdel Nasser in Yemen and in support of the Imam during the early 1960s through the good offices of Kamal Adham, head of Saudi intelligence. Another is his assertion that the same Adham told Iranian officials the date of the Syrian-Egyptian attack on Israel in 1973 but that the Iranians did not pass the news along to their purported ally. Sobhani's reliance on Amir Taheri's *Spirit of Allah* for nearly all his information about the Ayatollah Khomeini is unfortunate given the book's limited perspective and Sobhani's own language skills in Farsi.

In short, this book is an apparently reliable survey of Israeli-Iranian relations in their narrowest framework, with little interest in broader perspectives other than anti-Arab activities. Scarcely any attention is given to American foreign policy interests. The American embassy documents used pertain to Central Intelligence Agency analyses of Israeli ties to Iran, not to Washington's support of or alarm at the ramifications of these ties. Some statements must be taken as unverified and tantalizing gossip, albeit worthy of further inquiry, and others have basic textbooks as their inspiration.

Tanter's study is equally problematic. Tanter served as senior staff member for the Near East and South Asia on the National Security Council during 1981 and 1982, and this book is a paean to Alexander Haig's tenure as secretary of state; the fact that Haig provides a blurb for the book on the back cover does not inspire confidence. What Tanter does do is illustrate the in-fighting between globalists—including himself—and regionalists for control of Middle East policy during the critical period when Syrian-Maronite friction led to Israeli intervention and when PLO-Israeli military exchanges resulted in a July 1981 truce that encouraged Ariel Sharon to plan for an assault that resulted in the June 1982 invasion.

The details of the arguments are fascinating if bewildering because Tanter, as participant, is an advocate of the globalist perspective while never explaining its merits or the implications of its policy suggestions. Rather, Tanter argues ad infinitum for the creative use of diplomacy coordinated with force. He contends—as did Haig, according to Tanter—that the United States should have used Israeli force against the PLO and the Syrians to create new opportunities for American diplomacy. Just what these opportunities were, and how the United States could have wrung concessions from Israel after relying on its military to destroy the PLO, are never explained; contentions without explanations carry the day.

Equally disconcerting are Tanter's selective use of sources and the naïveté of his assertions. He assumes that Israel's pursuit of "lasting peace" meshed with that of the United States while noting elsewhere that Begin and Sharon wanted to destroy the PLO in order to secure the West Bank, not what Washington had in mind. He accepts Sharon's version of Israel's excuse for attacking the PLO in June 1982—that they would break the cease-fire—and ignores Schiff and Ya'ari's *Israel's Lebanon War* (1984), though he uses it elsewhere, which in effect calls Sharon a liar and accuses him of seeking to provoke such a violation in order to have a reason for an attack.

If Tanter had limited himself to bureaucratic infighting and policy debates, his text would have had a consistency and a logic underlying its approach. The book is worth reading for its details of Washington's competing visions of the world it sought to dominate. But Tanter's attempt to integrate that argument with his own explanation of events in the region and his advocacy of the globalists against the regionalists undermine his narrative. Indeed, his effort ultimately illustrates the illogic of the globalist approach better than any other source I have seen. One has no doubt as to the villains either, but they are not regionalists. They are Ronald Reagan, who refused to take control of competing branches of government—presumably for globalist benefit—and Robert McFarlane, who exceeded his responsibilities and manipulated intelligence information to the detriment of American interests.

Nevertheless, the attempt at a theoretical patina comparing management styles cannot hide the book's weaknesses, which include discussion of departmental authority. Tanter demonstrates on several occasions how Haig was frustrated by the State Department bureaucracy, but only to complain about it, not to investigate the nature of bureau management and the problems of interdepartmental coordination of policy. Finally, Tanter's repeated calls for the creative use of force to prepare the way for new diplomacy without giving any idea of what that combination entails and what its likelihood of success may be only bring to mind the fallout from our current involvement in Kuwait and Iraq, not only in those countries but with respect to Arab-Israeli matters as well. *Plus ça change.* . . . But at least we used our own force.

CHARLES D. SMITH

San Diego State University
California

TEIWES, FREDERICK C. *Politics at Mao's Court: Gao Gang and Party Factionalism in the Early 1950s.* Pp. xvi, 326. Armonk, NY: M. E. Sharpe, 1990. $45.00.

In 1953-54, an acute leadership conflict rocked the Chinese Communist Party (CCP) hierarchy and resulted in 1954-55 in a high-level purge of two ranking leaders, Gao Gang and Rao Shushi, and their associates. Gao was a CCP Politburo member, the party leader of Manchuria, and a vice-chairman of the People's Republic of China, and he chaired the powerful State Planning Commission, an agency that was equal in status to that of Government Administrative Council, or cabinet, headed by Premier Zhou Enlai. Rao was a CCP Central Committee member, party leader of East China and director of the Central Committee Organization Department.

The book by Frederick Teiwes, a veteran American China scholar teaching in Australia, reexamines the Gao-Rao affair in light of newly available Chinese sources. According to Teiwes, the nature of the Gao-Rao alliance was a factional power play, as Gao recruited supporters to oppose not Chairman Mao himself but his two top lieutenants, Liu Shaoqi and Zhou Enlai, in order to become CCP vice-chairman and the premier, and schemed to control the succession after Mao. These findings confirm much that has already been written; however, Teiwes refutes a thesis advanced by some writers that Gao's fatal error was that he maintained illicit relations with Moscow and gave inner-party secrets to the Soviets.

In addition to examining in detail CCP factionalism in the early 1950s, Teiwes's painstaking study also sheds light on the nature of the Chinese leadership system and the relations between Mao and his powerful associates. Thus Teiwes states:

The one indisputable conclusion to emerge from this study is the central role of Mao Zedong. In a classic case of an unchallenged authoritarian leader surrounded by deferential subordinates, Mao's words and actions shaped the Gao Gang-Rao Shushi affair from start to finish. Other leaders on all sides of the conflict reacted to Mao, hung on his often ambiguous words, and anticipated his moves and objectives (p. 142).

Is the Gao-Rao affair an exception to the often repeated myth about CCP lead-ership cohesion? How does the episode fit into the recurring pattern of CCP leadership factionalism and elite conflicts since the late 1950s? Teiwes, like other scholars, sees the Gao Gang affair as "an aberration in the general high level of Party unity in the early and mid-1950s," but he concedes that "it was an aberration rooted in court politics where final power was in the hands of one man and other leaders sought to divine his intent" and that the affair "brings clearly into view the nature of court politics under Mao in the early 1950s, when the successful functioning of the system was so dependent on one man's opinions, and one man's self-restraint."

The Gao-Rao case shows that the preconditions for a subsequent bitter factional split and leadership turmoil were already present. As Mao lost control and could no longer restrain himself in the 1960s, he would unleash the factional rivalry and smash the leadership hierarchy that the world witnessed during the Cultural Revolution.

PARRIS H. CHANG

Pennsylvania State University
University Park

EUROPE

KATSENELINBOIGEN, ARON J. *The Soviet Union: Empire, Nation, and System.* Pp. xx, 471. New Brunswick, NJ: Transaction, 1990. $42.95.

LAQUEUR, WALTER. *Soviet Realities: Culture and Politics from Stalin to Gorbachev.* Pp. xix, 231. New Brunswick, NJ: Transaction, 1990. $34.95.

Emphasizing their Jewish identity, the authors of the two books under review agree that the restructuring of Soviet culture, society, and economy will be difficult and take time. They both acknowledge the existence in Russian and Soviet history of a reform movement that repeatedly has been put down. While admitting that *glasnost* was part of Aleksandr Herzen's vocabulary as early as 1849, Laqueur believes that the concept is "a specifically Russian phenomenon: the attempt to combine a non-democratic or antidemocratic mode of government with a certain degree of cultural freedom, with accountability (especially on the lower levels of the administration), and with 'transparency.'" Closer during the decade before World War I than at any other time to constituting a "civil society," Russia failed to rid itself of what Katsenelinboigen calls its "one-dimensional" political and economic systems, a heritage maintained by the Soviet Union. At the same time, he contends, the "process of pluralization," of creating "a multidimensional system" with emphasis on democracy, pluralism, separation of powers, and openness, enters a particularly dangerous phase as it proceeds, as it has done since the late 1980s, "from the publication of ideas and their discussion by political groups, to the creation of popular organizations and the staging of massive demonstrations in support of these ideas." The attempt to democratize too quickly may culminate in mob rule. Finally, both authors see as one of the main obstacles to civility or multidimensionality what Katsenelinboigen calls the "real-life doppelganger" of Russian tradition, anti-Semitism. The latter is the subject of at least three of Laqueur's 16 chapters and of more than a third of Katsenelinboigen's work.

A Soviet émigré to the United States and by profession an economist, Katsenelinboigen believes that the Russian and Jewish cultures may be incompatible. In a chapter on Solzhenitsyn, he associates Russian tradition with Slavophilism, Orthodoxy, and anti-Semitism and deprecates its predilection for rural culture. Believing that tradition to be monolithic,

he underestimates its diversity and overlooks how both of its two main orientations—land and people—may serve as a foundation for an appreciation of ecology.

Except incidentally, Chernobyl apart, ecology is an important concern of neither author. Laqueur's Soviet realities revolve around culture and politics—the meanings of *glasnost* and totalitarianism, the Soviet book trade and Soviet literature, Stalinism and the cult of the individual, an illuminating analysis of the purges, U.S.-Soviet relations, and spies and police action as seen through the novels of British author John Le Carré and Soviet writer Julian Semyonov.

Despite a chapter on inflation in Katsenelinboigen's book, neither author raises the question of the relationship between Soviet economic stagnation or decline and the energy crisis and world stagflation, or of the feasibility, since the acceleration of the communications revolution, of existence as a closed state, especially for a people that aspires to political and cultural greatness. But Katsenelinboigen engages in a fine analysis of an appropriate approach to economic systems, especially the Soviet system. A certain number of economic invariants—prices, money, profit, inflation, competition—he affirms, characterize every economic system. The economic invariants operate, however, in the framework of national or cultural variables, including both horizontal and vertical, centralized and decentralized, command and market mechanisms, by means of which the economic invariants are allowed to function. Distinguishing between legal and illegal markets—exchange-distributive systems—he identifies in the Soviet Union at least four legal types, differing from each other on the basis of the nature of the command function to which they are subject and the degree to which they are subject to it and for which his names are violet, red, pink, and white.

Using different approaches but reaching several similar conclusions, the two books complement each other well.

TRAIAN STOIANOVICH
Rutgers University
New Brunswick
New Jersey

UNITED STATES

BOND, JON R. and RICHARD FLEISHER. *The President in the Legislative Arena.* Pp. xi, 259. Chicago: University of Chicago Press, 1990. $47.00. Paperbound, $16.95.

Research on the presidency has come of age. *The President in the Legislative Arena* by Jon R. Bond, professor of political science at Texas A&M University, and Richard Fleisher, associate professor of political science at Fordham University, is one of the quantitative analyses that puts the presidency in perspective. It does so by demonstrating how limited presidents are in securing victories on Capitol Hill.

The old saw, "The President proposes, the Congress disposes," comes through in all its glory here. At the core of the Bond-Fleisher thesis is that Congress truly rules. Presidential success on Capitol Hill has less to do with chief executives' popularity or personal skills than with the hand that presidents are dealt. Presidential success ultimately depends upon two interrelated factors largely beyond the presidents' own control: the size of their legislative contingents and the ideological makeup of the congressional parties. An important, if subsidiary, role is played by party and committee leaders in the House and the Senate.

These are the central findings of the book. It would add little to expand on them in this review, for the book is chock full of findings of great interest. What is most attractive about the book are the forthright proposal of a counterintuitive hypothesis—presidents do not matter as much as Congress does—and a straightforward, even if novel, methodology. Bond and Fleisher stick by their thesis and find strong support for it. They also criticize—with considerable justification—previous analyses of legislative-executive conflict and consensus on roll calls and propose a neat solution. Presidents start out with a base of support from members of their own party who agree with them on issues and with a core of opponents at the opposite ideological pole from the other party. How much can they mobilize the former and neutralize the latter? How can a Democratic president gain support from one cross-pressured group—conservative Democrats—without antagonizing the other—liberal Republicans? The task for presidents is daunting, and it turns out to be largely beyond the capacity of most chief executives to help themselves. Instead, each bloc responds primarily to the strategic situation defined by the voting strength and coherence of the others.

This contextual view of the world makes a lot of sense. It is nicely executed, especially when Bond and Fleisher take a detour in chapter 6 to reexamine the two-presidencies thesis—it works for Republicans, but not Democrats, but it does not seem to work for either party on the most important votes. The analyses are largely convincing. The prose sometimes gets bogged down in a morass of numbers. Yet, even as *The President in the Legislative Arena* is not ready for serialization in the *New Yorker*, Bond and Fleisher generally write well, often quite well.

While I find their book very impressive, I do have some reservations. For my taste, they put too much emphasis on the current topic *du jour* in American politics research, divided government. In so doing, they ignore other analyses of legislative-executive policy formation—Mark Peterson's *Legislating Together* and David R. Mayhew's work in progress on divided government—that suggest a far more limited impact of split party control than they offer. The difference largely stems from alternative conceptions of policymaking. Mayhew focuses on major policy innovations, while Peterson distinguishes between large and small policy decisions on the one hand and old and new programs on the other.

Let me pick two small nits. While Bond and Fleisher present a novel and indeed useful measure of presidential skills, Peterson's measures—presidential speeches, addresses to special interest groups, and television appearances—are more convincing. Asking Bond and Fleisher to compute such measures for so much larger a data base than Peterson's may be far too demanding, but differences between the two works will thus not be readily resolvable. Peterson's measure has greater depth, but Bond and Fleisher's covers far more cases. Second, the authors early on set up a straw man that they later find easy to knock down. On page 37 they argue that many observers fault Carter for not getting his energy program through in 1977. This view is entirely too simpleminded. Even Reagan could not prevail on energy issues—natural gas deregulation in 1982-83—so complex were the crosscutting cleavages on energy issues. Yet, Bond and Fleisher are just as wrong when they state that Carter got most of what he wanted on energy. To be sure, Congress passed an energy bill in 1978 with most of the same titles, but the bill bore little resemblance to what the president had originally proposed.

These objections, large and small, do not obviate my admiration for what Bond and Fleisher have accomplished. Theirs is a very important book. It will change much of the way we think about legislative-executive relations. The authors take a controversial thesis, stand by it, and support it. Hooray!

ERIC M. USLANER
University of Maryland
College Park

BROESAMLE, JOHN J. *Reform and Reaction in Twentieth Century American Politics*. Pp. xvi, 481. Westport, CT: Greenwood Press, 1990. $49.95.

Reform and Reaction in Twentieth Century American Politics explores a large and significant subject—the dynamic of domestic reform movements in the United States from populism in the 1890s to the diffuse "movement for a new America" in the 1960s. Since the populist movement was effectively spent by 1900, the book's reach is even broader than its title suggests. Moreover, since Broesamle is concerned with the decline of reform movements as well as with their rise, he covers here an entire century of American political history, from the presidency of Grover Cleveland through that of Ronald Reagan.

A book so inclusive cannot be expected to add anything novel to our understanding of any one of the four great reform eras of modern, industrial America. Historians of populism, progressivism, the New Deal, and the 1960s will not find new material here. They may even be expected to complain that the nuances of the specialist literature of their own periods are not adequately presented. But that is not Broesamle's purpose. He is interested in the big picture of how American reform movements have come and gone—their dynamic, or, as he prefers to put it, their life cycle. Indeed, his ambitious quest for the underlying structure of reform and reaction takes him well beyond the writing of American historians, to the professional literature of political science and sociology. Here, I think, lies the strength of his effort. Whether or not we conclude that its reach somewhat exceeds its grasp, the book deserves to be seen as a big-minded and challenging attempt to understand the dynamic of American domestic policymaking over the entire sweep of the industrial and postindustrial eras.

While Broesamle rejects theories of rigid periodic cycles in American history, he does argue that there is a similar structure to the coming and going of reform movements. As different as were the four great reform periods and their aftermaths, he sees in them a common life cycle. Each involved a widespread perception of the need for reform that reached from intellectuals and other elite actors to the general public. During each of these periods, public concerns displaced private ones; in effect, the polity took primacy over civil society. In each case, domestic, not foreign policy, concerns were at the forefront of the reform agenda. Each reform era similarly generated idealism and moral energy on a massive scale. In each case, the relatively disadvantaged came into vogue and were idealized by the intellectuals. Each era produced—by American standards—peak levels of political polarization around issues of class, ethnicity, race, and sex. And each produced similar reactions of red-baiting, nativism, and fundamentalism that cut into the movements "like an ax."

The decline phase of the four reform movements, Broesamle argues, is yet more impressively patterned. In each case, the common sense of reform purpose faded, and intellectuals and the public lost interest. Private interests and concerns once again came to the forefront. The intended beneficiaries of reform quickly lost their charm. In every case foreign/military policy concerns displaced domestic ones. In the reaction to each reform movement, a politics of cultural questions replaced the politics of class. Each reform era ended in considerable disillusionment with the polity and the public life. Each period ended with the ascendancy of business-oriented conservatism and the return of extreme suspicion of the realm of politics and the state.

While he might have made a great deal more of it, Broesamle is aware that this dynamic is uniquely American. It takes place wholly within a capitalist consensus. The American party system has been at all times dependent on individual presidents and presidential candidates for leadership and direction. Always, reform era or not, Americans have manifested a relatively weak sense of social class and a robust affirmation of "the American dream," which has no counterpart anywhere else in the world. Perhaps most important of all, our deepest political values—as political scientists have it, our political culture—have disposed us to be suspicious of state authority and to affirm individualism as our ultimate political goal.

If one were inclined to pick, considerable fault could be found with this book. Even for its huge and significant subject, it is too long. It contains a fair amount of redundancy that should have been excised by a good editor. Nevertheless, it deserves praise for its reach and synthetic grasp. Even if it does not entirely succeed, it should provoke scholars in the social sciences to think about American politics in big-minded terms. It should be especially useful for undergraduates, who now more than ever need a sense of the American past and its meaning for our own time. Finally, it should console liberals, among whom Broesamle is clearly to be counted, that their seemingly endless contemporary agony will pass. Everything we know from the past suggests that the dynamic of American politics described here will persist. If we cannot now see when or how the next era of reform will begin, we should remember that none of the previous reform eras was easy to see coming on. Broesamle impressively argues the case for their common pattern, but their causation remains quite mysterious.

W. WAYNE SHANNON

University of Connecticut

Storrs

EAGLES, CHARLES W. *Democracy Delayed: Congressional Reapportionment and Urban-Rural Conflict in the 1920s.* Pp. xiv, 173. Athens: University of Georgia Press, 1990. $25.00.

At some point between 1910 and 1920, America's dynamic urban population at last caught up with, and quickly surpassed, its more staid rural counterpart. In the landmark census of 1920, cities and towns with at least 2500 residents claimed over 51 percent of the nation's people, reversing an urban-to-rural ratio that had stood at 46:54 just 10 years earlier. This fundamental demographic shift, with all its dire implications for a nation steeped in frontier and small-town values, seemed both to contemporaries and to later historians to underlie the divisive and highly charged social issues that helped enliven the Roaring Twenties. Walter Lippmann, Lewis Mumford, and H. L. Mencken were just a few of the keen observers who perceived an urban-rural fault line running through the decade's heated debates over Prohibition, Sunday laws, immigration restriction, Darwinism, Fundamentalism, and the Ku Klux Klan. Later, beginning in the 1950s, historians also took up the urban-rural theme to explain the turbulent politics of the 1920s and, despite subsequent revisions and more recent challenges, it remains a favorite lens through which to view and understand the period.

In *Democracy Delayed*, Charles Eagles examines the surprisingly neglected issue of congressional reapportionment to test the validity of the urban-rural thesis. This is a logical approach since the results of the fourteenth census touched off an intense struggle that appeared to pit the nation's rising metropolitan centers against a selfish and unyielding agrarian rear guard desperately intent on preserving its power, even if that meant thwarting democratic principles of equal representation. In the end, opponents of redistricting succeeded in blocking reapportionment and delaying democracy for 10 years. The unprecedented impasse marked the first and only time in American history that Congress ever failed to reapportion itself after the decennial census. Only after the next count was taken in 1930, did Congress finally fulfill its constitutional duty, in 1931.

To determine whether the reapportionment deadlock reflected an urban-rural standoff, Eagles subjects eight roll-call votes taken in the House of Representatives to careful quantitative analysis. His findings provide aid and comfort to both proponents and critics of the urban-rural model. Overall, and not surprisingly, the most influential factor determining the votes cast by House members was pure political self-interest, namely, a judgment as to whether or not they expected their home states to gain or lose from redistricting. "Urban-rural influences," says Eagles, "would seem to have been at best secondary." Nevertheless, Eagles demonstrates clearly that many congressmen viewed and debated reapportionment in urban-rural terms and that a sharp urban-rural cleavage did in fact separate Democrats who hailed from the 29 states unaffected by redistricting. Urban-rural tensions seem to provide a "vital explanation" for their voting behavior.

Though clearly argued and presented, Eagle's intriguing conclusions are not as convincing as they easily could have been. In an article published in the *Jour-*

nal of American History in 1989, Eagles found strong urban-rural divisions running through House—and especially Democratic—votes on Prohibition and immigration restriction. His failure to incorporate and build upon those findings here is a curious omission that flaws an otherwise useful and interesting book. Much greater clarity might have been achieved had Eagles taken the next logical step and correlated reapportionment balloting with immigration and Prohibition votes. Perhaps divisions over those controversial issues did more to deadlock congressional reapportionment than more vaguely defined urban-rural differences. As Eagles readily concedes, "more work needs to be done" to "confidently evaluate the importance and validity of the urban-rural thesis" for the politics of the 1920s.

MICHAEL MAGLIARI

California State University
Chico

MEYER, DAVID S. *A Winter of Discontent: The Nuclear Freeze and American Politics.* Pp. xx, 294. New York: Praeger, 1990. $47.95. Paperbound, $16.95.

With insight and detail, David Meyer examines the rise and decline of the American nuclear freeze movement. He offers more than a useful history and suggests lessons for other mass political movements, contributing to an understanding of organizational change, political mobilization, and the democratic process.

Meyer traces the freeze from local origins in New England town meetings to a national forum in the U.S. Congress. He shows the freeze evolving from a grassroots effort that piggybacked on other local groups to a centralized, national campaign that relied on conventional lobbying, petitioning, and target voting. He

tells a story of coalition building around the political center—of using the freeze (a "simple and salable idea") to appeal to mainstream opinion, in the face of demands for a broader humanitarian, economic, or disarmament agenda.

But Meyer does not offer a happy ending for freeze activists. He makes his greatest contribution in revealing the weaknesses of the freeze movement. In expanding support and moving beyond local politics, the freeze was consumed by the political process; in sacrificing substance to national political acceptability, it became a political lowest common denominator. In Meyer's words, "the movement endorsed a tactical and political timidity, ultimately separating the freeze from the forces that gave it life" and "virtually abandoned long-range goals in favor of short-term support." The freeze is undone by friends as much as by adversaries, and "opponents of the movement were far less effective and dangerous . . . than apparent allies, who redefined the freeze to allow strategic nuclear modernization, for example, or to be nothing more than a plea for traditional arms control." Perversely, the freeze could gain support because it lacked meaning; and, for many, it was more an expression of discontent with the Reagan administration than a commentary on the arms race. In the end, congressional supporters would vote for a freeze and strategic weapon funding with no apparent contradiction.

If the book has a fault, it is that Meyer leaves a theoretical question unanswered. He draws from the theoretical literature on organizations and social change in rejecting theories that emphasize the constraints placed on social mobilization by the state, yet he does not fully reconcile his findings with theory. One is actually struck more by the political constraints in the freeze story than by the opportunities. Meyer suggests that an alternative freeze strategy could have been more effective, but, without theoretical guidance, he has not established this. Still, this book is a significant accomplishment and deserves to be read both by political activists and students of politics.

JAMES H. LEBOVIC

George Washington University
Washington, D.C.

WILSON, JAMES R. *Landing Zones: Southern Veterans Remember Vietnam.* Pp. xvi, 267. Durham, NC: Duke University Press, 1990. $21.95.

"You could ask twenty different people about Vietnam and hear about twenty different wars," James Wilson writes in *Landing Zones.* Change "twenty" to "twenty-four" and one has a perfect description of the contents of this volume. Wilson, a Vietnam veteran himself, has compiled the recollections of two dozen Vietnam veterans from across the Confederacy: male and female; military and civilian; black, white, and Hispanic; Army, Navy, Air Force, and Marines; rich and poor; general and tunnel rat. These recollections are preceded by a brief introduction, where Wilson elucidates his rationale for focusing on southerners, based on the disproportionate number who served in country, who were killed, and who won Medals of Honor.

Despite Wilson's attempt to provide a regional perspective on the war, about the only thing these veterans commonly report is the overwhelming first impression that Vietnam was permeated with a scent most graphically described as a combination of "diesel fuel and shit." Beyond this common thread, variety reigns. Some of the veterans draw parallels to the U.S. Civil War, reminding us of how imbued some southerners were with the mystique of the conflict of a century ear-

lier. Beyond the limited number of people who refer to this staple of southern consciousness, however, it is not clear that a collection of memories from nonsouthern Vietnam veterans would differ greatly from the ones presented here. Some of Wilson's respondents wanted to go to Vietnam; others dreaded the assignment. Some returned permanently disabled; others, unscratched. Some were imprisoned; others seldom encountered the enemy. Some could not wait to leave; others took on second tours of duty. Some learned that bullets do not respect skin color; others entered and emerged from the war as racists. Quite simply, different people brought different attitudes and skills to their different assignments, reacted differently to war, and, upon returning home, again reacted differently. Only on the last point should the differences not be overstated. Many veterans, regardless of their experiences in Vietnam, report alienation from those who did not share their experiences and difficulty with posttraumatic stress disorder.

The contributions are well edited, easily read, and absorbing. Wilson's book should be a popular addition to the literature telling the story of the war in Vietnam. Although modestly priced by today's standards, for a hardback, a paperback edition would be welcome. This volume could be of value to anyone interested in the Vietnam war.

JOSEPH STEWART, Jr.

University of Texas at Dallas
Richardson

SOCIOLOGY

CHUBB, JOHN E. and TERRY MOE. *Politics, Markets and American Schools.* Pp. xi, 317. Washington, DC: Brookings Institition, 1990. $28.95. Paperbound, $10.95.

Beginning with the *Nation at Risk* report in 1983, there has been a concerted effort at educational reform in the United States, including greater state regulation and control, the professionalization of teaching, school-based management, and, most recently, increased parental involvement. In *Politics, Markets and American Schools*, however, John E. Chubb and Terry Moe of the Brookings Institution argue that reforms such as these are problematic as long as schools as institutions remain subject to democratic control. According to them, schools cannot address the problem of educational reform because "they *are* the problem—and . . . the key to better schools is institutional reform."

Chubb and Moe are essentially concerned with what makes an effective school. Theoretically, they link the organization and performance of schools to their institutional environments and then, drawing on data from the national High School and Beyond survey, try to define "what effective schools look like, what conditions promote or inhibit their development, and how these conditions reflect the institution in which schools operate."

Chubb and Moe conclude from their data that school organization plays a critical role in school effectiveness—that taken alone it "is capable of shifting student achievement gains by more than one full year during four years of high school." Autonomous schools that are subject to less bureaucratic control function significantly better than do schools that are less autonomous. The authors conclude that the structure of school control not only affects a school's autonomy but determines the extent to which it will be successful.

Politics, Markets and American Schools maintains that effective school characteristics are achieved more consistently by market control than through direct democratic control. In this context, private schools as products of school competition and parental choice provide "clear academic goals, strong educational leadership, professionalized teaching, ambitious academic programs and teamlike organizations." These schools are important models for public schools, while public schools are controlled by the politics of democratic control. As a result, Chubb and Moe conclude that "success is built into the institutional structure of private education. As public education is now structured, institutions make success almost unnatural."

This book is a significant work in light of not only the recent reform movement in education but also the entire debate over the role of public and private education in American society. Ironically, it maintains that public education needs to reform itself by adopting the institutional structures of private schooling, ones that are subject more to market forces than to the forces of democratic control. Such an interpretation is obviously threatening to entrenched bureaucratic and political forces and will undoubtedly lead the findings of this study to be hotly debated and discussed.

EUGENE F. PROVENZO, Jr.

University of Miami
Coral Gables
Florida

DUFFY, JOHN. *The Sanitarians: A History of American Public Health*. Pp. 316. Champaign: University of Illinois Press, 1990. $32.50.

Over seventy years ago, Dr. Charles-Edward Amory Winslow defined the nature and scope of the "science and art of public health." Winslow's definition has stood the test of time remarkably well and even today it remains the most frequently quoted delineation of the parameters of the field of public health.

Forty years ago, I was introduced to the history of medicine as a first-year graduate student in the Yale Department of Public Health in a course taught by Winslow. Though retired and well over 70 years of age, he had retained his infectious enthusiasm and tack-sharp intellect to present a series of brilliant lectures designed to whet the appetites of newcomers to the discipline he helped shape and pioneer. The course was a truly delightful and unforgettable experience.

In the forty-year interim, during which I have been exposed to perhaps fifty-plus medical or public health histories, I can state unequivocally that I have not found one to be as enjoyable as John Duffy's *Sanitarians*!

Most medical or public health histories are, quite frankly, tedious, boring recitations of persons, dates, and events within precise, chronological time frames. Duffy, on the other hand, has masterfully woven 350 years of the disparate, though related, threads of the American public health movement into a beautiful, colorful, integrated fabric. Although there is some inevitable overlapping of the diverse time frames of the individual chapters, the final product is a powerful confluence of the concurrent evolutions of the myriad American public health practices over three and a half centuries. The volume begins with the advances in the sanitation of the environment and the conquest of the epidemic and communicable diseases and ends with our current conflicting advances toward the corporatization and governmentalization of health care services.

Duffy's title, *The Sanitarians*, while catchy and totally in keeping with the title of his previous history of American medicine, *The Healers*, is an immoderate understatement of the true breadth of this extraordinary book. While sanitarians have played important and vital roles in the development of American public health—and Duffy narrates their contributions most eloquently—this book also gives force to the efforts of the many other disciplines and specialists who played substantive roles in the history of American public health: bacteriologists, physicians, nurses, biostatisticians and epidemiologists, educators, social workers, program administrators, legislators, and all the other leaders involved in the "organized community efforts" directed toward preventing disease, prolonging life, and promoting physical, mental, and social well-being.

Duffy has produced a document that is not just another medical history. *The Sanitarians* is, in fact, a well-organized, well-written, easily readable, thorough, and nearly flawlessly accurate chronicle of the development of American public health. It is a fun book; it is an outstanding contribution to our medical and public health literature, perhaps the best of its kind to date; it is so good that I wish I had written it!

CHARLES NEWTON POSKANZER
State University of New York
Cortland

GATEWOOD, WILLARD B. *Aristocrats of Color: The Black Elite, 1880-1920.* Pp. xii, 450. Bloomington: Indiana University Press, 1990. $39.95.

Willard Gatewood examines the black social elite in the United States in the years from the end of Reconstruction through the growth of Jim Crowism at the turn of the century. While Gatewood takes as a unifying thread the history of the family of Blanche K. Bruce, a black senator from Mississippi, his emphasis is on the social, not the political, elite. The black political and social elite were often one and the same, but not always, as is evident from Gatewood's neglect of Hiram Revels, Mississippi's other black senator. Gatewood concentrates on Washington, D.C., where most of the black elite were found, although he briefly describes the black elite of other cities. Some of the black elite were clergymen, others were physicians, and still others were civil servants. Some of the black elite had substantial wealth; others had their good name but little else. Many were related, and almost all were set apart by the light color of their skin and their attitude of superiority regarding their fellow blacks.

Gatewood provides a description of the life of the "upper tens" that depicts them as living a life distinct from that of most other blacks, yet not wholly of white society even though many of them displayed the same characteristics as the white elite of the same period. Throughout, Gatewood contends that the black elite were concerned with the lot of their fellow blacks. Admittedly, some had a strange way of showing this concern, since they contended that many of their fellow blacks were not capable of entering polite society or even of exercising the franchise. The irony of this situation, portrayed in the last two chapters, is that, after the turn of the century, even the black elite had to confront the fact of their race. Their social position did not make them immune to the new Jim Crow legislation and social rules.

Aristocrats of Color is a thoroughly researched work displaying Gatewood's usual capable style. While he avoids the hazard of producing a gossipy account with no substance, some readers might wish for more analysis in places. Gatewood documents the often uneasy relationship of the black elite to Booker T. Washington, but he does not devote much attention to the elite's efforts to uplift their brothers and sisters. What about the views of the black elite regarding poor whites, or the views of the white social elite, particularly in Washington, concerning their black counterparts? Gate-

wood alludes to these themes in passing; perhaps more attention might have been helpful.

This is not to say that *Aristocrats of Color* is a flawed book; it is not. It is a book that scholars and other will turn to for information and to help them pose additional questions concerning race relations in the United States.

JOHN M. THEILMANN

Converse College
Spartanburg
South Carolina

GINZBERG, ELI. *The Medical Triangle: Physicians, Politicians and the Public.* Pp. xii, 314. Cambridge, MA: Harvard University Press, 1990. $27.50.

In this book of 20 chapters, Ginzberg has pulled together articles and papers he wrote for journals, edited books, or conferences during the period from 1985 to 1989. The chapters vary in length from 5 pages to 34 pages and reflect little editing of their original construction. The book's general focus is on health care policy and the major issues and actors involved in hammering out decisions in this area. It is divided into five sections of uneven size; they range from rather universal national questions about health care in America to parochial interests such as the health care system in New York City.

The first section, "The Changing Health Care System," is composed of five chapters. Respectively, they look at factors that destabilized the health care system, the rise of for-profit medicine, and the shift of power away from physicians to those third parties, especially government, that over time have come to foot a larger share of the cost of health services. In this section Ginzberg also has chapters on private versus public financing as well as on quality-of-care concerns evolving with high-tech medicine. This section reflects Ginzberg's mature wisdom about major policy issues.

The book's second section, entitled "Important Subsystems," is composed of four chapters, which respectively, deal with academic health centers, foundations, community health care centers, and health care in New York City. These chapters have a more parochial focus that does not measure up to the more universal questions treated in the rest of the book.

The third section deals with medical education, the question of the surplus of doctors, and the shortage of nurses. As a manpower-policy specialist, Ginzberg writes knowledgeably here, although no new ground is broken in these chapters.

The fourth section, "Patients' Needs and Resources," concentrates on clinical decision making in catastrophic situations, the rationing of cancer care, providing care for the elderly, the undersupport and policy confusion in the care of the mentally ill, and the problems we have in providing care for the poor. These chapters reflect a humane pragmatism in dealing with sensitive issues. The concluding section, "Health Agenda Issues," discusses balancing the quality of care with limited dollars, the history and outcomes of cost-containment efforts, and a rather dismal forecast for reaching consensus on how to deal with escalating health care costs.

On one hand, the book is uneven in the citations it gives, it would benefit from the inclusion of tables, and it sometimes seems to be dated. Nonetheless, for the newcomer it provides a wealth of insights into major health policy issues that our society is facing.

DUANE STROMAN

Juniata College
Huntingdon
Pennsylvania

YOUNG, I. M. *Justice and the Politics of Difference.* Pp. viii, 286. Princeton, NJ: Princeton University Press, 1990. $45.00. Paperbound, $12.95.

This is the big book from the Left for the 1990s. It must be read. Even those who are not of Young's political and moral persuasion will come away changed.

In each chapter, Young describes how those outside the white male bond suffer a vocabulary of indecencies and indignities in their everyday life. As a rainbow coalition of stigmatized others, nonwhite male individuals become collateral damage amid the underdogs of the larger society.

At first, readers will find themselves in familiar territory that harkens back to the late 1960s. This, however, is political and social discourse that was battered and bruised by Reaganomics and survived.

Young describes an economic paradigm created, argued, reshaped, and reconstituted by white males for white males. There is a concrete description of socially approved, often unnoticed forms of oppression that impale the others to become the dramaturgical backdrop to the white male bond. The point is made that welfare capitalism, Western and supposedly objective impartiality, and meritocracy do not or will not take into account differences that include specificity, variation, and heterogeneity of humankind.

For each major question addressed in the book, Young provides practical and workable political strategies and arrangements, often in the tradition of the social democrats.

One should read the book for no other reason than to gain insight into the latest secular mantras, including "deconstruction," "commutarianism," and "empowerment."

The text is tightly woven and integrated. Readers will always know to what part of the trail the author has led them.

Kudos to Iris Marion Young and her *Justice and the Politics of Difference*. She writes as an outsider who asks all of us to rethink the social and political boundaries of inclusion. As a white male, I was indeed convinced.

JOEL C. SNELL

Kirkwood College
Cedar Rapids
Iowa

ECONOMICS

ALLEN, ROBERT LORING. *Opening Doors: The Life and Work of Joseph Schumpeter*. Vol. 1, *Europe*. Pp. xxi, 314. Vol. 2, *America*. Pp. xxi, 348. New Brunswick, NJ: Transaction, 1991. No price.

This study of an economist widely regarded at his death as second only to J. M. Keynes in the 1900-1950 is written by an admiring former student, who paints the picture—good and bad—as he sees it. It is a picture of an extraordinarily complex human being, one with seeming serenity outwardly but with intense inner torment.

Born in Austria in 1883, Schumpeter attended the Faculty of Law at the University of Vienna. He joined a law firm in Cairo, here producing *The Nature and Principal Content of Theoretical Economics*, a book marrying marginal utility to Walras's general equilibrium. In 1909, Schumpeter entered academia at the University of Czernowitz, moving to Gratz in 1911, meanwhile producing his celebrated *Theory of Economic Development*, in which the entrepreneur-innovator and his innovations are seen as the source of modern economic development; *The Past and Future of Social Science*; *Epochs in Doctrinal and Methodological History*; and many articles.

Schumpeter entered politics in 1916; he was minister of finance briefly in 1919.

In 1925, after a failed fling in banking and industry, Schumpeter joined the University of Bonn. In 1932, he moved to Harvard.

Keynes's *General Theory* appeared in 1936, and Schumpeter reviewed it negatively, objecting to its attack on savings, its short-run focus, and its tying theory to policy. Moreover, Schumpeter "was unhappy that so many of his colleagues paid serious attention to it."

In 1939, Schumpeter's *Business Cycles* was published, offering a short cycle of about forty months, a major cycle of 8 to 11 years, "the only one required in Schumpeter's analysis," and a long wave of fifty to sixty years. Innovation was at center stage in the latter two. In 1942 came *Capitalism, Socialism and Democracy*, reaching the same conclusion as Marx on the future of capitalism but viewing capitalism's successes as leading to its destruction, whereas Marx cited the failures of capitalism.

In 1947, Schumpeter was elected president of the American Economic Association and in 1949 he was nominated to be president of the International Economic Association. He died in 1950, leaving an incomplete manuscript, which his widow edited. It was published with the title *History of Economic Analysis* and was reviewed with near-universal acclaim.

Economists largely ignored Schumpeter for many years, but, Allen argues, as Keynesianism lost some of its aura, Schumpeter's stock rose. Certainly in the recent business and government worlds there has been adulation of entrepreneurs. Related to this has been the rising popularity of laissez-faire and the declining popularity of government intervention. In 1981, the University of Vienna created an honorary Schumpeter professorship and several years later the International Schumpeter Society was founded. Schumpeter's current active legacy continues mainly, however, in the vigorous field of business history, with its scholarly journals here and abroad and large outpouring of scholarly books. In economics programs at universities, the neglect continues.

Opening Doors is a masterful biography. Allen has exploited archives worldwide and Schumpeter's vast diary and quasi-diary materials. He has consulted ex-students, ex-colleagues, and others around the globe who had some connection with Schumpeter or his family. The result is an intellectual, professional, personal biography painted against prevailing intellectual currents.

ERVIN MILLER

University of Pennsylvania
Philadelphia

JANOSKI, THOMAS. *The Political Economy of Unemployment: Active Labor Market Policy in West Germany and the United States.* Pp. xxvi, 351. Berkeley: University of California Press, 1990. $34.95.

Despite a rhetorical adherence to the work ethic, most nations except Sweden devote far more resources to cash payments and services for those who are jobless but employable than to helping them earn a living. "Active labor market policy" refers to policies that directly or indirectly promote employment, in contrast to cash or in-kind assistance. The persistence of unemployment and poverty, exacerbated during recessions, provides a powerful justification for vigorous employment policies.

Janoski has written a comprehensive comparison of education and training, job creation, and employment service programs in the United States and the former West Germany. To my knowledge, no other book within the last decade has attempted to analyze U.S. policy in this area comprehensively. For this reason, and the importance of the subject, Janoski's book deserves a wide readership.

The Political Economy of Unemployment has serious flaws, however. Most of the data are no later than 1980, especially for Germany. Janoski repeats much of the information from the introductory historical review in an analysis of the development of legislation. Although he has evidently put much effort into the work, the topic is insufficiently researched because Janoski has examined published material only. The U.S. government—and perhaps the government of Germany—invariably contracts with private research organizations to study or formally evaluate employment programs. In addition, program administrators themselves often collect a wealth of information. Knowledge of unpublished reports is essential for an accurate understanding of employment policy, but this book is deficient on that score. Finally, the exposition is remarkably uneven. Some difficult topics, such as Germany's educational system, are presented with clarity and finesse, while in other sections the reader will never see the forest for the trees.

Nevertheless, many of the principal conclusions of this book seem sound. Vigorous employment policies have proved dramatically effective, ironically by history's greatest destroyer of freedom, Adolf Hitler. Nazi job creation programs reduced unemployment by two-thirds in 1933 alone, pulling Germany out of the depression and helping to secure Hitler's domestic and international position. Currently, U.S. employment programs could benefit from adopting the more centralized administration used in Germany. Despite the current fashion of block grants, the idea that Washington is the problem rather than the solution is belied by the experiences of our education and criminal justice systems, both of which are managed locally but are in a disastrous condition.

FRANK GALLO

George Washington University
Washington, D.C.

KLAMER, ARJO and DAVID COLANDER. *The Making of an Economist.* Pp. xvi, 216. Boulder, CO: Westview Press, 1990. $48.00. Paperbound, $16.95.

BLOCK, FRED. *Postindustrial Possibilities: A Critique of Economic Discourse.* Pp. ix, 227. Los Angeles: University of California Press, 1990. $35.00. Paperbound, $12.95.

The Making of an Economist is an important book for the economics profession to ponder. Its central purpose is to report the results of a study of graduate economics education in six top programs—those at the Massachusetts Institute of Technology (MIT), Harvard, Columbia, Stanford, and Yale universities, and the University of Chicago. It does so from the perspective of the students in the program. The instruments used for the study include a detailed questionnaire—the results of which are discussed in chapters 2 and 3—and in-depth interviews with students at MIT, Harvard, Columbia, and Chicago—discussed, with ample quotes, in chapters 4-6. Klamer and Colander discuss the implications of their findings in chapters 9 and 10. Faculty with Ph.D. programs in economics and wanting to study the attitudes of their own students will find the questionnaire reproduced in an appendix of chapter 2.

Readers familiar with what has been happening in academic economics should not be surprised at Klamer and Colander's findings. The elite students at the elite graduate programs, who will proba-

bly dominate the profession within a few years, are receiving educations that will continue the technocratic trend that has dominated academic economics over the past two decades. Academic economists have closeted themselves in their ivory towers and are producing new generations of narrowly educated nerds.

This is a strange development. In earlier years, economists who tussled with the social and economic problems of their times were highly respected in the profession. The great economists who are studied in courses in the history of economic thought—for example, Adam Smith, Ricardo, Mill, Marx, Menger, Alfred Marshall, Veblen, Keynes, (and today) Hayek, and Milton Friedman—made their marks both in the development of new concepts and in their desire and ability to address policy issues. This is no longer the case in the Econ Tribe.

Students, most of whom are attracted to graduate study in economics by broadly conceived undergraduate courses that use relatively simple analytical techniques to deal with a variety of practical issues, are shocked to find what first, and perhaps permanently, appears to be a totally different subject. The stress in graduate work, particularly at places like MIT, is not on a broad economics education and an exploration of a variety of schools of economic thought but is, instead, on using high-powered mathematics and econometrics to develop and test rigorous and narrowly focused models based upon the neoclassical paradigm. Students spend their first year or two honing their technical abilities with problem sets. Their courses in applied aspects of the field are frequently presented as theoretical exercises. Institutional and historical materials take a back seat to modeling.

This activity does a good job of indoctrinating fledglings into academic economics. Most aspire to be economics professors. Sixty-five percent of the students surveyed believe that success in the profession requires good problem-solving skills, and 57 percent believe that knowledge of mathematics is essential. Forty-three percent believe that a broad knowledge of the economics literature is unimportant—their professors tend to assign only the most recent articles in academic journals, many of which they themselves have written—and 68 percent feel that a thorough knowledge of the economy is unimportant. The in-depth interviews conducted by Klamer and Colander also reveal that many of the students have learned to disdain economists who write for the public or draw upon sociology or anthropology for insights.

Getting a respectable job at a top research university is the ambition of most of the students. They do not regard a job at a good liberal arts college or a job in the public sector as an attractive alternative. This attitude is clearly approved of by their teachers.

Klamer and Colander say that the interviews with the students suggest a "definite tension, frustration, and cynicism" that went well beyond the normal graduate-student blues. There was a strong sense that economics was a game, that analytically neat modeling is more valued by the profession than relevant models that provide deeper understandings of institutions. The facade, not the depth of knowledge, is what is important.

Not all students share these attitudes. Indeed, students at Chicago tend to believe that their training is relevant to policy issues, even if it is not always useful in actually solving policy problems. Even so, for someone like me, who in the 1950s entered the profession in the belief that its purpose was to serve society by at least helping it to understand itself, *The Making of an Economist* is a depressing book.

Fred Block's *Postindustrial Possibilities* contains an elaborate critique of narrowly focused economic discourse. Block rightly points out that the highly abstract neoclassical model of the economy is not a good description of the real world and that realistic economic analysis must take into account "background factors" such as family, property rights, organizational structures, contractual relationships, expectations of economic actors, and the like. (Economists call most of these things "structural factors.") Changes in these factors can undermine all of the positive theories of the real world that assume the factors to be constant.

Block is particularly critical of the application of the neoclassical economic theory of markets to what he calls our "postindustrial" society, a society he defines as one in which the idea of an "industrial society" no longer applies. Negative definitions are usually unhelpful in scientific discourse. In Block's case, however, he seems to mean that our postindustrial society is characterized by the massive movements of women into the labor force that have resulted in the breakdown of the traditional patriarchal family, the arrival of computer-based automation, and the growing importance of services relative to manufacturing as the main source of employment.

Why is neoclassical market theory unhelpful in the analysis of Block's postindustrial society? Block seems to have two answers to this question. The first is that the theory assumes a manufacturing-based "industrial society." The second is that the theory is too abstract to be used as a tool to describe the actual workings of the economy.

Most economists would reject the first answer—primarily because they accept the second answer. As it is usually taught, the neoclassical theory of markets is a highly abstract model designed to study the behavior of a competitive free market system based upon private property in which profit-maximizing producers sell goods to utility-maximizing households that, in turn, finance their purchases with the proceeds from sales of labor and other factor services to the firms. The model is not designed to describe a real-life industrial economy, or any other real-life economy, for that matter. Its purpose is to provide a benchmark—a way to make predictions about how a market economy would behave when one or several of its assumptions is removed and replaced with other assumptions. Thus it is used to examine the consequences for the economy of price controls, of different kinds of taxes, of various government subsidies, and so forth. The model, properly adjusted for different legal frameworks, has also been used to analyze the behavior of not-for-profit enterprises, cooperatives, and even worker-council-type enterprises such as those that dominate the Yugoslavian economy.

Moreover, as Block himself acknowledges, economic thinking has invaded fields traditionally claimed by others. One need only think of the work of Gary Becker on the economics of the family, of James Buchanan, Anthony Downs, and Gordon Tullock, who created the field of public choice, or of Richard Posner and the field of law and economics. Some writers have applied economic thinking to the behavior of body cells and to ecological systems.

Thus the thrust of Block's critique is somewhat puzzling and one that I find difficult to accept. Many economists have refused to study the economy as an entity hermetically sealed from the society in which it operates. Indeed, a great deal of the work of modern economists—other than those enchanted with narrowly conceived mathematical models—is directed at the interactions between changes in legal and social conditions and the econ-omy. They are, even if they do not admit it, actually practicing economic sociologists or, to use a more ancient term, political economists.

BARRY N. SIEGEL

University of Oregon
Eugene

LAZONICK, WILLIAM. *Competitive Advantage on the Shop Floor*. Pp. x, 419. Cambridge, MA: Harvard University Press, 1990. No price.

This volume's central thesis is that the social relations of production on the shop floor are a critical and too frequently neglected determinant of labor productivity, capital accumulation, and competitive advantage in the global economy. While acknowledging that this aspect is but one piece of the total puzzle, Lazonick contends that the quantity and quality of effort expended by production workers is a consequence of their productive relations with employers, other workers, and their work, and in turn this effort underlies any coherent explanation of the success or failure of the capitalist enterprise.

Lazonick employs historical argument to explain the succession of English enterprise by American, and of American enterprise in turn by Japanese, over the course of the nineteenth and twentieth centuries. In a richly detailed mural, Lazonick demonstrates that a factor that originally led to the dominance of the English cotton industry, the incorporation of skilled craftsmen in the wage labor relations, also eventually led to its demise, as the workers' control and reproduction of craft skills limited the productivity in the English mills. The English capitalists were superseded by their U.S. competitors, who introduced technology in order to separate workers from their skills and thereby reasserted control of the work process on the shop floor. Lazonick then avers that these contrasting relations of production in cotton spinning serve as a microcosm that illustrates the entire ascendancy of U.S. capitalism over its English predecessor. Painting with an even broader brush, Lazonick then argues that while stripping workers of their skills explains the rise of U.S. capitalism, it also sets the stage for the eclipse of U.S. firms by Japanese capitalists. The Japanese increased productivity by instilling skills in the shop floor operatives, simultaneously ensuring worker effort by means of an elevated institutional commitment by the firm to the workers. This approach used the carrot in contrast to the stick that is predominantly utilized to extract worker effort in the United States. Lazonick firmly roots these alternative relations of production in the particular histories of the nations under examination.

Competitive Advantage on the Shop Floor bears a close resemblance to recent work on the social structures of accumulation within capitalist economies, though Lazonick focuses on the national as well as the temporal dimension of the evolution of productive relations. In the English case, we see a period of primitive accumulation of capital, followed by the movement to homogenization and eventual segmentation of labor in the United States. The Japanese case provides yet another set of relations of production. As has been done for the social structure of accumulation work, Lazonick posits the first two phases in a life-cycle model, where the characteristics responsible for the ascendancy of one set of productive relations eventually become an impediment to further productive development. Curiously, Lazonick appears to abandon this evolutionary model when he examines the contemporary Japanese rela-

tions of production. Unlike its predecessors, the Japanese case is portrayed more as an ideal, optimal set of productive relations, without much sense that they may also embody the seeds of their own inadequacy. Perhaps Lazonick's de-emphasis of other aspects of the Japanese economy, including its profound duality, the extensive use of subcontracting, the aggressive role of the state in capital accumulation, and cultural underpinnings, lead him to neglect this possible analogue to previously dominant relations of production.

In the context of his discussion, Lazonick also provides the reader with critical insights into both the Marxian and the neoclassical paradigms. Although methodologically more indebted to Marx, Lazonick argues that Marx erred in placing the forces of production in the predominant analytical role—instead of in Lazonick's relations of production—casting technology in the role of the instrument capitalists wielded to unilaterally forge productive relations with workers. As for the neoclassicists, Lazonick argues persuasively that the choice of technology cannot be understood simply in terms of relative factor prices. In an elegant yet concrete discussion, Lazonick demonstrates that production functions depend not only upon the available productive forces but also upon the particular social relations of production. The analysis also finds expanded support for the Schumpeterian hypothesis that instituting competitive measures in order to promote static efficiency may well impede the dynamic process of economic development.

Whether or not the reader is persuaded that an analysis of the social relations of production provides the best approach to understanding the internal development and succession of dominant national economies over the past two centuries, the reader will be convinced that this aspect of the historical process cannot be neglected.

ALEXANDER M. THOMPSON III
Vassar College
Poughkeepsie
New York

MARGO, ROBERT A. *Race and Schooling in the South, 1880-1950: An Economic History.* Pp. x, 164. Chicago: University of Chicago Press, 1991. $24.95.

In *Race and Schooling in the South, 1880-1950: An Economic History*, Robert Margo attempts to explain why the economic well-being of blacks was worse than that of whites in the South during the Jim Crow era, the period of government-sanctioned racial discrimination and segregation lasting from the end of Reconstruction (1866-77) to the close of the civil rights movement (1954-68). Margo begins by noting that the racial wage gap—the earnings differential between the races—for adult men closed by only 3 percent between 1900 and 1940 and by a dramatic 13 percent between 1940 and 1980. Accordingly, earnings of black males were 48 percent of white male earnings in 1940 and 61 percent in 1980. Margo is primarily interested in explaining the 3 percent figure, that is, the relative lack of black economic progress between 1900 and 1940.

Margo's explanation is a synthesis of three economic theories. The first is that large and persistent differences in the "quantity"—for example, the number of years spent in school—and "quality"—for example, the rate of illiteracy and test scores—of elementary and high school education between blacks and whites account for the racial wage gap. Essentially, blacks were unqualified to work outside the farm industry. Because the first theory focuses on deficiencies in the supply of labor, it is called a "supply-side," or "human capital," model. The second theory is that racial discrimination and segregation in labor markets kept black wages low, and no amount of educational equality could have overcome such barriers. This theory, which emphasizes deficiencies in the demand for labor, is called a "demand-side," or "institutionalist," model. Margo argues that both supply-side and demand-side forces converged to depress the economic status of blacks; neither model alone sufficiently explains the racial wage gap. The final theory states that equalizing educational and employment opportunities would not have eliminated the racial wage gap, because poverty and high rates of adult illiteracy among blacks—that is, "intergenerational drag," or family background—kept black children on the farm and out of the classroom.

Significantly, the phenomenon of racial oppression ties together Margo's three-part argument. Poor schooling—including shifting funds from black to white schools, limiting the number of black public high schools, and closing black elementary and high schools—poor employment opportunities, and poor family background were the intended socioeconomic effects of white supremacy—the desire of white southerners to create and maintain a social order in which they dominated blacks.

ROY L. BROOKS
University of Minnesota
Minneapolis

OTHER BOOKS

ALEXANDER, ROBERT J. *Venezuela's Voice for Democracy: Conversations and Correspondence with Rómulo Betancourt*. Pp. 184. Westport, CT: Greenwood Press, 1990. $37.95.

ALKULA, TAPANI. *Work Orientations in Finland: A Conceptual Critique and an Empirical Study of Work-Related Expectations*. Pp. 203. Helsinki: Finnish Society of Sciences and Letters, 1990. Paperbound, no price.

ALTER, MAX. *Carl Menger and the Origins of Austrian Economics*. Pp. viii, 256. Boulder, CO: Westview Press, 1990. $65.00.

APPIAH, JOSEPH. *Joe Appiah: The Autobiography of an African Patriot*. Pp. 400. Westport, CT: Greenwood Press, 1990. $39.95.

BARNEY, GERALD O. et al., eds. *Managing a Nation: The Microcomputer Software Catalog*. 2d ed. Pp. xvi, 338. Boulder, CO: Westview Press, 1991. Paperbound, $48.50.

BLACK, JAY KNIPPERS, ed. *Latin America: Its Problems and Its Promise*. 2d ed. Pp. xii, 627. Boulder, CO: Westview Press, 1991. $65.00. Paperbound, $24.95.

BLOOM, ALLAN, ed. *Confronting the Constitution: The Challenge to Locke, Montesquieu, Jefferson, and the Federalists from Utilitarianism, Historicism, Marxism, Freudianism, Pragmatism, Existentialism* .... Pp. 608. Washington, DC: AEI Press, 1990. $24.95.

CHRISTIAN, DAVID. *Living Water: Vodka and Russian Society on the Eve of Emancipation*. Pp. x, 447. New York: Oxford University Press, 1990. $74.00.

COHEN, ELIOT A. *Citizens and Soldiers: The Dilemmas of Military Service*. Pp. 227. Ithaca, NY: Cornell University Press, 1990. Paperbound, $12.95.

COHEN, SHELDON M. *Arms and Judgment: Law, Morality, and the Conduct of War in the Twentieth Century*. Pp. xiii, 226. Boulder, CO: Westview Press, 1989. $38.50. Paperbound, $16.95.

CONLAN, TIMOTHY. *New Federalism: Intergovernmental Reform from Nixon to Reagan*. Pp. xxii, 274. Washington, DC: Brookings Institution, 1988. $34.95. Paperbound, $15.95.

CORNWELL, TERRI LYNN. *Democracy and the Arts: The Role of Participation*. Pp. 232. New York: Praeger, 1990. $45.00.

CRANE, JOHN O. and SYLVIA CRANE. *Czechoslovakia: Anvil of the Cold War*. Pp. xxvi, 352. New York: Praeger, 1990. $45.00.

CROUCH, COLIN and RONALD DORE, eds. *Corporatism and Accountability: Organized Interests in British Public Life*. Pp. x, 294. New York: Oxford University Press, Clarendon Press, 1990. $55.00.

DAVIS, DAVID BRION. *Revolutions: Reflections on American Equality and Foreign Liberations*. Pp. viii, 130. Cambridge, MA: Harvard University Press, 1990. $19.95.

DONOVAN, RONALD. *Administering the Taylor Law: Public Employee Relations in New York*. Pp. 264. Ithaca, NY: ILR Press, 1990. $32.00. Paperbound, $14.95.

DOWNS, DONALD ALEXANDER. *The New Politics of Pornography*. Pp. xxiv, 266. Chicago: University of Chicago Press, 1990. $42.00. Paperbound, $14.95.

EASTON, DAVID and CORINNE S. SCHELLING, eds. *Divided Knowledge: Across Disciplines, across Cultures*. Pp. 261. Newbury Park, CA: Sage, 1991. $36.00. Paperbound, $17.95.

ELLIOTT, EUEL W. *Issues and Elections: Presidential Voting in Contemporary America—A Revisionist View*. Pp. xi, 140. Boulder, CO: Westview Press, 1989. Paperbound, $28.50.

ENTMAN, ROBERT M. *Democracy without Citizens: Media and the Decay of*

American Politics. Pp. xii, 232. New York: Oxford University Press, 1991. Paperbound, $11.95.

FALCOFF, MARK. *Modern Chile, 1970-1989: A Critical History*. Pp. xiii, 327. New Brunswick, NJ: Transaction, 1989. $32.95.

FERNÁNDEZ, DAMIÁN J., ed. *Central America and the Middle East: The Internalization of the Crises*. Pp. viii, 239. Miami: Florida International University Press, 1990. $26.95. Paperbound, $14.95.

FRANCO, PAUL. *The Political Philosophy of Michael Oakeshott*. Pp. vii, 277. New Haven, CT: Yale University Press, 1990. $30.00.

FREEDMAN, LAWRENCE, ed. *Europe Transformed: Documents on the End of the Cold War*. Pp. 512. New York: St. Martin's Press, 1990. $45.00.

FULLER, TIMOTHY, ed. *The Voice of Liberal Learning: Michael Oakeshott on Education*. Pp. 169. New Haven, CT: Yale University Press, 1990. Paperbound, $9.95.

GEER, JOHN G. *Nominating Presidents: An Evaluation of Voters and Primaries*. Pp. 176. Westport, CT: Greenwood Press, 1989. $37.95.

GILBERG, TROND. *Nationalism and Communism in Romania: The Rise and Fall of Ceausescu's Personal Dictatorship*. Pp. x, 289. Boulder, CO: Westview Press, 1990. $39.50.

GOLDIN, IAN and ODIN KNUDSEN, eds. *Agricultural Trade Liberalization: Implications for Developing Countries*. Pp. 488. Washington, DC: World Bank, 1990. No price.

HARAF, WILLIAM S. and THOMAS D. WILLETT, eds. *Monetary Policy for a Volatile Global Economy*. Pp. 216. Lanham, MD: AEI Press, 1990. $24.95.

HEARDEN, PATRICK J., ed. *Vietnam: Four American Perspectives: Lectures by George S. McGovern, William C. Westmoreland, Edward N. Luttwak, and Thomas J. McCormick*. Pp. xi, 112.

West Lafayette, IN: Purdue University Press, 1990. $17.50. Paperbound, $9.95.

HEILKE, THOMAS W. *Voegelin on the Idea of Race: An Analysis of Modern European Racism*. Pp. xiii, 161. Baton Rouge: Louisiana State University Press, 1990. $22.50.

HEPWORTH, MARK. *Geography of the Information Economy*. Pp. xix, 258. New York: Guilford Press, 1989. $30.00.

HERSPRING, DALE E. *The Soviet High Command, 1967-1989: Personalities and Politics*. Pp. xv, 322. Princeton, NJ: Princeton University Press, 1990. $39.50. Paperbound, $14.50.

HOLDEN, GERARD. *The Warsaw Pact: Soviet Security and Bloc Politics*. Pp. 227. Cambridge, MA: Basil Blackwell, 1989. No price.

HOLLWECK, THOMAS A. and PAUL CARINGELLA, eds. *The Collected Works of Eric Voegelin*. Vol. 28, *What Is History? And Other Late Unpublished Writings*. Pp. xxxvi, 256. Baton Rouge: Louisiana State University Press, 1990. $22.50.

JOHNS, SHERIDAN and RICHARD HUNT DAVIS, Jr., eds. *Mandela, Tambo, and the African National Congress*. Pp. xvii, 353. New York: Oxford University Press, 1991. $35.00. Paperbound, $13.95.

JONES, ANTHONY et al., eds. *Soviet Social Problems*. Pp. ix, 337. Boulder, CO: Westview Press, 1991. $52.00. Paperbound, $19.95.

KERBER, LINDA K. *Women's America: Refocusing the Past*. 3d ed. Pp. xii, 588. New York: Oxford University Press, 1991. $45.00. Paperbound, $18.95.

KODIKARA, SHELTON U., ed. *South Asian Strategic Issues*. Pp. 204. New Delhi: Sage, 1990. No price.

KUBEY, ROBERT and MIHALY CSIKSZENTMIHALYI. *Television and the Quality of Life: How Viewing Shapes Everyday Experience*. Pp. xvii, 287.

Hillsdale, NJ: Lawrence Erlbaum, 1990. $39.95. Paperbound, $19.95.

LEVITAN, SAR A. *Programs in Aid of the Poor.* 6th ed. Pp. viii, 189. Baltimore, MD: Johns Hopkins University Press, 1990. Paperbound, no price.

LIPSCHITZ, LESLIE and DONOGH McDONALD, eds. *German Unification: Economic Issues.* Pp. xv, 171. Washington, DC: International Monetary Fund, 1990. Paperbound, $10.00.

MANNING, PETER K. *Symbolic Communication: Signifying Calls and the Police Response.* Pp. xvii, 309. Cambridge, MA: MIT, 1989. $35.00.

McCAULEY, MARTIN, ed. *Gorbachev and Perestroika.* Pp. xii, 222. New York: St. Martin's Press, 1990. $45.00.

McLAUGHLIN, JUDITH BLOCK and DAVID RIESMAN. *Choosing a College President: Opportunities and Constraints.* Pp. xxxvi, 377. Princeton, NJ: Carnegie Foundation for the Advancement of Teaching, 1991. Paperbound, $8.00.

MESSERLIN, PATRICK A. and KARL P. SAUVANT, eds. *The Uruguay Round: Services in the World Economy.* Pp. 220. Washington, DC: World Bank, 1990. Paperbound, no price.

MITCHELL, NEIL J. *The Generous Corporation: A Political Analysis of Economic Power.* Pp. x, 163. New Haven, CT: Yale University Press, 1989. $18.50.

NEILSON, KEITH and RONALD G. HAYCOCK, eds. *The Cold War and Defense.* Pp. 216. New York: Praeger, 1990. $45.00.

OTTAWAY, MARINA, ed. *The Political Economy of Ethiopia.* Pp. 264. New York: Praeger, 1990. $42.95.

OTTO, JOHN SOLOMON. *The Southern Frontiers, 1607-1860: The Agricultural Evolution of the Colonial and Antebellum South.* Pp. 192. Westport, CT: Greenwood Press, 1989. $37.95.

PAEHLKE, ROBERT and DOUGLAS TORGERSON, eds. *Managing Leviathan: Environmental Politics and the Administrative State.* Pp. 320. Peterborough, Ontario: Broadview Press, 1990. Paperbound, $16.95.

PERETZ, DON. *Intifada: The Palestinian Uprising.* Pp. ix, 246. Boulder, CO: Westview Press, 1990. $38.50. Paperbound, $14.95.

PHADNIS, URMILA. *Ethnicity and Nation-Building in South Asia.* Pp. 328. Newbury Park, CA: Sage, 1990. $29.95.

PLISCHKE, ELMER, ed. *Contemporary U.S. Foreign Policy: Documents and Commentary.* Pp. xlv, 843. Westport, CT: Greenwood Press, 1991. $85.00.

PUTNAM, HILARY. *Realism with a Human Face.* Pp. lxxiv, 347. Cambridge, MA: Harvard University Press, 1990. $30.00.

RIZOPOULOS, NICHOLAS X., ed. *Sea-Changes: American Foreign Policy in a World Transformed.* Pp. 304. New York: Council on Foreign Relations Press, 1990. Paperbound, $14.95.

ROAZEN, PAUL, ed. *Louis Hartz: The Necessity of Choice—Nineteenth-Century Political Thought.* Pp. 215. New Brunswick, NJ: Transaction, 1990. $24.95.

ROBERTSON, A. H. and J. G. MERRILLS. *Human Rights in the World: An Introduction to the Study of the International Protection of Human Rights.* 3d ed. Pp. vi, 314. New York: Manchester University Press, 1990. $49.95.

ROSEN, STANLEY. *The Ancients and the Moderns: Rethinking Modernity.* Pp. x, 236. New Haven, CT: Yale University Press, 1991. $27.50. Paperbound, $12.95.

RUNCO, MARK A. and ROBERT S. ALBERT, eds. *Theories of Creativity.* Pp. 276. Newbury Park, CA: Sage, 1990. $36.00. Paperbound, $17.95.

SAGAN, SCOTT D. *Moving Targets: Nuclear Strategy and National Security.* Pp. xiii, 237. Princeton, NJ: Princeton University Press, 1989. Paperbound, $9.95.

SALMÓN, GARY PRADO. *The Defeat of Che Guevara: Military Response to Guerilla Challenge in Bolivia.* Translated by John Deredita. Pp. 304. New York: Praeger, 1990. $45.00.

SAMMETT, GEORGE, Jr. and DAVID E. GREEN. *Defense Acquisition Management.* Pp. xii, 498. Boca Raton: Florida Atlantic University Press, 1990. $59.95.

SANDERCOCK, LEONIE. *Property, Politics, and Urban Planning: A History of Australian City Planning, 1890-1990.* 2d ed. Pp. 302. New Brunswick, NJ: Transaction, 1990. No price.

SANDILANDS, ROGER J. *The Life and Political Economy of Lauchlin Currie: New Dealer, Presidential Advisor, and Development Economist.* Pp. xi, 441. Durham, NC: Duke University Press, 1990. $57.50.

SANDOZ, ELLIS, ed. *The Collected Works of Eric Voegelin.* Vol 12, *Published Essays 1966-1985.* Pp. xxii, 416. Baton Rouge: Louisiana State University Press, 1990. $32.50.

SCHIVE, CHI. *The Foreign Factor.* Pp. xiv, 138. Stanford, CA: Hoover Institution, 1990. $20.95. Paperbound, $15.95.

SCHMÄHLING, ELMAR, ed. *Life beyond the Bomb: Global Stability without Nuclear Deterrence.* Pp. xi, 207. New York: St. Martin's Press, 1990. $39.95.

SHEA, JOHN C., ed. *Arguments on American Politics.* Pp. xxi, 320. Pacific Grove, CA: Brooks/Cole, 1991. Paperbound, $17.00.

SHOVEN, JOHN B. and JOEL WALDFOGEL, eds. *Debt, Taxes, and Corporate Restructuring.* Pp. 210. Washington, DC: Brookings Books, 1990. $28.95. Paperbound, $10.95.

SINCLAIR, BARBARA. *The Transformation of the U.S. Senate.* Pp. vii, 233. Baltimore, MD: Johns Hopkins University Press, 1989. Paperbound, no price.

SKIDELSKY, ROBERT, ed. *Thatcherism.* Pp. ix, 214. Cambridge, MA: Basil Blackwell, 1990. Paperbound, $18.95.

SMITH, M. ESTELLIE, ed. *Perspectives on the Informal Economy.* Pp. 364. Lanham, MD: University Press of America, 1990. $35.50. Paperbound, $20.75.

SMITH, MICHAEL JOSEPH. *Realist Thought from Weber to Kissinger.* Pp. xii, 256. Baton Rouge: Louisiana State University Press, 1990. Paperbound, $9.95.

SMITH, MICHAEL PETER, ed. *Breaking Chains: Social Movements and Collective Action.* Pp. 218. New Brunswick, NJ: Transaction, 1991. Paperbound, $19.95.

SOLOW, ROBERT M. *The Labor Market as a Social Institution.* Pp. xviii, 116. Cambridge, MA: Basil Blackwell, 1990. $54.95.

STARZINGER, VINCENT E. *The Politics of the Center: The Juste Milieu in Theory and Practice, France and England, 1815-1848.* Pp. xxi, 160. New Brunswick, NJ: Transaction, 1991. Paperbound, $19.95.

STEBBINS, ROBERT A. *Sociology: The Study of Society.* 2d ed. Pp. xvii, 652. New York: Harper & Row, 1990. Paperbound, no price.

STETSON, DOROTHY McBRIDE. *Women's Rights in the U.S.A.: Policy Debates & Gender Roles.* Pp. xvii, 265. Pacific Grove, CA: Brooks/Cole, 1991. Paperbound, $16.25.

SWARTZ, THOMAS R. and JOHN E. PECK, eds. *The Changing Face of Fiscal Federalism.* Pp. x, 181. Armonk, NY: M. E. Sharpe, 1990. $39.95. Paperbound, $16.95.

TAYLOR, PETER J. *Britain and the Cold War: 1945 as Geopolitical Transition.* Pp. xiii, 153. New York: Guilford Press, 1990. $30.00.

TOLZ, VERA. *The USSR's Emerging Multiparty System.* Pp. xvi, 223. New York: Praeger, 1990. $35.00. Paperbound, $11.95.

TONRY, MICHAEL and JAMES Q. WILSON, eds. *Drugs and Crime.* Pp. x,

574. Chicago: University of Chicago Press, 1990. $39.95.

TSAKOK, ISABELLE. *Agricultural Price Policy: A Practitioner's Guide to Partial-Equilibrium Analysis.* Pp. xx, 305. Ithaca, NY: Cornell University Press, 1990. $54.50. Paperbound, $19.95.

VEIT, HELEN E. et al., eds. *Creating the Bill of Rights.* Pp. xxiv, 323. Baltimore, MD: Johns Hopkins University Press, 1991. $42.50. Paperbound, $10.95.

VETTER, HAROLD J. and GARY R. PERLSTEIN. *Perspectives on Terrorism.* Pp. xx, 268. Pacific Grove, CA: Brooks/Cole, 1991. Paperbound, $24.50.

WANG, YU SAN, ed. *Foreign Policy of the Republic of China on Taiwan: An Unorthodox Approach.* Pp. 240. New York: Praeger, 1990. $45.00.

WARD, KATHRYN. *Women Workers and Global Restructuring.* Pp. 272. Ithaca, NY: ILR Press, 1990. $32.00. Paperbound, $14.95.

WILK, STAN. *Humanistic Anthropology.* Pp. xii, 148. Knoxville: University of Tennessee Press, 1991. $22.50.

WILSON, GRAHAM K. *Interest Groups.* Pp. xii, 198. Cambridge, MA: Basil Blackwell, 1990. $47.95. Paperbound, $14.95.

WOLFF, KURT H. *Survival and Sociology: Vindicating the Human Subject.* Pp. xi, 119. New Brunswick, NJ: Transaction, 1991. No price.

WOODS, RANDALL B. and HOWARD JONES. *Dawning of the Cold War: The United States' Quest for Order.* Pp. xiii, 335. Athens: University of Georgia Press, 1991. $35.00. Paperbound, $14.95.

WOOLARD, KATHRYN A. *Double Talk: Bilingualism and the Politics of Ethnicity in Catalonia.* Pp. xiv, 183. Stanford, CA: Stanford University Press, 1989. $29.50.

WORLD BANK. *Argentina: Reforms for Price Stability and Growth.* Pp. xxxii, 290. Washington, DC: World Bank, 1990. Paperbound, no price.

WORLD BANK. *Poverty: World Development Report 1990.* Pp. xii, 260. New York: Oxford University Press, 1990. Paperbound, $14.95.

YORK, HERBERT F. *The Advisors: Oppenheimer, Teller and the Superbomb.* Pp. xiv, 201. Stanford, CA: Stanford University Press, 1989. $32.50. Paperbound, $8.95.

YOUNG, T. R. *The Drama of Social Life: Essays in Post-Modern Social Psychology.* Pp. xiii, 367. New Brunswick, NJ: Transaction, 1990. No price.

ZASLAVSKAYA, TATYANA. *The Second Socialist Revolution: An Alternative Soviet Strategy.* Pp. 264. Bloomington: Indiana University Press, 1990. $35.00. Paperbound, $14.95.

ZEITLIN, MAURICE. *The Large Corporation and Contemporary Classes.* Pp. 306. New Brunswick, NJ: Rutgers University Press, 1989. $42.00. Paperbound, $15.00.

INDEX

Asian Affairs:
An American Review

Asian Affairs: An American Review focuses on U.S. policy in Asia, as well as on the domestic politics, economics, and international relations of the Asian countries. Written primarily for readers wanting relevant information about a part of the world that is of vital importance to American interests, it is also a valuable resource for teachers, political analysts, and those involved in international business. The journal is published under the sponsorship of the Contemporary U.S.-Asia Research Institute in New York.

Executive Editors

- *Stephen P. Cohen*, University of Illinois, Department of Political Science, Urbana, IL
- *James C. Hsiung*, New York University, Department of Politics, New York, NY
- *Donald E. Weatherbee*, University of South Carolina, Department of Government and International Studies, Columbia, SC

Order Form

❏ YES! I would like to order a one-year subscription to *Asian Affairs*, published quarterly. I understand payment can be made to Heldref Publications or charged to my VISA/MasterCard (circle one).

❏ $29.00 for individuals ❏ $57.00 for institutions

ACCOUNT # _____ EXP. DATE _____

SIGNATURE _____

NAME/INSTITUTION _____
ADDRESS_____
CITY/STATE/ZIP _____
COUNTRY_____

ADD $9.00 FOR POSTAGE OUTSIDE THE U.S. ALLOW SIX WEEKS FOR DELIVERY OF FIRST ISSUE.

SEND ORDER FORM AND PAYMENT TO:
Heldref Publications, *Asian Affairs*, Department A
1319 Eighteenth Street, NW, Washington, DC 20036-1802

(202) 296-6267 FAX (202) 296-5149
Customer Service/Subscription Orders 1 (800) 365-9753

A